DRAWING THE LINE

just ideas

transformative ideals of justice in ethical and political thought

series editors
Drucilla Cornell
Roger Berkowitz

DRAWING THE LINE

TOWARD AN AESTHETICS OF TRANSITIONAL JUSTICE

Carrol Clarkson

FORDHAM UNIVERSITY PRESS

NEW YORK 2014

Copyright © 2014 Fordham University Press

All rights reserved. No part of this publication may be reproduced, stored in a retrieval system, or transmitted in any form or by any means—electronic, mechanical, photocopy, recording, or any other—except for brief quotations in printed reviews, without the prior permission of the publisher.

Fordham University Press has no responsibility for the persistence or accuracy of URLs for external or third-party Internet websites referred to in this publication and does not guarantee that any content on such websites is, or will remain, accurate or appropriate.

Fordham University Press also publishes its books in a variety of electronic formats. Some content that appears in print may not be available in electronic books.

Library of Congress Cataloging-in-Publication Data

Clarkson, Carrol, 1968–
  Drawing the line : toward an aesthetics of transitional justice / Carrol Clarkson.
    page cm. — (Just ideas)
  Includes bibliographical references and index.
  ISBN 978-0-8232-5415-6 (cloth : alk. paper) — ISBN 978-0-8232-5416-3 (pbk. : alk. paper)
  1. Justice in literature. 2. Law and aesthetics. 3. Law and ethics. 4. Transitional justice—South Africa. 5. Authors, South African—Aesthetics. I. Title.
  PN56.L33C58 2014
  809.933554—dc23

                                                                2013009209

Printed in the United States of America

16 15 14   5 4 3 2 1

First edition

In memory of my father, Robert Cox, who always drew the line, and my mother, Marguerite, who always encouraged me to draw

Contents

	Acknowledgments	xi
	Introduction	1
PART I	Drawing the Line	
	1. Drawing the Line	25
	2. Redrawing the Lines	46
PART II	Crossing the Line	
	3. Justice and the Art of Transition	65
	4. Intersections: Ethics and Aesthetics	88
	5. Poets, Philosophers, and Other Animals	107
PART III	Lines of Force	
	6. Visible and Invisible: What Surfaces in Three Johannesburg Novels?	137
	7. Who Are We?	161
	Conclusion	181
	References	187
	Index	199

Acknowledgments

My first thanks go to Peter Fitzpatrick and Drucilla Cornell: At Peter's generous invitation I presented a paper at a Critical Legal Studies Conference in Johannesburg in 2003. My disciplinary base is in English literature, but in preparing for this conference, new lines of enquiry were suddenly open to me, and I realized that I could participate in different kinds of conversation—conversations to cherish for a lifetime. It is thanks to Drucilla Cornell's revelatory suggestion that I could see my way clear to integrating a few articles I had written into a larger book project. Drucilla has been a continual source of encouragement and inspiration to me, often at critical moments.

My heartfelt thanks go out to those with whom I have had life-enhancing conversations while writing this book: Emilios Christodoulidis, Scott Veitch, Johan van der Walt, Oren Ben-Dor, Hans Lindahl, Bert van Roermund, Natalie Pollard, Louis Blond, and Willem Boshoff. The artwork on the cover of this book is by Willem Boshoff. Thank you to François du Bois and Antje du Bois-Pedain, who invited me to write a chapter for their book *Justice and Reconciliation in Post-Apartheid South Africa*: This is the essay in which I first started thinking about the concept of drawing the line. Special thanks, too, to Kjetil Enstad, who invited me to present a keynote address at the conference "Crossing Boundaries," which was hosted by the School of Advanced Study at the University of London in September 2009. I received invaluable input from Kjetil and other participants at this conference and would especially like to thank Hillis Miller for memorable conversations about drawing lines, about Thomas Hardy, and about the lifelines and deadlines of scholarly writing.

In April 2012 I had the privilege of visiting the University of Stockholm for a month. In the seminar series I presented I had the opportunity to speak about the ideas in this book; I benefited enormously from conversations with colleagues and students who attended the seminars. My special thanks go to Claudia Egerer for her extraordinary hospitality and generous intellectual engagement, to Stefan Helgesson, and to Richard Begam, who was visiting the University of Stockholm at the time.

Alex d'Angelo, subject librarian at the University of Cape Town, helped me to track references and sources that I was beginning to think had no material existence in this world. I would also like to thank Daniella Cadiz Bedini—my research assistant at the University of Cape Town and the first person to read the manuscript in its entirety. My sincere thanks go out to the readers at Fordham University Press. Their generous, insightful, and expansive engagement with my work remains a source of inspiration to me.

Stephen, Jacob, and Christopher Clarkson have read and commented on parts of this manuscript in truthful, thought-provoking, imaginative, incisive, and entertaining ways. I'm more appreciative of this, and of so much else besides, than I know how to say.

Throughout this book the discussions are based on somewhat different, in some cases shorter, versions of essays that have been published elsewhere. I thank the editors and publishers for permission to draw on this material for the present project:

> 2005. "Embodying You: Levinas and a Question of the Second Person." *Journal of Literary Semantics* 34: 95–105.
>
> 2005. "Visible and Invisible: What Surfaces in Recent Johannesburg Novels?" *Moving Worlds* 5 (1): 84–97.
>
> 2007. "The Time of Address." In *Law and the Politics of Reconciliation*, edited by Scott Veitch, 229–40. Aldershot: Ashgate.
>
> 2007. "Who Are We? 'Don't Make Me Laugh.'" *Law and Critique* 18 (3): 361–74.
>
> 2008. "Drawing the Line: Justice and the Art of Reconciliation." In *Justice and Reconciliation in Post-Apartheid South Africa*, edited by François du Bois and Antje du Bois-Pedain, 267–88. Cambridge: Cambridge University Press.
>
> 2008. "Ancient Antagonisms." *English Academy Review* 25 (2): 101–10.

2008. "Locating Identity in Phaswane Mpe's *Welcome to Our Hillbrow*." In *Connecting Cultures*, edited by Emma Bainbridge, 65–73. Abingdon: Routledge.

2009. "Photo Essay: Welcome to Our Hillbrow." *Safundi: The Journal of South African and American Studies* 19 (2): 215–22.

2010. "Fences." In "Current Writing: Text and Reception in South Africa." Special issue, *Law and South African Literature* 22 (2): 83–100.

2012. "'The Obliging Etymology of *Nomos*'": Peter Fitzpatrick and the Aesthetics of Law." In *Reading Modern Law: Critical Methodologies and Sovereign Formations*, edited by Ruth Buchanan, Stewart Motha, and Sundhya Pahuja, 165–77. New York: Routledge.

The work on the cover of this book is by Willem Boshoff, 2003: *Neves I*, etching on paper, 52 × 64 cm. My thanks to Willem for granting permission to use this work.

DRAWING THE LINE

Introduction

1

"Art, like morality, consists of drawing the line somewhere," G. K. Chesterton wrote in 1928, insisting on the necessity—if also the contingency—of marking a limit in the act of making an ethical decision (Chesterton 1928, 780). Yet the act of drawing this line is an art as much as it is a question of morality. A line drawn reconfigures space: It divides yet juxtaposes two entities; it connects two distant points. Figuratively, it includes some and excludes others; it marks a boundary between standing for and standing against, or it traces a path along which places are invested with significance, words are understood, and lives are lived.[1] All of these lines could have been drawn somewhere else.

---

1. See Tim Ingold's seminal work *Lines: A Brief History*, which aims to "lay the foundations for what might be called a comparative anthropology of the line" (Ingold 2007, 1). The last phrase of my sentence echoes Ingold: "Life is lived . . . along paths, not just in places, and paths are lines of a sort" (Ingold 2007, 2).

In this book I am interested in the way in which lines of thought are materialized in the world of sensory perception: in the visual arts, literature, and other forms of cultural production. At the same time, lines of thought—and in *Drawing the Line* I am preoccupied with thoughts of transitional justice—seem to be generated by what is depicted, uttered, or written, and (facing the other way now) by what is seen, heard, and read. In the relations that arise between artist and viewer, speaker and listener, writer and reader, this book explores the different ways in which cultural, political, and legal lines are imagined, drawn, crossed, erased, and redrawn in postapartheid South Africa.

My use of the term "aesthetics" is not restricted to its more colloquial sense of "study of the beautiful."[2] In ancient Greek philosophy, *aesthesis* refers to "lived, felt experience, knowledge as it is obtained through the senses" (Cazeaux 2000, xv); one of the originary meanings of "aesthetics" (dating back to 1803) is "the science of the conditions of sensuous perception" (*OED*). A leading preoccupation in the discussions to follow is the way in which a social setting is calibrated so that some people (or other animals, or things) are seen, or heard, or valued as significant while others are not. What does it take to recalibrate the settings so that what has been unseen, or unheard, or devalued before can now be perceived as worthy of attention?

For the most part my discussions are sparked by what might traditionally be considered works of art (that is to say, literature and the visual arts), but throughout the book I use Jacques Rancière's phrase "aesthetic act" to refer to any event, or speech, or encounter that makes it possible to reset social perceptions of what counts and what matters, especially in relation to questions of social justice and to questions of political and legal identity. In his seminal work *The Politics of Aesthetics*, Rancière speaks in specific terms of "aesthetic acts" as "configurations of experience that create new modes of sense perception and induce novel forms of political subjectivity" (Rancière 2004b, 9). In the course of this book, then, I take an aesthetic act to be an incident that brings about a different perception of one's standing in relation to others. My points of reference—the "incidents" or "aesthetic acts" in

---

2. The *OED* tells us that the term "aesthetic" was "misapplied in G[erman] by Baumgarten to 'criticism of taste,' and so used in Eng[lish] since 1830." The question of aesthetic taste is taken to another level in the feud between Apple and IBM. "The only problem with Microsoft is they just have no taste, they have absolutely no taste," says Steve Jobs in the early 1990s, about a decade after the launch of Windows. He goes on to explain: "I don't mean that in a small way. I mean that in a big way, in the sense that they don't think of original ideas and they don't bring much culture into their product" (Isaacson 2011, 179).

this book—include encounters with works of South African writers and artists (Phaswane Mpe, Marlene van Niekerk, Zoë Wicomb, Ivan Vladislavić, William Kentridge and Willem Boshoff, among others), but my discussions also reflect on momentous historical events, such as Mandela's statement from the dock at the Rivonia Trial in 1964, and the building and opening of South Africa's new Constitutional Court, in Hillbrow in March 2004, on the ground of the Old Fort where many of the 156 treason trialists had been held. In what ways and under what conditions do these aesthetic acts lead to a different way of perceiving the relation between the actual and the possible, say, or to a radically different appreciation of what counts as perceptible, or intelligible, or legitimate in a social order?[3] What interests me is the context in which certain works, acts, or encounters, by creating a new field of sensory perception, have the potential to bring about shifts in the way a community delineates itself in terms of what it *perceives* to be significant, or even noticeable at all. To what extent does an aesthetic act have the ethical potency to redraw the lines, altering the margins of exposure of one to the other, thereby recalibrating the terms of cultural, political, and legal interactions? These are the central preoccupations of my book.

To a certain extent, then, my leading line of enquiry can be understood to resonate with Benedict Anderson's *Imagined Communities*. Anderson's point of departure "is that nationality, or, as one might prefer to put it in view of that word's multiple significations, nation-ness, as well as nationalism, are cultural artefacts of a particular kind" (Anderson 2006, 4). "The nation," Anderson writes, "is an imagined political community," and, he goes on to say, "all communities larger than primordial villages of face-to-face contact (and perhaps even these) are imagined. Communities are to be

---

3. Judith Butler writes in her 1999 preface to *Gender Trouble*: "No political revolution is possible without a radical shift in one's notion of the possible and the real. And sometimes this shift comes as a result of certain kinds of practices that precede their explicit theorization, and which prompt a rethinking of our basic categories: what is gender, how is it produced and reproduced, what are its possibilities" (Butler 1999, xxiv). In *Precarious Life*, Butler takes up related questions within the context of a post-9/11 America: "The line that circumscribes what is speakable and what is livable also functions as an instrument of censorship.

"To decide what views will count as reasonable within the public domain, however, is to decide what will and will not count as the public sphere of debate. And if someone holds views that are not in line with the nationalist norm, that person comes to lack credibility as a speaking person, and the media is not open to him or her (though the internet, interestingly, is)" (Butler 2004, xx).

Although she does not mention Rancière specifically, her discourse is clearly resonant with the concept of the "distribution of the sensible": "To produce what will constitute the public sphere, however, it is necessary to control the way in which people see, how they hear, what they see. . . . The public sphere is constituted in part by what can appear, and the regulation of the sphere of appearance is one way to establish what will count as reality, and what will not" (Butler 2004, xx).

distinguished, not by their falsity/genuineness, but *by the style in which they are imagined*" (Anderson 2006, 6, my emphasis).[4]

Anderson offers the definitions above in "anthropological spirit" and, with attentiveness to historical, geographic, and political specificity, pivots his argument on what he takes to be a decisive moment in the birth of the imagined community of the nation: that is, the coming into being of the novel and the newspaper (Anderson 2006, 25). This book takes its cue from Anderson in its attention to the different styles and modes of imagining a South Africa in the time of its transition to democracy. Each chapter starts out with reference to a South African text or context, but the tenor of the discussion throughout is more broadly philosophical. Rather than analyzing literary and other works in South Africa through a *given* theoretical or philosophical lens, my discussions use South African texts as points of departure, suggesting how these works might challenge *and hence contribute to* debates in contemporary Continental aesthetics and critical theory and, perhaps even more specifically, to debates in the field of law and literature.[5]

I take Jacques Rancière's politico-aesthetic philosophy, and especially his notion of the "distribution of the sensible," to be one of the most important voices in these contemporary debates, and one that is of particular relevance to South Africa in the time of its social, political, and legal transitions. Starting out from Aristotle's *Politics*, Rancière's *Disagreement* defines political justice: It is "not simply the order that holds measured relationships between individuals and goods together. It is the order that determines the partition of what is common" (Rancière 1999, 5). Politics begins when those "who have no part in anything" protest, in the name of an overarching community, against the wrong inflicted by other parties. A community becomes a political community when the part that has no part announces itself to be "the people." In Rancière's deft formulation,

> the struggle between the rich and the poor is not social reality, which politics then has to deal with. It is the actual institution of politics itself. There is politics when there is a part of those who have no part, a part or

---

4. For a thought-provoking critique of Anderson's thesis, see Peter Fitzpatrick's *Modernism and the Grounds of Law* (Fitzpatrick 2001b, 116–20).

5. Gary Boire (2004) provides a deft but nuanced account of developments in the "Law and Literature" movement in "Symbolic Violence: Law, Literature, Interpretation," the afterword to "Law, Literature, Postcoloniality," a special issue of *Ariel*. With specific reference to a South African context, see Mark Sanders's *Ambiguities of Witnessing: Law and Literature in the Time of a Truth Commission* (2007). In his introduction to "Law and South African Literature" (2010), a special issue of *Current Writing*, Patrick Lenta offers a summative account of Law and Literature scholarship in South Africa.

party of the poor. Politics does not happen just because the poor oppose the rich. It is the other way round: politics (that is, the interruption of the simple effects of domination by the rich) causes the poor to exist as an entity.

Rancière 1999, 11

For Rancière, then, politics has to do with the "partition of what is common," and in his elaboration of the "distribution of the sensible," his understanding of politics is carried across to the realm of sensory perception. The distribution of the sensible is "the system of self-evident facts of sense perception that simultaneously discloses the existence of something in common and the delimitations that define the respective parts and positions within it" (Rancière 2004b, 12). It is an appreciation of the way in which a world of sensory perception is partitioned and shared within a social structure. Some things will be made visible in one segment of society, for example, but not another; some things will be actively silenced—or given the chance to be heard—in different spaces of a social organization. The distribution of the sensible is thus a way of dividing up the world, and people, as Rancière puts it in *Dissensus* (Rancière 2010, 36). It is a partitioning that separates and excludes as much as it creates certain spaces for participation. It is in this sense that aesthetics and politics for Rancière are inextricably tied. He writes that

> aesthetics can be understood in a Kantian sense—re-examined perhaps by Foucault—as the system of *a priori* forms determining what presents itself to sense experience. It is a delimitation of spaces and times, of the visible and the invisible, of speech and noise, that simultaneously determines the place and the stakes of politics as a form of experience.
>
> Rancière 2004b, 13

Thus, "figures of community are aesthetically designed"; "the important thing is that the question of the relationship between aesthetics and politics be raised at this level, the level of the sensible delimitation of what is common to the community, the forms of its visibility and of its organization" (Rancière 2004b, 18). Through the creation and partitioning of worlds of sensory experience, meaningful social engagements become possible; and aesthetic experience can thus be appreciated as intrinsic to our everyday relation to the world.

Part of the project of this book is to develop a discourse that understands better what is at stake in these aesthetic experiences and to question the role that aesthetic acts may have to play in our relations with others and in the creative projection of a more just future. Aesthetic acts—acts of law and acts of literature, as the chapters to follow demonstrate[6]—have the potential to bring new cognitive possibilities to light, challenging and reimagining existing lines of division and limitation, breaking new paths of meaning and communication, and initiating new lines of inquiry.

II

A negative tension, rather than the productive relation I have begun to develop in the first section of this chapter (that is, the relation between politics and aesthetics, or, differently put, the relation between philosophy and the creative arts, between the rational rule of law and the affective force of literature), has fueled dominant discourses around these topics for centuries. This has much to do with the long-standing influence of Plato's *Republic*, with its engaging discussion of the "ancient antagonism" between the philosophers and the poets (Plato 2003, §607b). In this section of the introduction I track contemporary aesthetic preoccupations back to Plato's dialogue, highlighting just a few aspects of a philosophical conversation (spanning more than two thousand years) in ways that inform my discussions in other parts of this book.

It is perhaps Kant who did most to bring aesthetic concerns within reach of serious ethical and political philosophical enquiry, but the view commonly attributed to Plato, thanks to the turn of the conversation in book 10 of the *Republic*, has held sway for centuries: that is to say, the view that the poets have nothing to contribute to matters of serious philosophical concern. Socrates and his friends, in their quest for an understanding of justice, sketch out a fanciful vision of an ideal social order; they reach the conclusion that poetry ought to be banished from the state, as it has yet to be proved that the arts "have a place in a well-run society" (Plato 2003, § 607c). The ills that the arts might bring to bear on a just state are numberless: "All the poets from Homer downwards have no grasp of truth but merely produce a superficial likeness of any subject they treat" (Plato 2003, § 600e); the artist makes his representations not "by reference to the object

---

6. "Acts of Literature" is the title of a book of essays by Jacques Derrida (1992a), edited and introduced by Derek Attridge.

as it actually is" but to its "superficial appearance"—his representation is "one of an apparition" and not of the truth (Plato 2003, § 598b). Socrates continues:

> But you will know that the only poetry that should be allowed in a state is hymns to the gods and paeans in praise of good men; once you go beyond that and admit the sweet lyric or epic muse, pleasure and pain become your rulers instead of law and the rational principles commonly accepted as best.
>
> Plato 2003, § 607a

This last argument—that the only poems to be admitted in a just state are hymns and paeans in praise of the gods and good men and that other forms of literature have the potential to derail the rule of law—has a particular poignancy in a history of South African letters: It has to do with the contested boundaries of the literary as much as it does with those of the law. In 1824, two Scottish settlers in the Cape Colony, John Fairbairn and the poet Thomas Pringle, asked the governor of the Cape, Lord Charles Somerset, for permission to launch the first literary journal in South Africa. Somerset, after some hesitation, granted his approval, on condition that nothing published should be "detrimental to the peace and safety of the Colony" (Robinson 1974, first page). The journal had ambitions of establishing a "Republic of Letters," and, in keeping with literary tastes of the time, foregrounded poetry over other genres. It also aimed to include articles ranging through topics such as natural science, moral philosophy, and "the principles of society."[7] But the journal was short-lived. After only two issues, Lord Somerset objected to "On the present state and prospects of the English emigrants in South Africa," an article sympathetic to the plight of British settlers on the eastern boundary line of the Colony, and the publication of the English edition of the journal ceased. In a letter dated August 16, 1824, Somerset argued that "he should greatly deviate from his duty, in giving countenance to an Establishment conducted by persons, who have *wilfully* paid so little regard to the Authorities and established Regulations of the colony" (cited in McDonald 2009, 9).

---

7. Peter McDonald offers an illuminating discussion of the *South African Journal* in his groundbreaking book *The Literature Police: Apartheid Censorship and its Cultural Consequences*. See McDonald's introduction, especially pages 2–15.

Later Somerset reiterated that he could not allow the founding of "an association which might have the tendency to produce political discussion" (cited in McDonald 2009, 9). In its incipient stages in South Africa, then, the promotion of the literary is associated with a dangerous politics—one that threatens the rule of law. Just over a century later, the complex relation between literature and censorship would have a definitive impact on the South African literary scene during the apartheid years.[8]

But where the *South African Journal* was an acknowledged threat to Somerset's authority in its capacity to disseminate empathetic knowledge of those living on the tenuous and threatened borderline of the Colony, Socrates and his friends are insistent that the poets know nothing and that their work has no serious value—yet this comes in the teeth of ordering their banishment from the just state. "We seem to be pretty well agreed," says Socrates in conclusion, "that the artist knows little or nothing about the subjects he represents and that the art of representation has no serious value; and that this applies above all to tragic poetry, epic or dramatic" (Plato 2003, § 602b).

Nevertheless, it is not without some reluctance that poetry and the dramatic arts are to be banished from the ideal state: "Even the best of us enjoy it," admits Socrates (Plato 2003, §605d), "especially when it's Homer" (Plato 2003, § 607d)—and should a poet visit the just state,

> we shall treat him with all the reverence due to a priest and giver of rare pleasure, but shall tell him that he and his kind have no place in our city, their presence being forbidden by our code, and send him elsewhere, after anointing him with myrrh and crowning him with fillets of wool.
>
> Plato 2003, § 398a

As the discussion draws to a close, Plato's characters seem increasingly reluctant to banish the poets forever—"let us freely admit that if drama and poetry written for pleasure can prove to us that they have a place in a well-run society, we will gladly admit them, for we know their fascination only too well ourselves" (Plato 2003, § 607c), and, further still,

> we should give [poetry's] defenders, men who aren't poets themselves but who love poetry, a chance of defending her in prose and proving

---

8. This is the terrain of Peter McDonald's sociohistoric study *The Literature Police*. The literary and visual works I have chosen to discuss in this book are for the most part created or set in the time of South Africa's transition to democracy. My project enters more explicitly into contemporary theoretical and philosophical debates than McDonald's does.

that she doesn't only give pleasure but brings benefit to human life and human society. And we will listen favourably, as we shall gain much if we find her a source of profit as well as pleasure.

Plato 2003, § 607d–e

In the language of *The Republic*, poetry has no serious value because the arts constitute "representations at the third remove from reality" (Plato 2003, § 598e); the subject of a painting or a poem is not the truth itself. It is not even a material object in the world but a representation of a perspectival aspect of something visible. Further, these representations are "easy to reproduce without any knowledge of the truth, because they are appearances and not realities" (Plato 2003, § 598e), and, as a result, they have "no serious value" (Plato 2003, § 602b).

This epistemological question is pivotal in John Locke's *An Essay Concerning Human Understanding* (first published in 1690). Locke's engagement with problems of representation in language is important: It makes us uneasy about any outright segregation of the philosophers and the poets, not so much in terms of what it says about the poets but because of the implications for any philosophical discourse. Locke mounts a carefully staged argument: Knowledge is not innate, and although sensory experience is vital, forming "*the materials of thinking*," knowledge is not reducible to perception (Locke 1997, 2.1.2, emphasis in the original, here and following). Reflection, the reasoned working out of connections and differences between experience-based ideas, grounds knowledge too. So far, so good, as far as the philosophers in Plato's *Republic* are concerned. But in "Of Words," book 3 of *An Essay Concerning Human Understanding*, Locke speaks about language in ways that foreground the *mediation* of words: Even the philosophers, through language, have questionable access to "the truth," "realities," in the terms of Plato's dialogue. Again, Locke presents his argument in careful steps: The "far *greatest part of words*," he writes, "*are general terms*" (3.3.1); "*it is impossible, that every particular thing should have a distinct peculiar name*" (3.3.2), and, third, "*a distinct name for every particular thing, would not be of any great use for the improvement of knowledge*" (3.3.4). What this amounts to is that words do not stand for "real essences." Instead, they stand for "nominal essences"—abstract, *generalizing* ideas in the mind that we construct ourselves for convenience. These nominal essences, with names annexed to them, are "creatures of our own making": "*general and universal,* belong not to the real existence of things; but *are the inventions* and *creatures of the understanding*, made by it for its own use, *and concern only signs*, whether words, or ideas" (3.3.11).

The radical move here (one that would be at the core of twentieth-century Saussurean linguistics) is to disaggregate words and things and to key language into a creative conceptual field. But it is perhaps Locke's presentation of his entire *approach* to the question of human knowledge that has the most far-reaching implications for the discussions in the rest of this book.

In the opening paragraphs of *An Essay Concerning Human Understanding*, Locke announces his project to be an inquiry into the origins, certainty, and extent of human knowledge, together with "the grounds and degrees of belief, opinion, and assent." He presents his project as having a "historical, plain method"; his is an attempt to give an "account of the ways, whereby our understandings come to attain those notions of things we have, and can set down any measures of the certainty of our knowledge, or the grounds of those persuasions, which are to be found amongst men, so various, different, and wholly contradictory." How does one account for *contradictory* views that can equally be "asserted somewhere or other with such assurance, and confidence," and embraced with "fondness, and devotion," and maintained with "resolution and eagerness"? We "may perhaps have reason to suspect," Locke continues, "that either there is no such thing as truth at all; or that mankind hath no sufficient means to attain a certain knowledge of it" (Locke, 1.1.2).

Presented this way, Locke's project holds out the tantalizing promise of the kind of radical postmodern philosophical investigation one would more readily associate with the likes of a Michel Foucault, and, indeed, Locke's philosophical resonance with Foucault is one that the contemporary philosopher Ian Hacking registers. Hacking points out that this foremost empiricist philosopher of the seventeenth century "thought that we understand concepts and knowledge better when we understand what puts them in place, what brings them into being." He goes on to speak insightfully of what he calls "the Lockean imperative"—that is, the injunction "to understand our thoughts and beliefs through an account of origins" (Hacking 2002, 63). This is how the first chapter of this book opens—with its consideration of *nomos*, the Greek word for "law."

The philosophy of human cognition, and the attempt to represent its object, takes another revolutionary turn in Immanuel Kant's *Critique of Pure Reason*, published in 1781. In the preface to the second edition (1787),

Kant announces his work to be tantamount to a Copernican revolution in philosophy:

> Up to now it has been assumed that all our cognition must conform to the objects; but all attempts to find out something about them *a priori* through concepts that would extend our cognition have, on this presupposition, come to nothing. Hence let us once try whether we do not get farther with the problems of metaphysics by assuming that the objects must conform to our cognition, which would agree better with the requested possibility of an *a priori* cognition of them, which is to establish something about objects before they are given to us. This would be just like the first thoughts of Copernicus, who, when he did not make good progress in the explanations of the celestial motions if he assumed that the entire celestial host revolves around the observer, tried to see if he might not have greater success if he made the observer revolve and left the stars at rest.
>
> Kant 1998, 110

A central preoccupation for Kant throughout his lifework is to ask how an objective universal claim might be possible, given that subjectivity is the basis of experience.[9] Judgment, in Kant, becomes a question of how we choose to represent the relation between the particular and the universal or (in more specifically Kantian terms) between intuition and concept. He makes a distinction between determinate and reflective judgments. A determinate judgment sees an object as a particular kind of thing ("this is a tomato"), but a reflective judgment, such as a judgment of taste, does not assign to an object properties that would easily place it empirically. The concept at work is indeterminate in the moment of our saying, "This is beautiful"; it is a judgment that has reference not to the empirical properties of the object—for example, the landscape or painting—under discussion but to the realization that "the order we perceive in the world is a reflection of the order we require for meaningful, intelligible experience" (Cazeaux 2000, 5). That is to say, as Clive Cazeaux deftly elucidates, "moments of beauty, for Kant, are moments when we glimpse the conditions for the possibility of experience" (Cazeaux 2000, 5).

---

9. For a succinct account of Kant's influence on philosophical aesthetics, see Clive Cazeaux's introduction to the section on nineteenth-century German aesthetics in *The Continental Aesthetics Reader* (Cazeaux 2000, 4–6).

An aesthetic experience, then, is fundamental to any intelligible engagement with one's world, and since "appearances are not things in themselves," as Kant observes in the *Critique of Pure Reason*, "but rather the mere play of our representations, which in the end come down to determinations of the inner sense" (Kant 1998, 230), then the development of that "inner sense" is what will enable a different appearance of the world.

The section "On Words" in Locke's *An Essay Concerning Human Understanding*, and Kant's Copernican Revolution in the *Critique of Pure Reason*, could perhaps be taken as implicit philosophical scaffolding for Ferdinand de Saussure's early-twentieth-century theory of the linguistic sign. "The linguistic sign unites, not a thing and a name," Saussure writes, "but a concept and a sound-image" (Saussure 1960, 66). On the one hand, Saussure's self-regulating linguistic system of differences is often (but mistakenly) taken to mean that reference to the world does not take place. Christopher Norris, for example, is not alone in his view that "the referential function" is "denied to language in all varieties of post-Saussurean discourse" (Norris 1984, 169).[10] On the other hand, Saussure has tempted those in his wake to reduce the world to textual construct, and one might be forgiven for thinking that the epitome of such a view is Derrida's scandalous assertion that "*il n'y a pas de hors-texte*" (Derrida 1967, 227)—"there is nothing outside the text" or, as I prefer to translate it, "there is no outside-text."

Turning to Derrida now (Derrida is an important figure in many of the chapters to follow): Careful attention to the paragraphs in which "*il n'y a pas de hors-texte*" appears makes for a more nuanced reading than is generally the case. For the English speaker the trouble begins with the usual translation, "there is nothing outside the text." The translation is misleading because it relies on the unquestioned assumption of an easy opposition between inside and outside—but it is precisely a philosophical *challenge* to the logic of an opposition like this one that is at the core of Derrida's lifework and that is also activated in the assertion "*il n'y a pas de hors-texte*." There is nothing that can be *signified, in and of itself*, without some sedimentation in a language, a concept, an image, a gesture, a text—in short (to use a characteristically Derridean phrase), in writing in general. One cannot do away with the text altogether, and still have a legitimate idea of what the text signifies as dif-

---

10. I have spoken about this in my article "'By Any Other Name': Kripke, Derrida, and an Ethics of Naming." But see especially David Schalkwyk's essay "Saussure, Names, and the Gap between Word and World."

ferent from itself. Writing stages the disappearance of a presence that could never have existed purely in its own terms anyway:

> For we have read *in the text* that the absolute present, nature, that which words like "real mother," etc., name, have always already slipped away, have never existed; that what opens meaning and language is writing as the disappearance of natural presence.
>
> Derrida 1967, 228, my translation; emphasis in the original[11]

Years later Derrida would provide a commentary on "there is nothing outside the text," glossing it as "there is nothing outside context" (Derrida 1988, 136). "In this form, which says exactly the same thing," Derrida tells us, "the formula would doubtless have been less shocking." But, he goes on to say, "I am not certain that it would have provided more to think about" (Derrida 1988, 136).

This reminds me of the preface to Wittgenstein's *Philosophical Investigations*: "I should not like my writing to spare other people the trouble of thinking. But, if possible, to stimulate someone to thoughts of his own" (Wittgenstein 2001, x^e). Yet further still, the juxtaposition of these two major twentieth-century philosophers is one route to thinking about a symbiotic, rather than an antagonistic, relation between philosophy and literature.[12] "What is the meaning of a word?" Wittgenstein asks as a way of opening the lectures published under the title *The Blue and Brown Books*—the lectures that would form the basis of *Philosophical Investigations*. The next sentence comes as a surprise: "Let us attack this question" (Wittgenstein 1994, 1). "We are up against one of the great sources of philosophical bewilderment," Wittgenstein explains in parenthesis, "a substantive makes us look for a thing that corresponds to it" (Wittgenstein 1994, 1). And it is this "looking for a thing" that makes literature—and especially fiction—come off second-best in the philosophy/art antagonism. Perhaps Bertrand Russell is the one who most spectacularly evinces the standoff between the philosophers and the poets with this conversation-stopper about Shakespeare's *Hamlet*: "The propositions in the play are false because there was no such man" (Russell 1940, 294).

---

11. "Car nous avons lu *dans le texte*, que le present absolu, la nature, ce que nomment les mots de 'mère réelle,' etc., se sont toujours déjà dérobés, n'ont jamais existé; que ce qui ouvre le sens et le langage, c'est cette écriture comme disparition de la presence naturelle" (Derrida 1967, 228, emphasis in the original).

12. See Henry Staten's seminal work *Wittgenstein and Derrida*.

That is why the language philosophy of the later Wittgenstein rather than, say, of Bertrand Russell is more congenial to the literary critic. The Wittgenstein of *Philosophical Investigations* has a completely different angle of approach: "The meaning of a word is its use in the language" (Wittgenstein 2001, § 43). Thus, in the Wittgenstein of *Philosophical Investigations*, the emphasis does not fall on questions about the truth conditions of a proposition (as it often does in analytic philosophies of language) or on the abstract relation between sign and referent (as in many post-Saussurean theories of language). Instead, language is considered as a social practice, in which the contingencies of cultural, historical, political, and other contexts are *actively brought to bear*. The supposed alternative of world *or* word is thus effectively bypassed by both Derrida and Wittgenstein, so that their philosophies of language have a condign application in literary studies. Further, literature is an instance of a highly sophisticated and specialized use *of* our everyday language; it is not an aberrantly different language altogether—"as though literature, theater, deceit, infidelity, hypocrisy, infelicity, parasitism, and the simulation of real life were not part of real life!" writes Derrida in *Limited Inc.* (Derrida 1988, 90).

Now back to Plato—and Wittgenstein. "So great is the natural magic of poetry," says the Socrates of the *Republic*. "Strip it of its poetic colouring, reduce it to plain prose, and I think you know how little it amounts to" (Plato 2003, § 601a–b). This can be taken in two ways (I am putting it in an outrageously rudimentary way):

1. The poets have nothing to say.
2. Poetic language enables something to be said.

Certainly, the tenor of the discussion in *The Republic* is (1). But (2) leads to interesting insights. Wittgenstein once said that his philosophical method could be summed up as being the "exact opposite of that of Socrates" (Monk 1990, 337–38). Plato's Socrates will initiate a discussion by asking a question such as "What is justice?" "What is knowledge?"—and then proceeding to seek an ideal essence common to all examples of justice or knowledge. Wittgenstein, on the other hand, looks *at*, rather than *past*, each instance of the use of a word as a way of speaking about its meaning. For Wittgenstein, then, "*essence* is expressed by grammar" (Wittgenstein 2001, § 371, Wittgenstein's emphasis) and "grammar tells us what kind of object anything is" (Wittgenstein 2001, § 373). "Grammar," in Wittgenstein's sense, is a way of speaking about meaning that is implicated within a network of sociocultural human interactions. Further, and picking up on (2) above, it is this Wittgensteinian understanding of grammar that, as David Schalkwyk usefully phrases it, "construes both the limits and the possibilities of the sayable" (Schalkwyk 1996, 92). Now, literature and other forms of aesthetic production can each be understood as constituting different grammars in this sense, so that the question arises in this form: What does a literary or an artistic grammar *enable* us to say? The question needs to be asked of philosophy as much as it does of literature and the arts more generally.

Throughout his writings, Wittgenstein is vigilant with regard to the limits set by his own mode of expression. In his preface to the *Tractatus*, he announces that the book will "draw a limit to thinking, or rather—not to thinking, but to the expression of thoughts; for, in order to draw a limit to thinking we should have to be able to think both sides of this limit (we should therefore have to be able to think what cannot be thought)" (Wittgenstein 1922, 27). The *Tractatus* is stylistically innovative: It consists of a series of meticulously numbered paragraphs, where the numbering orchestrates a complex hierarchy of emphasis, and a set of intricate relations between the propositions. Wittgenstein explains this in a footnote:

> The decimal figures as numbers of the separate propositions indicate the logical importance of the propositions, the emphasis laid upon them in my exposition. The propositions *n*.1, *n*.2, *n*.3, etc., are comments on proposition No. *n*; the propositions *n.m*1, *n.m*2, etc., are comments on proposition No. *n.m*; and so on.
>
> Wittgenstein 1922, 31

Again, but this time in the preface to *Philosophical Investigations*, Wittgenstein tells us about his philosophical method: He had intended, initially, that his "thoughts should proceed from one subject to another in a natural order, and without breaks," but "the best that I could write would never be more than philosophical remarks; my thoughts were soon crippled if I tried to force them on in any single direction against their natural inclination.— *And this was, of course, connected with the very nature of the investigation*" (Wittgenstein 2001, ix^e, my emphasis).

If, following the *Tractatus* now, "*The limits of my language* mean the limits of my world" (Wittgenstein 1922, § 5.6, Wittgenstein's emphasis), then any challenge to, or extension of, that linguistic limit constitutes a shift in the limit of what can be thought. Even though Socrates is all for "plain prose" (Plato 2003, § 601b) and what we would call third-person, reported speech

(Plato 2003, § 393a–98b), *The Republic* (like Plato's other writings) takes the form of a spirited dialogue, with Socrates, Glaucon, Adeimantus, and others all speaking in the first person. What would the Socratic method in philosophy have amounted to had Plato himself stuck to "plain prose" instead of using the genre of dramatic dialogue? Similar questions of other branches of philosophy could be asked: Where would existentialism be without the novel? What would have become of analytic philosophy without Russell's formulation of the mathematical language of formal logic? "A good route to philosophical fame is to found a *method*," says the entry for Russell in the *Oxford Companion to Philosophy* (Honderich 1995, 782, my emphasis).[13] For Russell, everyday language—"plain prose"—is crude to the extent of enshrining the "savage superstitions of cannibals" (cited in Honderich 1995, 782); the new language of formal logic enabled him to refine and shift the boundaries of philosophical thought.

In summary, then: This second section of the introduction brings us to a point of heightened awareness about the ways in which the lines, or limits, of our thought can be shifted and set by the modes of our discursive and artistic engagements with the world. What possibilities for thinking about a more just future are opened by these creative engagements with our world and by the philosophical discourses we use to talk about that engagement? These concerns inform the discussions throughout the book.

III

Before sketching out the main themes of each chapter, as I will do in section IV, let me return briefly to a question that underwrites all of the discussions to follow—namely, what value is there in an *aesthetic* discourse with reference to what is arguably the most significant moment in South Africa's legal and political history? Later chapters highlight contributions made by South African writers—such as Phaswane Mpe, Njabulo Ndebele, J. M. Coetzee and many others—but in beginning to address this question I find it helpful to refer to the Kantian inspiration of Drucilla Cornell's political philosophy, whose work in philosophies of *ubuntu*, in turn, becomes pertinent toward the end of this book. For the characters in Plato's *Republic*, as we have seen, the conclusion that "all the poets from Homer downwards

---

13. Pertinent to the discussion here, of course, are the methodological innovations of deconstruction.

have no grasp of truth but merely produce a superficial likeness of any subject they treat," and that the artist knows nothing about what he represents, entails the view that the arts have "no serious value" (Plato 2003, § 600e, § 602b). But in Kant, it is the recognition of the *limit* of human knowledge that provides a valuable basis for ethical thinking and that keeps open the possibility of an idea such as freedom. Cornell puts this across clearly:

> The critical philosophy of Immanuel Kant begins with a . . . humble understanding of the notion of the limit of theoretical knowledge, suggesting to us that the world as we know it is the world as we have represented it to ourselves; there is no beyond that the mind can reach out and grasp, and as Kant famously tells us, what we know in reality as scientific law is what we have put there.
>
> Cornell 2008, 3

That we cannot explain or grasp cognitively that which lies beyond our given conceptual scheme does not necessitate the view that intimations of freedom, or justice, or truth, are "obsolete" (Cornell 2008, 72). In fact, quite the contrary, as we read in Kant's "Fundamental Principles of the Metaphysics of Morals":

> We can explain nothing but what we can reduce to laws the object of which can be given in some possible experience. Freedom, however, is a mere idea, the objective reality of which can in no way be presented in accordance with laws of nature and so too cannot be presented in any possible experience; and because no example of anything analogous can ever be put under it, it can never be comprehended or even only seen. . . . Now, where determination by laws of nature ceases, there all *explanation* ceases as well, and nothing is left but *defense*, that is, to repel the objections of those who pretend to have seen deeper into the essence of things and therefore boldly declare that freedom impossible.
>
> Kant 1996, § 4:459

This is the way in which Cornell, via Kant, links the aesthetic and the political: First, "the future, as what is *other* to our present social reality, cannot be known in advance and already foreclosed by some grand theory" (Cornell 2008, 3). But then, if critical philosophy begins with the understanding that "we can never get beyond our own representations and the world as it is given to us by the imagination" (Cornell 2008, 4), it is both a feat and a responsibility of the imagination to begin to effect political change by recognizing the contingency of one's historical situation, and by trying to imagine it otherwise. Cornell's *Moral Images of Freedom* thus constitutes a sustained defense of "the role of the imagination and, more specifically, aesthetic ideas in political philosophy" (Cornell 2008, 11).

Ironically, this is precisely what Plato's *Republic* performatively *affirms*, despite its explicit, constative arguments to the contrary. The dialogue comprises an imaginative and intricate vision of an ideal state; Socrates and his interlocutors (as much as Plato himself) perform a strategic act of the imagination—which is to say, an aesthetic act—in order to come to a better understanding of the concept of justice. Years later, in the *Laws*, Plato would revisit the question about whether the "serious" poets should be granted entry into the state, and here the response to the poets is rather different from the one explicitly articulated in the *Republic*:

> Most honoured guests, we're tragedians ourselves, and our tragedy is the finest and best we can create. At any rate, our entire state has been constructed so as to be a "representation" of the finest and noblest life—the very thing we maintain is most genuinely a tragedy. So we are poets like yourselves, composing in the same *genre*, and your competitors as artists and actors in the finest drama, which true law alone has the natural power to "produce" to perfection (of that we're quite confident).
>
> Plato 1970b, § 817

In their efforts to imagine and to project the idea of a just social order, the lawgivers and the philosophers in Plato's later text become "poets" themselves.

IV

A reading of Plato's dialogues, alongside Chesterton's pronouncement that "art, like morality, consists of drawing the line somewhere," leads to the thought that an ethical world, like an artwork, is something that needs to be *created*; it is not a natural given. In the chapters to follow I examine the creative forces at work in imagining, drawing, and redrawing the lines in postapartheid South Africa.

Each chapter can be read as a freestanding essay, and the chapters do not need to be read in sequence. Nevertheless, I have divided the book into three parts—"Drawing the Line" (chapters 1 and 2), "Crossing the Line" (chapters 3, 4 and 5), and "Lines of Force" (chapters 6 and 7). Read in sequence, the chapters develop a sustained appreciation of the *aesthetic acts* (in Rancière's sense of the term) that are integrally part of recalibrating a socio-legal order. Throughout the book, my discussions refer to texts explicitly discussing lines and borderlines—texts by prominent philosophers, writers, and other thinkers, such as Heidegger's "Uber 'die Linie'" (literally, "Concerning 'the Line'" but more usually translated as "On the Question of Being"); Carl Schmitt's *Nomos of the Earth*; Paul Celan's "The Meridian"; Hillis Miller's *Ariadne's Thread: Story Lines*; Tim Ingold's *Lines: A Brief History*; Drucilla Cornell's *Philosophy of the Limit*; Njabulo Ndebele's *Fine Lines from the Box*. Perhaps what is most important is that each chapter *tests* the value of Euro-modern discourses within the context of aesthetic acts in South Africa's time of transitional justice. Yet each chapter also explores the active contribution that works from South Africa could make to Continental debates in contemporary aesthetics. Thus, chapter 1 ("Drawing the Line"), following what Ian Hacking would call a "Lockean imperative," places the term *nomos* under semantic and etymological pressure. How does a reading of Carl Schmitt's *The Nomos of the Earth* alongside Martin Heidegger's "The Origin of the Work of Art" lead to a nuanced reflection on contemporary literatures representing—and challenging—the legacy of fences and boundaries from a time of European colonial expansion? But *in turn*, what contribution do writers from South Africa, such as Herman Charles Bosman and J. M. Coetzee, make to a "philosophy of the limit"? The texts discussed in this chapter provoke further questions about the borderlines between law and literature, with specific reference to images of arrogations of land—and authorship. Chapter 2 ("Redrawing the Lines") asks how the linguistic theories of Roman Jakobson and Mikhail Bakhtin could lead to a clearer understanding of the way in which Nelson Mandela's Rivonia Trial statement was able to transform the oppressive language of apartheid law into a medium for active and radical political protest. The chapter also explores in some depth how Mandela's statement leads us to question assumptions we may have had about the boundaries between law and politics. Chapter 3 ("Justice and the Art of Transition") reads Derrida's "Force and Signification" and "Force of Law"—essays written nearly thirty years apart—alongside each other, exploring the force of art and the force of law at work in the building (both literal and metaphorical) of South Africa's new Constitutional Court. The chapter examines the relation between law and justice with reference to the Derrida essays and to artworks by Willem Boshoff, William Kentridge, and others involved in aesthetic and political decisions about the architectural design of the Constitutional Court building in Hillbrow. Chapter 4 ("Intersections: Ethics and Aesthetics") sets out with a reflection on an everyday encounter in South Africa—the purchasing of a craft item from a street hawker at a traffic-light intersection—and goes on to ask to what extent the ethical philosophy of Emmanuel Levinas might be helpful in a daily practice of an ethics of address. Chapter 5 ("Philosophers, Poets, and Other Animals") sets out with a reflection on a comment made by Lucy Lurie in J. M. Coetzee's novel *Disgrace*. "On the list of the nation's priorities," says Lucy, "animals come nowhere" (Coetzee 1999a, 73). The chapter pays particular attention to J. M. Coetzee's *The Lives of Animals* and to another contemporary philosophical dialogue, Paola Cavalieri's *The Death of the Animal*, and takes Levinasian ethics further in relation to questions about "natural law": What does Levinas have to offer when we are confronted with post-Darwinian thoughts of extinction (of languages, cultures, and peoples) and with thoughts of all-too-entrenched racial lines and the readily assumed lines segregating humans from other animals? What does literature have to offer in these ethical debates usually considered to be the domain of philosophy? Chapter 6 ("Visible and Invisible: What Surfaces in Three Johannesburg Novels?") explores the extent to which Merleau-Ponty's phenomenology offers valuable insights in a reading of contemporary South African novels representing the palimpsestic city of Johannesburg. A juxtaposition of novels by Ivan Vladislavić, Marlene van Niekerk, and Phaswane Mpe shows just how complex the "imagined communities" of Johannesburg are, troubling any assumptions about the ease with which Euro-modern discourses can be applied to a local context. Chapter 7 ("Who Are We?"), which opens onto the conclusion of this book, sets up a dialogue between Jean-Luc Nancy's *The Inoperative Community* and African communitarian philosophies of *ubuntu*. What contribution does *ubuntu* make to contemporary philosophies of community, and to what extent can works such as those by Jean-Paul Sartre (*What Is Literature?*), Jean-Luc Nancy (*The Inoperative Community*), and Benedict Anderson (*Imagined Communities*) help us to think through to possible postaparthied communities of listeners, viewers, and readers?

Taken together, these chapters invite reflection on a possible aesthetics of transitional justice. At the same time the book makes an appeal for the justice of a postapartheid *aesthetic* enquiry, as opposed to simply a political or legal one. If aesthetic acts can be understood to calibrate the terms of cultural, political, and ethical engagements in our world, what kind of critical discourse would be condign to appreciating such an understanding, and to what extent do the processes and practices of aesthetic acts themselves *generate* the discourses and modes of thinking more usually identified—and kept apart—as legal and political philosophy?

PART I

Drawing the Line

1

Drawing the Line

I

"In many ways law is colonialism's first language," writes Gary Boire in his afterword to the special edition of *Ariel: Law, Literature, Postcoloniality* (Boire 2004, 231). This chapter pays attention to this "first language"—the scene of the *nomos*, that very first significant plough line drawn in the ground, marking the boundary of an arrogated territory. This act of drawing the line is also an "aesthetic act" in the sense that Rancière gives to the term, and that I delineated in the introduction: an act that reconfigures perceptions of what counts, of what matters, and of what is allowed within a designated social order.[1] In *Modernism and the Grounds of Law*, social and legal philosopher

---

1. Englishmen Charles Mason and Jeremiah Dixon began surveying for the Maryland–Pennsylvania border in 1763. The Mason-Dixon line, as it became known, marked the boundary between the free and the slave states. At first it was thought "impossible for the Art of Man" to draw this line, but, as Edwin Danson tells us, it was after their successful astronomical expedition to South Africa that Mason and

Peter Fitzpatrick speaks of the "spatial locating of law's range via the obliging etymology of 'nomos'" (Fitzpatrick 2001b, 91, my emphasis). He goes on to cite Cornelia Vismann's essay, "Starting from Scratch: Concepts of Order in No Man's Land," which describes the "initial scene of the law":

> The primordial scene of the *nomos* opens with a drawing of a line in the soil. This very act initiates a specific concept of law, which derives order from the notion of space. The plough draws lines—furrows in the field—to mark the space of one's own. As such, as ownership, the demarcating plough touches the juridical sphere. . . . The primordial act as described here brings together land and law, cultivation and order, space and *nomos*.
>
> Vismann 1997, 46–47, cited in Fitzpatrick 2001b, 91–92

Vismann's paper constitutes a reading ("an enthralling account and analysis" in Fitzpatrick's terms [Fitzpatrick 2001b, 225]) of Carl Schmitt's influential *The Nomos of the Earth*, which, in turn, provides an extended reflection on the relation between the arrogation of land and legal title. Schmitt writes about "land appropriation as the primeval act in founding law" (Schmitt 2003, 45); the etymology of *nomos*—which in Schmitt's account refers to a boundary line drawn in the soil marking ownership of the land as much as it refers to the rule of law within a community—serves to justify his appeal for a return to a "normative order of the earth" (Schmitt 2003, 39) and as an elaboration of his leading thesis: "Law is bound to the earth and related to the earth" (Schmitt 2003, 42). Peter Fitzpatrick's nuanced discussion of *nomos* takes further Vismann's critique of Schmitt's relentlessly spatial account of the law, even while Fitzpatrick himself takes the "obliging etymology" of *nomos* on board. His notion of "the other, responsive dimension of space" (Fitzpatrick 2001b, 93) offers provocative commentary on Schmitt's understanding of the relation between *nomos* and the law defined as spatial orientation.

By way of an extended engagement with Fitzpatrick's reading of Schmitt's *Nomos of the Earth*, this chapter proposes what is perhaps a new field of

---

Dixon could begin their geodetic survey (Danson 2001, 1). Danson's wonderful book, *Drawing the Line: How Mason and Dixon Surveyed the Most Famous Border in America*, offers a revelatory insight: "The Greek Earth-centred universe within its celestial sphere, while erroneous, is for convenience still used today by surveyors and astronomers. Viewed from the Earth, the stars do seem to be wheeling endlessly across the sky from east to west; in reality, it is Earth turning from west to east. Centred on Earth, and of infinite radius, the celestial sphere is imagined as being a vast globe" (Danson 2001, 34–35).

enquiry, namely, an *aesthetics of law*. More specifically put: If the primordial scene of the law is the act of drawing the line (in both a literal and a figurative sense), then it becomes possible to think through what an aesthetics of law might entail. This chapter does just that, reading Carl Schmitt's *The Nomos of the Earth* alongside Martin Heidegger's "The Origin of the Work of Art," which was first presented as a lecture in Freiburg in 1935 and then later expanded into a tripartite lecture series delivered in Frankfurt in 1936.

My discussion in this chapter takes the concept of an "aesthetics of law" further than Fitzpatrick himself does in any substantive or explicit way, but at the same time my argument is inspired by an analysis of Fitzpatrick's literary style. A distinctive feature of this style is his extensive and creative use of quotations from a range of other sources. Literary, philosophical, psychoanalytic, anthropological, and critical-legal texts become the colorful and tightly woven-in threads that make up the fabrics of his own arguments. The sustained, and even foregrounded device of quoting and alluding to other works is characteristic, too, of several of the modernist literary texts to which Fitzpatrick himself refers with such insight.[2] In my discussions of Fitzpatrick's work, I play up this allusiveness, following through the aesthetic and ethical implications of the use of citation in his own critical-legal discourse. In his insistent responsiveness to—and incorporation of—the writings of others in his texts, Fitzpatrick not only speaks about but *performs* what he might call the disruptive ambivalence of instantiating a conceptual field that depends on what is ever beyond but, at the same time, incipient within it. Through its engagement with Fitzpatrick's writing, this chapter moves toward a philosophical consideration of the limit of the law and on toward a discussion of the relation between law and literature. Interleaving my discussions are references to works by South African writer Herman Charles Bosman (best known for his short stories set in the Marico district of the Transvaal) and to fiction and critical writings by Nobel Prize–winning author J. M. Coetzee.

But let us return to Carl Schmitt and that obliging etymology of *nomos*—the Greek word for law—which also quite literally refers to a drawing of the line in the soil.

---

2. A core preoccupation of Peter Fitzpatrick's writing is the relation between law and literature. The focus of my discussion in this chapter is Fitzpatrick's *Modernism and the Grounds of Law* but see also his "Juris-fiction: Literature and the Law of the Law" (Fitzpatrick 2004) and "Law Like Poetry: 'Burnt Norton'" (Fitzpatrick 2001a).

II

In this section I am concerned with the image of the law as fence or *nomos*, and I begin by picking out and following back to its source one of the citation threads in Fitzpatrick's *Modernism and the Grounds of Law*. The passage quoted from Cornelia Vismann's essay in the opening section of this chapter—and quoted in *Modernism and the Grounds of Law*—in its turn alludes to Carl Schmitt's extended reflection on the *nomos*, a reflection that brings *nomos* into the field of a philosophical, historical, and politically charged discourse.

In the foreword to *The Nomos of the Earth in the International Law of the Jus Publicum Europaeum*, Carl Schmitt presents the concept of *nomos* as having a primordial, foundational, and even chthonic quality. "Human thinking again must be directed to the elemental orders of terrestrial being here and now," he writes. "We seek to understand the normative order of the earth" (Schmitt 2003, 39). *Nomos*, for Schmitt, links order and orientation: "*Nomos* comes from *nemein*—a [Greek] word that means both 'to divide' and 'to pasture.' Thus, *nomos* is the immediate form in which the political and social order of a people becomes spatially visible" (Schmitt 2003, 70). The boundary line, or fence, or wall, for Schmitt takes on an unequivocally positive and spatially visible relation to what is enclosed and, hence, to the law: "The solid ground of the earth is delineated by fences, enclosures, boundaries, walls, houses, and other constructs. Then, the orders and orientations of human social life become apparent. Then, obviously, families, clans, tribes, estates, forms of ownership and human proximity, also forms of power and domination, become visible" (Schmitt 2003, 42).

Further, and importantly in Schmitt, the concrete historical event of land appropriation is intrinsically bound up in the concept of law. Schmitt speaks of land appropriation as being the "archetype of a constitutive legal process"; it "creates the most radical legal title, in the full and comprehensive sense of *radical title*" (Schmitt 2003, 47). Even further still, it is the historical act of land appropriation that grants conceptual legitimacy to the law: "We must take heed that the word not lose its connection to a historical process—to a constitutive act of spatial ordering" (Schmitt 2003, 71); "it is a constitutive historical event—an act of *legitimacy*, whereby the legality of a mere law first is made meaningful" (Schmitt 2003, 73). Carl Schmitt approvingly cites the German linguist Jost Trier: "In the beginning was the fence," says Trier. "Fence, enclosure, and border are deeply interwoven in the world formed by men, determining its concepts. The enclosure gave birth to the shrine by removing it from the ordinary, placing it under its own laws, and entrusting it to the divine" (cited in Schmitt 2003, 74). Thus *nomos* "is a fence-word" (Schmitt 2003, 75), and "every *nomos* consists of what is within its own bounds" (Trier 1942, 232, cited in Schmitt 2003, 75).

Schmitt sees the action of the *nomos* as having three stages: appropriation, division, and cultivation (Schmitt 2003, 351), and the emphasis of his inquiry is on what is inside the boundary, what the fence tells about the enclosed field it delineates. Hence, "this is the original meaning of *nomos*," writes Fitzpatrick, citing Dudley Young, "that portion of food-bearing land (we still call it 'keep') through which my sheep may safely graze" (Young 1992, 317, cited in Fitzpatrick 2001b, 92). Schmitt notes that from the sixteenth to the twentieth century, the cultivated, and—by extension—the civilized field demarcated by European International Law was taken to be representative of an order applicable to the whole earth. Further, "*Civilization* was synonymous with *European* civilization" (Schmitt 2003, 86), and the new world was considered not enemy territory but free space, open to European occupation. But the presumed spatial certainty of what is bounded, unequivocally circumscribed by the *nomos*, becomes more complex with colonial expansion in Africa. The "crucial distinction between European and non-European or colonial soil," writes Schmitt's translator, G. L. Ulmen, "was lost in Africa, and with it the meaning of the legal distinction of 'beyond the line,' which separated the reach of European public law from the sphere of lawlessness" (Ulmen 2003, 26–27).

If Carl Schmitt's thesis is right, then one can surely trace apartheid laws in South Africa back to the time of its colonial arrogations. And if Schmitt's translator is right, then one can also appreciate how European colonial lines would be far more difficult to draw, justify, and maintain—in spatial terms as much as in political or legal terms.[3] Ulmen's observation leads to the insight that in the colonies, the physical, geographic disaggregation of a single boundary line and the ambit of a jurisdiction brings with it the troubling of the conjunctive metaphoric force of drawing the line and laying down the law.

---

3. Social anthropologist Tim Ingold, in his innovative and engaging study *Lines: A Brief History*, has this to say about the drawing of colonial lines: "Colonialism . . . is not the imposition of linearity upon a non-linear world, but the imposition of one kind of line on another. It proceeds first by converting the lines along which life is lived into boundaries in which it is contained, and then by joining up these now enclosed communities, each confined to one spot, into vertically integrated assemblies" (Ingold 2007, 2–3).

Literary texts (in contrast to Carl Schmitt's thesis) offer an appreciation of a much more fraught relation between territorial boundaries and the limit of what is just, perhaps most especially in colonial and postcolonial contexts. My illustrative example here is from the short story "Unto Dust" by South African writer Herman Charles Bosman (1905–51). The story was first published in the journal *Trek* in February 1949—that is, just months after D. F. Malan's apartheid Nationalist Party came into power in 1948; the story's politically subversive undertow is perhaps best appreciated in that context. Although written in English, many of Bosman's stories capture the rhythms of the Afrikaans language and the practice and mindset of the everyday in the Groot Marico farming district in the Transvaal. Bosman's irony is deftly executed through the use of a first-person farmer-raconteur, Oom Schalk Lourens:

> Once, during the malaria season in the Eastern Transvaal [Oom Schalk relates], it seemed to me, when I was in a higher fever and like to die, that the whole world was a big burial-ground. I thought it was the earth itself that was a graveyard, and not just those little fenced-in bits of land dotted with tombstones in the shade of a Western Province oak-tree or by the side of a Transvaal koppie. This was a nightmare that worried me a great deal, and so I was very glad, when I recovered from the fever, to think that we Boers had properly marked-out places on our farms for white people to be laid to rest in, in a civilised Christian way, instead of having to be buried just anyhow, along with a dead wild-cat, maybe, or a Bushman with a clay pot, and things.
>
> Bosman 2006, 262–23

Oom Schalk mentions this to his friend, Stoffel Oosthuizen, who offers some comforting words against high-flown talk of death as the great leveller. "He would still like to see things proved," Oom Schalk reports Stoffel Oosthuizen as saying. Schalk continues: "The first time he heard that sort of talk about death coming to all of us alike, and making us all equal, Stoffel Oosthuizen's suspicions were aroused. It sounded like a speech made by one of those liberal Cape politicians" (Bosman 2006, 263). Stoffel goes on to tell a story (supposedly to "illustrate his contention" that death is *not* the great leveller) about Hans Welman's death and about the impossibility, six months later, of distinguishing his bones from those of the black man Oosthuizen killed in the same place in a bush skirmish in the Transvaal. Oosthuizen and his friends have the task of bringing Hans Welman's remains back to his

widow for Christian burial on the farm, which was named Nietverdiend—
"Undeserved." Long after the funeral, the black man's dog can still sometimes be seen in the vicinity of the graveyard on Hans Welman's farm. Once Stoffel Oosthuizen has told his story, Oom Schalk comments, "I don't know whether he told the story incorrectly, or whether it was just that kind of a story, but, by the time he had finished, all my uncertainties had, I discovered, come back to me" (Bosman 2006, 263).

Throughout Bosman's work, images of fences and graveyards are striking in that they invite thoughts of the mutability and contingency of the human boundaries they are meant to set and stabilize: barbed-wire fences sag and are corroded by rust; memories are obliterated by the erasure of names on stones bleached and weathered by sun, rain, wind, and sand. Traces of human passing are lost as cemetery plots and graves recede, indiscriminately, back into the landscape. Fences and tombstones are poignant reminders of the very phenomena they are meant to keep at bay, to the extent that "those little fenced-in bits of land" seem hardly up to the task of isolating and defining the perimeters of "Boer," "white people," "Christian," "civilised"—or even of human existence itself—as something assuredly different from other animal life. The *story* that Stoffel Oosthuizen relates, intended to illustrate and justify the idea of what is fenced in ("After all, that was one of the reasons why the Boers had trekked away into the Transvaal and the Free State . . . because the British Government wanted to give the vote to any Cape Coloured person walking about with a kroes head and cracks in his feet" [Bosman 2006, 263]), insists instead on the uncertainties it is meant to fence out.

Bosman's story, published in February 1949, is surely prescient and subversive in foregrounding the *insecurities* created by the attempt to explain and justify exclusionary racial, religious, and colonial lines. The magnitude of the apartheid government's self-constructed sense of threat, at the same time as the publication of Bosman's story, can surely be registered in the spectacularly divisive laws it instituted immediately upon coming into power: 1949 saw the Prohibition of Mixed Marriages Act; 1950, the Suppression of Communism Act, the Population Registration Act, the Group Areas Act, the Immorality Amendment Act, and the banning of the South African Communist party.

For Herman Charles Bosman's characters, their predicament is focused through a colonial lens: The "properly marked-out places on our farms for white people to be laid to rest in, in a civilised Christian way" (Bosman 2006,

263), do not seem able to sustain reference to colonial, let alone European soil. The loss of the distinction between the civilized and the uncivilized has an elemental quality beyond the reach of any politics in the thought that "the whole world was a big burial-ground," that "the earth itself . . . was a graveyard" (Bosman 2006, 263).

Taking the cue from Bosman: The complexity of our understanding of the spatial range of the *nomos* intensifies as soon as we undertake further serious thinking about the *logic* of the limit. In thinking the boundary, or the limit, or the fence, one is often led to think foremost of what is supposedly *excluded* or beyond the range of that limit. In Bosman's writing, the effect is to satirize racist and colonial attitudes in a localized setting, but in much contemporary legal and political philosophy, the question of the limit takes on a further, if more abstract ethical resonance. The "philosophy of the limit" (to use Drucilla Cornell's name-phrase for deconstruction), with reference to Derrida's "'logic of parergonality,' demonstrates how the very establishment of a system as a system implies a *beyond* to it, precisely by virtue of what it excludes" (Cornell 1992, 1). Moving away from Schmitt's resolutely spatially determined legal interiors, Fitzpatrick refers to Jorge Luis Borges's *Dreamtigers* and to Lewis Carroll's "The Hunting of the Snark" (in turn, examples both discussed by Boaventura de Sousa Santos, to whom Fitzpatrick also refers) and speaks of the irresolution of law's spatial determinations: "Whilst determination can never be completely spatially formed, responsiveness cannot be ever completely unformed" (Fitzpatrick 2001b, 90–91).

In the work of both Fitzpatrick and Cornell, the *irresolution* of what is inside the supposed boundary, thanks to its responsive relation to what is beyond it, takes on a positive ethical coloring. For Cornell reading Derrida, the "project is not only to show us why and how there is always the Other to the system; it is also to indicate the ethical aspiration behind that demonstration" (Cornell 1992, 2). Further, and more specifically, Cornell's undertaking is to

> show the significance for legal interpretation of Derrida's own understanding of justice as an aporia that inevitably serves as the limit to any attempt to collapse justice into positive law.
>
> Cornell 1992, 2

By way of a thinking-through of this philosophy of the limit in relation to the tensions and suspensions between justice and the law, both Fitzpatrick and Cornell offer a challenge to Schmitt's materially spatial conceptions. Fitzpatrick takes this further still: The content of the law is not only irresolute but vacuous.

III

In his nuanced discussion in *Modernism and the Grounds of Law*, Fitzpatrick demonstrates the ways in which the common law, "despite its vaunted and supposedly exceptional grounding, provides no alternative to law's vacuity" (Fitzpatrick 2001b, 93). This passage reminds me of Heidegger's discussion of art in his essay "The Origin of the Work of Art." In this section I bring aspects of Heidegger's aesthetic theory into conversation with Fitzpatrick's theory of law. The discussion ultimately brings Heidegger's use of the word *Riss* (a rift, a fissure, a scratch, and *also* a draft, a plan, a sketch, according to the *Langenscheidt Standard Dictionary*) into juxtaposition with the concept of *nomos* and the philosophy of the limit, as I have been sketching it out thus far. But first, let us consider the idea of law's vacuity in relation to Heidegger's discussion of art. What is the origin of the work of art? Heidegger asks. Is it the artist, or the work?

> The artist is the origin of the work. The work is the origin of the artist. Neither is without the other. Nevertheless, neither is the sole support of the other. In themselves and in their interrelations artist and work *are* each of them by virtue of a third thing which is prior to both, namely . . . art.
> . . . But can art be an origin at all? Where and how does art occur? *Art—this is nothing more than a word to which nothing actual any longer corresponds.*
>
> Heidegger 1993, 143 my emphasis (except the word "are")

Perhaps both the artist and the work have been vaunted as art's grounding, but just as Fitzpatrick registers law's vacuity, Heidegger draws attention to art's correspondence to "nothing actual." For Heidegger, "art is truth setting itself to work" (Heidegger 1993, 167)—and he goes on to discuss this idea in some detail with specific reference to the building of a Greek temple. I track this example here at least in part because of the kinetic relation Heidegger establishes between what he calls "world" and "earth"—which will bring me back to the concept of the *nomos* (recall Schmitt's *Nomos of the Earth*)—via the multivalency of Heidegger's term, *Riss*.

First to the temple: We are perhaps tempted to think that the temple is built as an act of portraying the prior existence of the gods in that place and that the ground there is already holy. However, in Heidegger's subtle account, a "building, a Greek temple, portrays nothing. It simply stands there in the middle of the rock-cleft valley," and yet, "by means of the temple, the god is present in the temple. This presence of the god is in itself the extension and delimitation of the precinct as a holy precinct" (Heidegger 1993, 167). Thus, even while it portrays nothing, it is the temple building that signifies the ground as sacred, that creates within it the shape of meaning and human destiny in acts of nature (birth, death, and other natural phenomena, such as the existence of other animals or the weather) that in themselves are void and heedless of any meaning that humans might attribute to them. This, in turn, makes me think of a conversation between two characters in Anne Michaels's novel *The Winter Vault*:

> A temple was the first power station. Think of the formulas invented,
> the physical achievement of thousands of men moving a mountain,
> hewing and hauling stone tonne by tonne, often hundreds of kilometres,
> to a site of precise coordinates—all in an attempt to capture spirits.
>   To define space. . . . No. Not to give shape to space, but to give shape to . . . emptiness.
>
> Michaels 2009, 9 (second ellipsis in the original)

The temple in Heidegger gives shape not only to the abstract emptiness of a human world with respect to the gods—but to the physical earth surrounding the building. The presence of a work of art, for Heidegger, is not simply a "bare placing"; it instantiates a site for human dedication to, and consecration of, a meaningful world where truth finds its opening. "Towering up within itself, the work opens up a *world* and keeps it abidingly in force" (Heidegger 1993, 169), and "To be a work means to set up a world" (Heidegger 1993, 170). At the same time, the ground on which the temple is built *becomes* "earth"—in Heidegger's special sense. The temple gives definition to the rocks on which it is built as sturdy foundation, say. It makes manifest the violence of the storm raging above it, or of the radiance of the light of day when the sun glints off its stones. In the natural phenomena that arise, thanks to the building of the temple, "earth occurs essentially as the sheltering agent," and so the "temple-work, standing there, opens up a world and at the same time sets this world back again on earth, which itself only thus emerges as native ground" (Heidegger 1993, 168).

What gradually comes into focus in Heidegger's essay is a vertiginous relation between "world" and "earth"—both of which are called forth in the creation of a work of art. What interests me here is the metaphor Heidegger uses to describe this relation—that is, the image of *Riss*. The German word *Riss* (as I have mentioned) designates a fissure, rift, or scratch, but it is also a design, draft, or drawing, and, even further still, it is worth noting that it is a cognate of the English word "writing" (see editor's note, Heidegger 1993, 188). Hillis Miller helpfully threads the etymological narrative this way:

> The word *write* itself comes from Old English *writan*, from Germanic *writan* (unattested), meaning to tear, scratch. All the *graph* words— graph itself, paragraph, . . . epigraph, . . . —go back to words meaning pencil, to inscribe, or the inscription itself: Latin *graphium*, pencil, from Greek *graphion*, pencil, stylus, from *graphein*, to write, derived from the root, *gerebh-*, scratch . . . "Sign" is from Latin *signum*, distinctive mark or feature, seal. "Glyph" is from Greek *gluphein*, to carve, from the root *gleubh-*, to cut, cleave. "Mark" comes from Old English *mearc*, boundary, hence landmark, sign, trace. The root is *merg-*, meaning boundary or border, that is, a line traced around the edges of a region.
>
> Miller 1992, 9

In Albert Hofstadter's translation of Heidegger's essay, *Riss* is often rendered as "rift-design" in English, and it is clear that Heidegger himself is playing up the multivalency of the term. "For in truth" writes Heidegger, "art lies hidden within nature; he who can wrest it from her, has it." Heidegger goes on to provide a gloss on his use of the word "wrest"—*Reissen*: "*Reissen heisst hier Herausholen des Risses und den Riss reissen mit der Reissfeder auf dem Reissbrett*"—in Hofstadter's translation: "'Wrest' here means to draw out the rift and to draw the design with the drawing-pen on the drawing-board" (Heidegger 1993, 195, German in the footnote). This rift, or design, for Heidegger, thus *puts into relation* what is simultaneously separated and joined on either side of the *Riss*—world and earth or, even more crudely put, art and nature: "This rift does not let the opponents break apart; it brings what opposes measure and boundary into its common outline"—and even further still: "The rift is the drawing together, into a unity, of sketch and basic design, breach and outline" (Heidegger 1993, 188). Thus the world of art is responsive to the earthly forms in nature; in fact, art discloses those forms—it does not exclude them, nor does it abstract or reduce them to the supposedly determinate limits of its own world.

Now the last sentence of the previous paragraph purposely carries verbal echoes of Peter Fitzpatrick's own way of writing about law. The alignment I am beginning to suggest between a philosophy of law and a philosophy of art may seem far fetched—but it is an alignment obligingly provided by Fitzpatrick himself (as we shall see in a moment) and also by Heidegger, in volume 1 of *Nietzsche: The Will to Power as Art*:

> The artistic states are those which place themselves under the supreme command of measure and law, taking themselves beyond themselves in order to advance.
>
> Heidegger 1991, 130

And further:

> Such states are what they essentially are when, willing out beyond themselves, they are more than they are.
>
> Heidegger 1991, 130

I read close parallels here in Fitzpatrick's accounts of the law in *Modernism and the Grounds of Law*:

> Determination itself depends integrally on law's responsiveness and this responsive dimension is always beyond the determinant.
>
> Fitzpatrick 2001b, 107

And:

> Even at its most settled, or especially at its most settled, law could not "be" otherwise than responsive to what was beyond its determinate content "for the time being," but neither could it dissipate in a pure responsiveness.
>
> Fitzpatrick 2001b, 104

What this amounts to, finally, is "the irresolution of law's dimensions" (Fitzpatrick 2001b, 107), to the extent that law's capacity for responsiveness, in Fitzpatrick's philosophy of law, is indeed part of what constitutes it in the first place. Bringing this finally back to the *nomos*, in Fitzpatrick's inimitable style:

> A return to that obliging etymology of nomos can now extend beyond the fixing of law in the bounded earth and unfold more of how the responsive may be "placed" in law: "with a supremely judicious sense

of metaphor, the Greeks also used '*nomos*' to designate song or melody, that portion of structured time through which my emotions . . . may safely range in search of nourishment without fear of being ecstatically carried away."

Fitzpatrick 2001b, 101, citing Young 1992, 317–18

There is a certain sense in Heidegger's work, as well as in Fitzpatrick's, that art/law does not simply exclude, but in fact makes possible, and even brings forth that other to which law is intrinsically responsive; the *nomos*, *Riss*, or outline evokes thoughts of what lies beyond it, unsettling complacent preconceptions of what is supposedly stabilized within its border. Further still, if part of what constitutes the law is its responsiveness to this other, then what is "other" to the law is not dispensable but a structural condition for law's being what it is. Within the specific context of Schmitt's rigidly spatial conception of *nomos* and other "talismanic spatial metaphors of inside and outside—of boundaries, terrain and atemporal demarcation" to posit the idea of autonomous law, Fitzpatrick's concern is "to show how the very effort at such determinant positing calls forth, or at least indicates the need of, the other, responsive dimension of space" (Fitzpatrick 2001b, 93, with reference to Davies 1996, 18, Davies 1998, 155–56, and Derrida 1992b, 6).

IV

Ever since Plato's *Republic*, poetry has been presented as law's other. In the dialogue, Socrates, Glaucon, Adeimantus, and others set out in detail their dream of a just state, and they decide that poetry and the dramatic arts ought to be excluded from it. Once you admit "the sweet lyric or epic muse," says Socrates, "pleasure and pain become your rulers instead of law and the rational principles commonly accepted as best" (Plato 2003, § 607a); the poet

> wakens and encourages and strengthens the lower elements in the mind to the detriment of reason, which is like giving power and political control to the worst elements in the state and ruining the better elements. The dramatic poet produces a similarly bad state of affairs in the mind of the individual, by encouraging the unreasoning part of it.
>
> Plato 2003, § 605b–c

If philosophy identifies the just state and its laws as being on the side of reason and identifies poetry and the arts generally as being on the side of "feelings" (§ 605d), "instinctive desires" (§ 606a), and "desires and feelings of pleasure and pain" (§ 606d), then the logical conclusion is that the arts have no place within the domain of the law.

Nevertheless, I would argue that the very core of Fitzpatrick's oeuvre consists in a sustained critique of the kind of mutually exclusive dualisms that are easy to find in Plato's dialogue.[4] In two of his papers, Fitzpatrick challenges a Manichean approach to law and its other with specific reference to law and poetry. In "Law like Poetry: 'Burnt Norton'" (2001a) and "Juris-fiction: Literature and the Law of the Law" (2004), Fitzpatrick argues that the logic at work in both law and literature is a responsiveness to what is supposedly beyond the limit of each respective discipline. In "Juris-fiction" Fitzpatrick states this explicitly: "Law and literature . . . share the same ambivalence between existent instantiation and what is ever beyond yet incipient in it" (Fitzpatrick 2004, 222)—even more radically, the "'disruptive ambivalence' that constitutes the law can be derived from a quality of literature" (Fitzpatrick 2004, 215). In its call for a *decision* in each legal case (the outcome of a case is not absolutely foreseeable in advance), "what is always involved with the law . . . is the creative reaching out to a possibility beyond its determinate existence, a beyond where law "finds itself" in being integrally tied to, and incipiently encompassing of, its exteriority" (Fitzpatrick 2004, 221).

Throughout his work, Fitzpatrick links law and literature through their responsiveness to what is yet to come as a possible constituent of them—which leads us to question complacent assumptions about where the borderlines of those disciplines really are. In his essays specifically focused on law and literature, Fitzpatrick's argument develops by way of philosophical reflections on—and incisive and sensitive close readings of—fiction and poetry, perhaps most notably the work of modernist and other twentieth-century poets: T. S. Eliot, Wallace Stevens, and W. H. Auden, to name just a few.

But increasingly what has come to interest me is not only what Fitzpatrick *says about* law and literature in his work but what he *does* in his own writing. A characteristic feature of his stylistic and conceptual approach (and this is a feature that I have foregrounded in this chapter) is an insistence on quoting, citing (that is, "to summon officially in a court of law," the *OED* tells us), invoking, drawing on, alluding to, borrowing from, referencing, and cross-

---

4. A careful reading of Plato's dialogue shows the relation between paired and opposed terms (such as philosophy and poetry, law and the creative arts) to be more intricate than I suggest here. I have discussed the dialogue in more detail in section II of the introduction.

referencing the innumerable other texts that are thereby threaded through the present piece of writing. The cumulative effect of these quotations is that, in reading Fitzpatrick's work, one develops a sense of not simply reading a monologic text in isolation. Instead the words become gateways onto a multivoiced philosophical conversation—a conversation that goes as far back as Plato and that includes voices such as those of Hobbes, Heidegger, T. S. Eliot, Wallace Stevens, Freud, Blanchot, Foucault, Derrida, and Beethoven, among countless others. The impact of all these references and quotations is that Fitzpatrick's own writing, like the law he writes about, *performs* the utter responsiveness that gives it an ethical orientation. Fitzpatrick's work is therefore not simply the product of one who writes but of one who *listens*, intently, to the voice of the other.

I would like to discuss this in detail; I restrict myself to just one example—that is, the first sentence of *Modernism and the Grounds of Law* . . . Actually, now that I come to it, let me cite the first two sentences, but I shall speak about the first sentence; even more specifically, my emphasis is on the first word. Here are the opening sentences of the introduction: "Extravagant as it may seem, this whole work is initially encapsulated in Freud's attempt to locate the origin of society in the primal parricide of *Totem and Taboo*. . . . Here Freud turned to 'the originary question of grounds', to borrow the phrase" (Fitzpatrick 2001b, 1, citing Derrida 1989, 60). At the back of my mind as I read this is the opening sentence of E. M. Forster's *A Passage to India*: "Except for the Marabar Caves—and they are twenty miles off—the city of Chandrapore presents nothing extraordinary" (Forster 1982, 31), but to return to *Modernism and the Grounds of Law*, "extravagant" also has an "obliging etymology," as *The Shorter Oxford English Dictionary* tells us:

> **Extravagant** (ekstræ·văgănt). ME. [*-extravagant-*, pres. ppl. stem of med.L. *extravagari*, f. *extra* EXTRA + *vagari* wander . . .
>
> That wanders out of bounds; vagrant; keeping no fixed place . . . "Roving beyond just limits or prescribed methods" (J.)

The first two sentences of *Modernism and the Grounds of Law*, with their reference to Freud as the impetus for the project and a borrowed phrase from Derrida, certainly are extravagant in their roving beyond the prescribed methods one would expect from a book in legal philosophy. The book announces itself as a response to Freud's *Totem and Taboo*—and thus the effect of "seem" (in "Extravagant as it may seem") gains its semantic force: What are the "bounds" of *Modernism and the Grounds of Law* if it is explicitly cast as having its origins in the work of Freud? Is Freud's "attempt" then not incipiently *within* the arguments of *Modernism and the Grounds of Law*, and is Fitzpatrick's supposed vagrancy in citing it not really a wandering out of bounds at all? Yet if the arguments of *Modernism and the Grounds of Law* are only "initially encapsulated" in Freud, then the book is not entirely in that keep either. Thus the citation in the very first sentence already raises unsettling questions in a thematic way, but, what is perhaps more important, it *performs* the "disruptive ambivalence" that Fitzpatrick locates in the responsiveness of law. Like the law of which it speaks, the book itself is only questionably contained within determinations one might traditionally set for a monograph written by a single author, as we shall see in the concluding section of this chapter.

But first let me reiterate that my interest in Fitzpatrick's work has not only to do with the ideas expressed but with the implications of his stylistic approach. I would argue that, far from being an irrelevant, if idiosyncratic, feature of his writing, Fitzpatrick's strategy of referencing, which it to say, his giving voice to the other, enacts the ethic of responsiveness that underwrites his legal philosophy.

I have spoken about what I called "the first sentence of *Modernism and the Grounds of Law*"—but of course, this is not strictly the first sentence. The real first sentence, after the list of contents, appears under the heading "Acknowledgements," and *this* first sentence reads, "Rarely can the arrogations of authorship have been so sorely tested" (Fitzpatrick 2001b, ix). In the acknowledgments Fitzpatrick elaborates on this idea: The "infinity of influence cannot be encompassed," he writes, and at a more radical level, any supposed containment of the book itself is open to question: "Its spurious self-sufficiency is also greatly challenged by the creative readings of previous drafts, or a chunk of them offered by . . ." A litany of names follows, each linked to an item in an enchanting list that includes "exuberance," "research on globalism," "poetry," "red pens," "intellectual companionship," an "exemplary index," "sustaining joy," a "Kentish-Brazilian garden," and "much everything" (Fitzpatrick 2001b, ix).

Returning specifically to the idea of the tested arrogations of authorship: The entire project of *Modernism and the Grounds of Law* is ostensively acknowledged and introduced by its author as being intimately engaged in conversation with other voices in creatively different ways—which reminds me of what I take to be a central ethical preoccupation throughout the writings of South African–born novelist J. M. Coetzee. "Writing is not free expression," says Coetzee in an interview with David Attwell. "There is a true sense in which writing is dialogic: a matter of awakening the countervoices in oneself and embarking upon speech with them. It is some measure of a writer's seriousness whether he does evoke/invoke those countervoices in himself, that is, step down from the position of what Lacan calls 'the subject supposed to know'" (Coetzee 1992, 65).

In a moment of the writer's utter responsiveness to the other, for Coetzee—and I would say that this holds for Fitzpatrick as well—one's authorship cedes ground to an internal dialogue that questions ideas about the writer's presumptive occupation of sites of authority and knowledge.[5] What this leads to is an argument that Fitzpatrick's sustained literary device of citation throughout his writing can be understood to take effect in the *Riss*, the fault line, the in-between (a word that Fitzpatrick often uses) that both separates and joins speaker and listener, writer and reader, me and you. A book like *Modernism and the Grounds of Law* is therefore the work not simply of a single author but of an interlocutor—that is to say, one who carries the ethical freight of participating in a conversation, of listening and responding, of questioning the grounds of one's authority, of rethinking and perhaps revising one's initial position. The ethical charge is activated, and measures a higher voltage, when the interlocutor assumes responsibility as the writer.

The performative effect of writing as response, even before the subsumptive themes and ideas are opened for analysis, is of particular interest to J. M. Coetzee. "Ideas are certainly important—who would deny that?" Coetzee writes, and then goes on to explain:

> Whereas a style, an attitude to the world, as it soaks in, becomes part of the personality, part of the self, ultimately indistinguishable from the self. To put it another way: in the process of responding to the writers one intuitively chooses to respond to, one makes oneself into the person whom in the most intractable but also perhaps the most deeply ethical sense one wants to be.
>
> Coetzee 1993, 7

---

5. The idea of responsiveness to other writers is one of the leading preoccupations in my book on Coetzee, *J. M. Coetzee: Countervoices* (2009).

V

In this closing section, I return briefly to images of fences in literary texts: "It is often our mightiest projects," says the unnamed narrator of W. G. Sebald's novel *Austerlitz*, "that most obviously betray the degree of our insecurity" (Sebald 2001, 16–17), and certainly this holds true of David Lurie's response to the attack in which his daughter, Lucy, is gang-raped on her farm in the Eastern Cape in J. M. Coetzee's novel *Disgrace*: "They ought to install bars, security gates, a perimeter fence, as Ettinger [Lucy's neighbor] has done," says Lurie. "They ought to turn the farmhouse into a fortress. Lucy ought to buy a pistol and a two-way radio, and take shooting lessons" (Coetzee 1999a, 113), but the trouble with the building of fortresses like these (as again the narrator in Sebald's novel observes) is that

> it ha[s] been forgotten that the largest fortifications will naturally attract the largest enemy forces, and that the more you entrench yourself the more you must remain on the defensive. . . . The frequent result, said Austerlitz, of resorting to measures of fortification marked in general by a tendency towards paranoid elaboration [is] that you [draw] attention to your weakest point, practically inviting the enemy to attack it.
>
> Sebald 2001, 19–20

Certainly this is a realization that David Lurie reaches in *Disgrace*,. "Even the days of Ettinger, with his guns and barbed wire and alarm systems, are numbered" (Coetzee 1999a, 134), Lurie thinks to himself, and later on, Lucy uses this argument to vindicate her decision to accept Petrus's proposal of marriage and to hand over the title deeds of her farm to him: "To whom can I turn for protection, for patronage?" Lucy says to her father. "To Ettinger? It is just a matter of time before Ettinger is found with a bullet in his back" (Coetzee 1999a, 204). Lucy's understanding of her own position is not contained by Western colonial conceptions of supposed legal boundaries, of land arrogation or proprietorship, which puts her views into stark contrast with those of her father. In some respects at least, Lucy's attitudes are reminiscent of those of Michael K in Coetzee's early novel *Life & Times of Michael K*. Having escaped from the camps (where, for a time, it was his job to repair fences), Michael K often turns in thought to fences, boundary markers, and other signs of human and animal passage through the landscape:

> Every mile or two there was a fence to remind him that he was a trespasser as well as a runaway. Ducking through the fences, he could feel a craftsman's pleasure in wire spanned so taut that it hummed when it was plucked. Nonetheless, he could not imagine himself spending his life driving stakes into the ground, erecting fences, dividing up the land. He thought of himself not as something that left tracks behind it, but if anything as a speck upon the surface of an earth too deeply asleep to notice the scratch of ant-feet, the rasp of butterfly teeth, the tumbling of dust.
>
> Coetzee 1983, 133

Michael K digs a burrow and sets up a makeshift shelter on the Visagies' farm, where his mother used to work; he chooses not to occupy the farmhouse, even though it has long since been abandoned, and he resists the temptation to carry utensils and other handy tools across from the Visagies' house to his "home in the earth": "The worst mistake, he told himself, would be to try to found a new house, a rival line, on his small beginnings out at the dam. Even his tools should be of wood and leather and gut, materials the insects would eat one day when he no longer needed them" (Coetzee 1983, 142–23).[6]

In *Disgrace*, Lucy becomes increasingly frustrated with Western conceptions that earth is to be owned, that growing plants is subject to legal title. The contrast in attitude between Lucy and David Lurie is all the more striking in Coetzee's verbal echo in the phrases "we both know that" and "you know that" in the two sentences below—

> Stop calling it *the farm*, David. This is not a farm, it's just a piece of land where I grow things—we both know that
>
> Coetzee 1999a, 200, emphasis in the original

and in Lurie's response to Lucy's unconventional marital and property negotiations with Petrus:

---

6. Coetzee's readers will surely be put in mind of the creature in Kafka's story "The Burrow." The creature is afraid that his burrow is not safe from outside attack, and for a time lives outside, keeping watch over the entrance, too anxious to return, lest he betray his keep. The thought occurs to him that "by now it is almost as if I were the enemy spying out a suitable opportunity for successfully breaking in" (Kafka 1988, 142). Yet even within his elaborately constructed burrow, the creature is driven to distraction by his own fearful imagination: "And it is not only by external enemies that I am threatened. There are also enemies in the bowels of the earth. I have never seen them, but legend tells of them and I firmly believe in them. They are creatures of the inner earth; not even legend can describe them" (Kafka 1988, 130).

> It's not workable, Lucy. *Legally* it's not workable. You know that
>
> Coetzee 1999a, 204, my emphasis

Taken together, these sentences seem to imply a disaggregation between what is workable and what is *legally* workable, where "legal" is considered in the strictly determinative mode that Schmitt would accord to it. To what extent does an understanding of Lucy's response demand a looking beyond the conventionally perceived limits of a Western law? Or to what extent does it simply fuel racial tensions in a fragile, postapartheid society? The publication of *Disgrace* led to heated critical controversy, largely thanks to the ANC's reference to the novel in its submission to the Human Rights Commission's Inquiry into Racism in the Media in April 2000.[7] Faced with all the ambiguities of the literary text, and in trying to make sense of Lucy's response in particular, the reader of Coetzee's novel may well be led to wonder (as Oom Schalk Lourens does at the end of Stoffel Oosthuizen's tale in Herman Charles Bosman's short story "Unto Dust"), "I don't know whether he told the story incorrectly, or whether it was just that kind of a story, but, by the time he had finished, all my uncertainties had, I discovered, come back to me" (Bosman 2006, 263). Has Coetzee told the story of Lucy, Petrus, David Lurie, and the dogs incorrectly? Is it just that kind of a story? A challenge is sent out to the reader to question long-standing ideas about the legitimacy of a colonial inheritance in Africa, *and further*, to question any assumptions one may have had about the semantic keep of the literary text. If, for Coetzee, the presumed authority of the writer is an assumption that he plays into,[8] the raising of the countervoice, the stepping down from a monologic and all-knowing authorial position, constitutes one of his leading ethical and political preoccupations. In an interview with Coetzee in February 1987, Tony Morphet speaks about *Foe* as a novel that "might be seen as something of a retreat from the South African situation." The novel is set, for the most part, on a desert island and actively invites the reader to think of Daniel Defoe's *Robinson Crusoe* as its intertext. Coetzee replies to Morphet's suggestion: "*Foe* is a retreat from the South African situation, but

---

7. For an illuminating discussion of the ANC's submission to the Commission, see Attwell's 2002 essay "Race in *Disgrace*."

8. Coetzee says of his book *Foe*: "My novel, *Foe*, if it is about any single subject, is about authorship: about what it means to be an author in the professional sense (the profession of author was just beginning to mean something in Daniel Defoe's day) but also in a sense that verges, if not on the divine, then at least on the demiurgic: sole author, sole creator" (Coetzee 2005a, 145).

only from that situation in a narrow temporal perspective. It is not a retreat from the subject of colonialism or from questions of power. What you call 'the nature and processes of fiction' may also be called the question of who writes? Who takes up the position of power, pen in hand?" (Coetzee and Morphet 1987, 462).

Bosman's "Unto Dust" and Coetzee's *Disgrace* and other critical writings raise unsettling questions about colonial arrogations of land as much as they do about the "arrogations of authorship" (Fitzpatrick 2001b, ix) and hence of supposedly stable, demarcated meanings encountered by the readers of law and of literature. The testing of these arrogations may be one way in which contemporary South African literature could contribute to a thinking through of a postapartheid jurisprudence. Further, if the boundary, or fence, or limit of the law invites us to think of what is beyond it, what would it take to redraw the lines? What possibility is there for rendering justice through laws grounded in colonial appropriations and the imposition of territorial boundaries? What forces, if any, would have the power to wrest a new constitutional and democratic law from the imperial ideologies that seem to have given rise to those laws in the first place? These are the topics of the next chapter.

2

Redrawing the Lines

I

In a striking passage from his autobiographical work, *Long Walk to Freedom*, Nelson Mandela gives his account of the initial hearings of the Rivonia Trial on October 15, 1962:

> I entered the court that Monday morning wearing a traditional Xhosa leopard-skin *kaross* instead of a suit and tie. The crowd of supporters rose as one and with raised clenched fists shouted *"Amandla!"* and *"Ngawethu!"* The *kaross* electrified the spectators. . . .
>
> I had chosen traditional dress to emphasize the symbolism that I was a black African walking into a white man's court. I was literally carrying on my back the history, culture and heritage of my people. That day, I felt myself to be the *embodiment* of African nationalism, the inheritor of Africa's difficult but noble past and her uncertain future. The *kaross* was also a sign of contempt for the niceties of white justice. I well knew that

the authorities would feel threatened by my *kaross* as so many whites feel threatened by the true culture of Africa.

Mandela 1994a, 311–12, my emphasis on "embodiment"

The emphasis on performance here is unmistakable. The public becomes a "crowd of supporters," the "spectators." Mandela in full traditional regalia "electrifies" the crowd: He is a spectacular "sign," a "symbol," an embodied cipher of more than could possibly be subsumed in a thematized, linear narrative. This is one way of understanding performance—that is to say, as theatre. But in this chapter I would like to link this notion of performance to the "performative" in language in its more specifically linguistico-philosophical sense, to show how Nelson Mandela's speech acts, most especially at the Rivonia Trial, opened a path for political appeal *within* the institutional edifice of apartheid law.[1]

In his seminal work *How to Do Things with Words*, J. L. Austin makes the distinction between constative and performative uses of language: constatives are propositions in a traditional philosophical sense—statements that can be deemed true or false. But performatives are speech acts that through their very utterance bring about a change in a state of affairs and are not verifiable in the way that propositions often are. To say "I forgive you," or "I pronounce you man and wife" within a particular social context is to *do* something; the words do not simply represent or describe some event external to the utterance. In Austin's words, a performative "is not to *describe* my doing of what I should be said in so uttering to be doing . . . or to state that I am doing it: it is to do it" (Austin 1965, 6). Austin's conception of the performative can thus be linked to the idea of "aesthetic acts" that I sketched out in the introduction to this book, in the sense that aesthetic acts (following Rancière) bring about a shift in perception or understanding on the part of those who encounter the artwork, or the speech, or the literary text.

In this chapter I examine closely a few excerpts from Mandela's speeches and writings at critical junctures in his career. Mandela's acute awareness of the performative effect of any speech utterance invites reflection on the ways in which the temporal and spatial dynamics of the situation of address subtend, and sometimes even usurp, the subsumptive content of what is

---

1. My discussion can be read as taking a cue from Judith Butler, who writes in her 1999 preface to *Gender Trouble*: "My theory sometimes waffles between understanding performativity as linguistic and casting it as theatrical. I have come to think that the two are invariably related, chiasmatically so, and that a reconsideration of the speech act as an instance of power invariably draws attention to both its theatrical and linguistic dimensions" (Butler 1999, xxvii).

said. In its irreducibility to the coordinates of the calendar or the map, what is the effect that the event or the site of address has on the interlocutors it instantiates? My point of departure is a discussion of the Rivonia Trial—the initial hearing was set for October 15, 1962, and Mandela read his statement from the dock on April 20, 1964. Through Mandela's appearance at the initial hearings in his traditional Xhosa *kaross* and the extraordinary performative force of his statement from the dock, the Rivonia Trial initiated a redrawing of the lines between law and politics: Mandela and the ANC, up till then, had been considered to operate beyond the boundaries of the law. But by giving Mandela a hearing (in both the legal and the ordinary sense of this word), the Rivonia Trial offered him a legal site from which to issue a political appeal, and as a result, the relation between law and politics in South Africa became irrevocably troubled: A political appeal to humanity's conscience suddenly had a spectacular and a *legitimate* place within the overall social configuration of apartheid South Africa. The "distribution of the sensible"—to borrow Rancière's phrase—would never be the same. Mandela's words radically altered the social system determining what could legitimately be seen and heard, and hence brought out starkly the oppressive delimitations that had prevented people from perceiving what they actually shared in common.

II

My discussion of performance in its linguistico-philosophical sense begins by referring to a handy distinction made by the linguist Roman Jakobson—the distinction between what he calls the "speech event" and the "narrated event" (Jakobson 1990, 390). The "speech event" is the situation of address: The accent is on the speaker and auditors, or on the writer and readers. It has to do with the sites of utterance and response in any discourse (spoken, written, depicted). The "narrated event" is the thematic content of the speech event—what is spoken about in the speech event. It is at the level of the narrated event that meaning is most commonly assumed to inhere, but in this chapter I focus on the meaningful inflections of the speech event itself. With regard to the excerpts from Mandela's speeches, the question is therefore not exclusively "What is Mandela talking about?" Rather, it has to do with an antecedent question of *whether* his speeches and writings are able to speak to his addressees in a meaningful way in the first place. To approach the question from this angle is to explore a fault line between the event of the saying and what is said, which reminds me of Rancière's characterization of a political work of art. "The dream of a suitable political work of art," writes Rancière, "is in fact the dream of disrupting the relationship between the visible, the sayable, and the thinkable without having to use the terms of a message as a vehicle. It is the dream of an art that would transmit meanings in the form of a rupture with the very logic of meaningful situations" (Rancière 2004b, 63).

It is in this context that I return to Mandela's account of the opening scene of the Rivonia Trial as Mandela describes it in *Long Walk to Freedom*. In this narrative about the initial hearings, and at the level of communicated content (that is, using "the terms of a message as the vehicle"), the binary oppositions could hardly be more clear-cut: Xhosa *kaross* versus Western "suit and tie"; "black African" versus "white man"; the "true culture of Africa" versus the "niceties of white justice"; "African nationalism" versus a "white man's court"; "my people" versus "the authorities"; the "noble past" versus an "uncertain future." Mandela's opposition to the apartheid laws is unambiguously stated, but to the extent that his forced presence in court, in his traditional regalia, amounts to an expression of contempt, Mandela's appearance *and audience* at the Rivonia Trial amount to a rupture in the very logic of apartheid law.

At the level of symbolic opposition in the narrative account of *Long Walk to Freedom*, Mandela makes a plea for what Derrida might call a "change of terrain"—a "placing oneself outside, . . . affirming an absolute break and difference" (Derrida 1982, 135). In Derrida's terms, this would be one way of effecting a deconstruction—and with specific reference to Mandela here—a way of dismantling the apartheid regime. But if Mandela's *kaross* is an emblematic protest, it is important to note that the protest is explicitly (in Mandela's own words) against "the *niceties of white* justice" and not against justice itself. This already begins to complicate any notion of an "*absolute* break" or change of terrain, which brings me to another crucial passage in *Long Walk to Freedom*, where, again, Mandela is as acutely sensitive to the event of his communication as he is to the communicated message itself. Mandela realized that his very appearance in his *kaross* in a white man's court "would transmit meanings in the form of a rupture with the very logic of meaningful situations"—to repeat Rancière's phrasing—even before anything was said in the form of a communicated message. When he first appeared in court before a magistrate for formal remand, Mandela noticed the embarrassment of the magistrate and others whom he knew as colleagues. He makes the following observation:

> at that moment I had something of a revelation. These men were not only uncomfortable because I was a colleague brought low, but because I was an ordinary man being punished for his beliefs. In a way I had never quite comprehended before, I realized the role I could play in court and the possibilities before me as a defendant. I was the symbol of justice in the court of the oppressor, the representative of the great ideals of freedom, fairness and democracy in a society that dishonoured those virtues. I realized then and there that I could carry on the fight even within the fortress of the enemy.
>
> Mandela 1994a, 304

It is here that one thinks of Derrida's description of another kind of deconstruction, a deconstruction that uses "against the edifice the instruments or stones available in the house, that is, equally, *in language*" (Derrida 1982, 135). A pattern is now beginning to emerge: Derrida speaks of two operative modes of deconstruction: "changing the terrain" and using "the instruments or stones available in the house"—a reciprocal language. "It also goes without saying," Derrida continues, "that the choice between these two forms of deconstruction cannot be simple and unique" (Derrida 1982, 135). What he calls for is a "new writing," one that "must weave and interlace these two motifs of deconstruction" (Derrida 1982, 135). What I am beginning to suggest is that Mandela effects precisely such a "new writing."[2] Clearly, the intention is not to trivialize Mandela's actions here, to read them as an allegory for an abstracted European philosophy that in itself has little, if anything, to do with political transformation in South Africa. Rather, to see Mandela as effecting this new kind of writing is to understand better the subtleties of a political strategy that, at once, operates both within and beyond the given order. But further still, Mandela's actions give point to Derrida's increasingly urgent appeal for philosophical praxis. It is not necessarily the "professional philosophers" who are best able to effect "transition towards political and international institutions to come," says Derrida in one of his later interviews:

---

2. In his essay "Writing the South African Treason Trial," Stephen Clingman makes an interesting and thought-provoking argument: "While the initial script was written by the prosecution, the task of the defence was to rewrite the trial while it was underway" (Clingman 2010, 37).

The lawyer or the politician who takes charge of these questions will be the philosophers of tomorrow. Sometimes, politicians or lawyers are more able to philosophically think these questions through than professional academic philosophers. At any rate, philosophy today, or the duty of philosophy, is to think this in action, by doing something.

Derrida 2004, 3–4

An extraordinary process of "thinking in action" takes place at the scene of the initial hearings of the Rivonia Trial. At the level of what is communicated or *said*, at the level of the "narrated event," Mandela calls for a change of terrain, an end to the apartheid laws, but in the event of the *saying*, that is, at the level of the "speech event" itself, Mandela uses the stones in the house to stand as a symbol of justice. Differently put: *What* it is that Mandela represents, in the white man's court, is *opposition* to the apartheid laws, but *how* he does that is to represent, to symbolize, to embody (these are Mandela's own terms) a justice that is ostensibly the cornerstone of the very house in which he stands.

Let me follow this through, with an emphasis on what is at stake in the conditions underwriting the symbolic. It is at this point that any notion of an *absolute* alterity or singularity has to be questioned. What Mandela symbolizes is opposition, but *that* he should be recognized as being symbolic of anything at all demands—and, in fact, instantiates—a relation to what he opposes. In the sense of Jean-Luc Nancy's *partage* (of both sharing and dividing), and taking the cue from Derrida, "an absolute, absolutely pure singularity, if there were one, would not even show up, or at least would not be available for reading. To become readable, it has to be *divided*, to *participate* and *belong*. Then it is divided and takes *its part* in the genre, the type, the context, meaning, the conceptual generality of meaning" (Derrida 1992a, 68, emphasis in the original).

The emphasis on readability and meaning is critical here.[3] To be readable, even as a symbol of opposition, presupposes a shared language; it instantiates a dialogic relation in its expectation and affirmation of a "responsive range" (the phrase is Peter Fitzpatrick's [Fitzpatrick 2004, 224]). Further, the readable sign is never the *first* word; "the speaker is not Adam," as Bakhtin points out (Bakhtin 1986, 94), "any speaker is himself a respondent to a

---

3. On the question of meaning and a "shared language" in relation to reconciliation and forgiveness, see Derrida, "On Forgiveness" in *On Cosmopolitanism and Forgiveness* (2001), especially pages 36 and 45–51.

greater or lesser degree. He is not, after all, the first speaker, the one who disturbs the eternal silence of the universe" (Bakhtin 1986, 69).

III

The time of address is thus deeply imbricated in the past: "Each utterance is filled with echoes and reverberations of other utterances to which it is related. . . . Every utterance must be regarded primarily as a *response* to preceding utterances" (Bakhtin 1986, 91).

Yet if the utterance responds to what precedes it, it is also a response to the future, in that it is oriented toward the audience it anticipates. Again following Bakhtin: "From the very beginning, the utterance is constructed while taking into account possible responsive reactions, for whose sake, in essence, it is actually created" (Bakhtin 1986, 94).

The address is therefore never simply a statement in a present, to those present, but a dialogic response, which is readable thanks to a relation to the past (we recognize the language) and to the future, by virtue of its orientation toward potential responsive reactions: "The temporality specific to the aesthetic regime of the arts," writes Rancière, "is a co-presence of heterogenous temporalities" (Rancière 2004b, 26). An account of the time of address therefore has to take cognizance of the implications of what is at stake in the instantiation of the responsive range of that address.

Mandela's statement from the dock is a response to the apartheid government that has occasioned his being in court in the first place, and it is also a response to the audiences it anticipates. ("Which ones?" I hear you ask. We are coming to this.) Any complacency about supposedly predetermined and static sites of response, however, is challenged—the "authorities," for example, are unseated from a presumed position of control. Mandela makes this clear in his retrospective account of the hearings: "I well knew the authorities would feel threatened by my *kaross*" (Mandela 1994a, 312). It is the audience, as active participant in the speech utterance, that generates what Mandela chooses to say and to symbolize: The auditors thus share the *responsibility* of what is said. Mandela's "moment of revelation" about the role he could play in court is well-attuned to his performative moral force, a force that resists containment either in the content of what he says (an expression of opposition) or in the event of his saying, because it presupposes a language *shared* with an audience that, as we shall see, infinitely exceeds the institutional confines of the courtroom. On the one hand, Mandela's role in court, as the defendant in a political trial, is rigidly defined: He is not there voluntarily; the speaking positions and "discussions" are determined in advance by rules of procedure that cannot be negotiated; the passing of sentence is inevitable.

But Mandela's own reflections on the event point to the ways in which the supposedly clear-cut mechanisms of the court of law are unhinged. This shift in the settings according to which legal procedure is played out is made clear in another excerpt from *Long Walk to Freedom*: "By representing myself I would enhance the symbolism of my role. I would use my trial as a showcase for the ANC's moral opposition to racism. *I would not attempt to defend myself so much as put the state itself on trial*" (Mandela 1994a, 304, my emphasis). In Mandela's *response* to the voice of oppression, the roles within the courtroom are reversed, and the sites of responsibility destabilized and reconfigured, through language, in such a radical way that the question of holding only the *speaker* to account for what is said becomes problematic: That Mandela chooses to say *this* in his statement, that he chooses to "put the state on trial," is the necessary consequence of his moral protest against the injustices of apartheid legislation. In that Mandela's statement is a response to the state. What he says cannot be accounted for without reference to what has occasioned his response. Refracted through Mandela's dialogic discourse, it is an institutionalized racism that now becomes the object of judgment—and not only for the official judges. Mandela's speech makes an ethical demand that exploits, but at the same time redirects, the lines of judgment and defense that trace out the legal space.

IV

Further still, and in turn, Mandela anticipates that his statement from the dock will be heard. The anticipation of an institutional hearing (in both a literal and a metaphoric, legal sense), and the ineluctable, institutional signal of being heard by the state, is something that was not there before the initial hearings of the Rivonia Trial. That the response (of passing sentence) is negative is, for the moment, of secondary consequence. In his distinction between reconciliation and forgiveness, Derrida makes this clear: "Even if I say 'I do not forgive you' to someone . . . whom I understand and who understands me, then a process of reconciliation has begun; the third has intervened" (Derrida 2001, 49). In the preparations for his defense at the Rivonia Trial, Mandela and the others accused took the decision that Mandela should read a statement from the dock instead of testifying and undergoing cross-examination. A statement from the dock does not carry the same legal weight as ordinary testimony, and Mandela's attorneys warned him about the precariousness of his situation: "Anything I said in my statement regarding my own innocence would be discounted by the judge," Mandela writes, and goes on to say: "But that was not our highest priority. We believed it was important to open the defence with a statement of our politics and ideals, which would establish the context for all that followed" (Mandela 1994a 347). Bram Fischer read the statement ahead of the defense and urged Mandela not to read his final paragraph, which, he felt, was sure to incur a death sentence, but Mandela was resolute: "I felt we were likely to hang no matter what we said, so we might as well say what we truly believed" (Mandela 1994a, 348). Mandela's statement would indeed bring about a different context for the voicing of the antiapartheid struggle. The statement took over four hours to read; it disarmed legal proceedings as the prosecution had anticipated an ordinary testimony in which Mandela would deny charges of sabotage and would be subject to cross-examination. Instead, his speech still stands as an incontrovertible statement of belief; it was not subject to verifiability in the limiting format of a legal interrogation. The statement received worldwide publicity and was published almost in its entirety in the *Rand Daily Mail*, even though all of Mandela's words at the time were banned. His statement recalibrated, in a radical way, the legal and political settings of the antiapartheid struggle.

Mandela's account of his first meeting with P. W. Botha in 1989 at Tuynhuys is once again an indication of a shift in the decades-long process of Mandela's being heard by the state. The performative force of the "speech event" itself, before any analysis of the content of what was said (the "narrated event"), stands out as memorable in Mandela's autobiographical account. The meeting was brief—less than half an hour long. Mandela describes the discussion as "friendly and breezy" throughout. On the one serious question raised—namely, the unconditional release of all political prisoners—Botha was intransigent. But Mandela ends his account with the following comment: "While the meeting was not a breakthrough in terms of negotiations, it was one in another sense. Mr Botha had long talked about the need to cross the Rubicon, but he never did it himself until that morning at Tuynhuys. Now, I felt, there was no turning back" (Mandela 1994a, 540). Botha's Rubicon, as Mandela reads it, is to choose to reposition himself within a responsive range; the content of what is literally *said* or negotiated, or resolved, within this dialogic frame is an entirely different matter and not as important as the fact that Botha invited Mandela to Tuynhuys for a conversation.

Rivonia had brought about a radical redistribution of the sensible: The political, antiapartheid protest had been voiced and heard in a court of law, making it possible for a self-designated nation to question and to reconsider its own delineations of what counted as legitimate and what did not. People and words—up to now relegated to a zone beyond the law—had been seen and heard within a new context of litigation. Thanks to a different articulation of a field of perception at Rivonia, an apartheid society was challenged to respond to something it had heard, and to create new thoughts about its laws.[4]

It is perhaps most importantly the instantiation of a response from "the authorities" that Mandela's appearance in court had effected. It is a response that Mandela had not been able to bring into being before that day, and it draws a subtle distinction, namely, between the *ir*responsible and the *non*-responsible. A striking instance of this is in the references Mandela makes to several letters he had written to the prime minister before the time of his imprisonment: The letters were never answered. Clearly, the government wished to position itself beyond Mandela's responsive range—to cast itself as "not responsible" rather than as "irresponsible." To be irresponsible is to affirm a responsibility that has been breached. To be nonresponsible is to deny that one falls within the ambit of a responsible field. In fact, it amounts to a denial that such a field exists at all. The refusal to respond to an appeal can be read as "not responding" or as "irresponsible," depending on the respondent's relation to the appeal.[5] Further, the reading can be affected by the perceived legitimacy of the appeal.

But now, in court, at the initial hearings of the Rivonia Trial, and with all the official legal trappings of a *hearing*, it is impossible to deny that some

---

4. In the back of my mind I have the words of Steven Corcoran's introduction to Rancière's *Dissensus*: "The dissensus by which the invisible quality subtending social distinction is made visible, and the inaudible speech of those rejected into the obscure night of silence audible, thereby enacts a different *sharing* of the sensible" (Corcoran 2010, 7). Judith Butler's work can also be read as being in conversation with that of Rancière. In the preface to *Gender Trouble* she writes: "What continues to concern me most is the following kinds of questions: what will and will not constitute an intelligible life, and how do presumptions about normative gender and sexuality determine in advance what will qualify as the 'human' and the 'livable'? . . . What is the means by which we come to see this delimiting power, and what are the means by which we transform it?" (Butler 1999, xxiii). See the related point I have made in endnote 3 of the introduction.

5. Derrida and Hillis Miller (in response to Derrida's *The Gift of Death*) approach the question of irresponsibility differently from the way I do here. See further reference to this in chapter 4.

appeal has been made. In Mandela's symbolic call for justice, it becomes increasingly difficult for the state to cast a refusal to respond to his statements as a simple nonresponse: An ethical demand has been made, irrevocably, and it has been given audience in court. At the very least, Mandela's appearance in a "white man's court" redraws a line: It situates the apartheid government within the boundaries of a responsible field. But the situatedness of Mandela's appeal "in court" brings about a different, if infinitely nuanced, set of conditions of response—on all sides.

In order to discuss these conditions of response, it is necessary to address the question of what it means to voice a political protest "in court." In a subtle and carefully argued paper, Emilios Christodoulidis makes the point that "activist and judge inhabit different 'universes' closed off to intertraffic meanings" (Christodoulidis 2004, 180). He goes on to argue that "'the objection that cannot be raised' is not merely one that is side-lined in official discourse; rather . . . the very possibility of raising it, *in the courtroom*, is structurally removed" (Christodoulidis 2004, 181, my emphasis).

Now seemingly this goes against my argument that Mandela's statement from the dock is *heard*, that it instantiates the apartheid government within responsive range. But what I want to suggest is that Mandela's statement is not made entirely "in court" and that it is precisely the inability, on the part of the government, to suppress "intertraffic meanings" (between law and politics, between what is inside and what is beyond the courtroom, between the present time of address and its chiasmatic relation to the past and the future) that does indeed constitute a responsive field.

What is Mandela's "responsive range" in the Rivonia Trial? In order to address this question, I want to jump forward in time to the speech Mandela delivered on February 11, 1990, after serving sentence for twenty-seven years. In his address to the gathered crowds in Cape Town, Mandela cites (let us say reiterates) part of the statement he had made in the Rivonia trial. The way in which he frames the citation already alerts us to his own awareness that his statement does not speak to only *one* time or space:

> In conclusion I wish to quote my own words during my trial in 1964. *They are true today as they were then*:
> "I have fought against white domination and I have fought against black domination. I have cherished the ideal of a democratic and free society in which all persons live together in harmony and with equal

opportunities. It is an ideal which I hope to live for and to achieve. But if needs be, it is an ideal for which I am prepared to die."

Mandela 1994b, 217, my emphasis

The time and the site of the text of the address are not restricted to particular coordinates of the calendar or the map—of which Mandela himself is acutely aware. Just before the end of the Rivonia Trial, in full knowledge that he would be found guilty and that sentence would be passed, in the here and now, Mandela concluded his statement with the following observation: "I have no doubt that *posterity* will pronounce that I was innocent and that the criminals that should have been brought before this court are the members of the government" (Mandela 1994a, 319, my emphasis). The time of address cannot be arrested in history: It is ever open to rereading, to countersignature. In Scott Veitch's deft formulation of the workings of amnesty, each utterance can be rewritten: "*That is what happened then and that is what happened then now*" (Veitch 2001, 36). Certainly this is an instance of Mandela's anticipation of a *future* "what happened then now," of a "justice to come" that would be recognized thanks to the iterability of the address in contexts never to be repeated in exactly the same way.

To add another layer of complexity: The symbol of the *kaross*, the leopard skin that Mandela wore at the Rivonia Trial, certainly speaks to those physically present in the room, but let us consider the language in which it speaks. Mandela, wearing his *kaross* during the trial, raises questions about the *justice* of the apartheid laws. He is the "embodiment of African nationalism" (Mandela 1994a, 312), the very "symbol of justice in the court of the oppressor" (Mandela 1994a, 304). He reiterates that he "had chosen traditional dress to emphasize the symbolism that [he] was a black African walking into a white man's court" (Mandela 1994a, 311). The symbol thus speaks on political and ethical levels not quite contained within the parameters of legal discourse and procedure, and of this the authorities were all too aware. The commanding officer, Colonel Jacobs, had tried to confiscate the *kaross*, but the best he could do was to insist that Mandela wear his traditional attire in the courtroom only and not on his way to and from the court, "for fear it would 'incite' other prisoners" (Mandela 1994a, 312). It is in this sense that Mandela's statement is not made only "in court." It is as if the symbolism of the *kaross* reconfigures the legal setting. The judge is an "oppressor," and Mandela himself is not reducible to the speaking position of defendant at trial. In addition to his being a symbol of justice, and an embodiment of African nationalism, he is "an ordinary man being punished for his beliefs" (Mandela 1994a, 304). With regard to his addressees, many of the people in the courtroom were Mandela's "friends and family, some of whom had come all the way from the Transkei" (Mandela 1994a, 311). Thus, it is not simply a question of speaking to those in legal office from an absolutely legally prescribed site and in an absolutely determinate role. Mandela's statement from the dock is not simply a case of "us[ing] the law to oppose the law" (Dyzenhaus 2001, 77).[6] As embodied symbol, Mandela speaks in the present, *but not only here, or now,* "in court." His appeal is to a justice that falls beyond the compass of apartheid law; his audience is wider than the one subscribing to these laws. In more complex and subtle ways, the appeal to the administrators of the law within the courtroom, if this appeal is to be *heard*, is one that bypasses the racist legislation that prescribes each individual's official role and interlocutory position. The appeal is heard by fellow human beings with a higher sense of justice than the apartheid laws they are legally bound to administer. The performative effect of his appearance "in court" was, at least in one sense, to effect a much wider responsive range.

Mandela's address upon his release from prison is a striking, performative instantiation of himself *insofar* as he stands in relation to his people: This is a moment in the "posterity" to which he refers in the Rivonia Trial; it is the audience Mandela anticipated in the 1960s—the one that would pronounce him innocent. Mandela's speech of February 11, 1990 pays elaborate attention to the inauguration of himself as speaking subject in intricately sophisticated relation to his addressees. Much of the speech consists of an extended greeting to a "you" variously inflected by the immediate past and in specific relation to the "I" instantiated by the discourse itself:

> Friends, comrades and fellow South Africans, I greet you all in the name of peace, democracy and freedom for all.
>
> I stand before you not as a prophet but as a humble servant of you, the people. Your tireless and heroic sacrifices have made it possible for me to be here today. I therefore place the remaining years of my life in your hands.
>
> Mandela 1994b, 214

---

6. David Dyzenhaus offers a philosophically rigorous and thought-provoking account of Bram Fischer's dilemma in relation to the law: the choice between going underground and using the law to challenge it (see especially pages 69–78).

The rhetoric of performative address becomes more insistent as the speech gathers momentum, as the following quotation demonstrates:

> I send special greetings to the people of Cape Town. . . . I salute the African National Congress. . . . I salute our President, Comrade Oliver Tambo. . . . I salute the rank and file members of the ANC. . . . I salute combatants of Umkhonto we Sizwe. . . . I salute the South African Communist Party. . . . I salute General Secretary Joe Slovo. . . . I extend my greetings to the working class of our country . . . I greet the traditional leaders of our country. . . . I pay tribute to the endless heroism of youth, you, the young lions. You, the young lions, have energised our entire struggle.
>
> I pay tribute to the mothers and wives and sisters of our nation. You are the rock-hard foundation of our struggle. Apartheid has inflicted more pain on you than on anyone else.
>
> Mandela 1994b, 214–16

Each specification of "you" extends the addressive range that radiates out from the "I"—an "I" in turn rendered more complex in each stated relation to an incremental and ever more nuanced "you." In his *Problems in General Linguistics*, Benveniste makes the following observation about the subject positions "I" and "you." "I" and "you" (unlike the grammatical position of the third person) always have reference to the present *utterance* and not to a stable referent outside of the context of the present situation of address. Thus, "*I* is 'the individual who utters the present instance of discourse containing the linguistic instance *I*,'" and similarly, "'*you* [is] the individual spoken to in the present instance of discourse containing the linguistic instance *you*'" (Benveniste 1971, 218). Further, the pronominal forms "I" and "you" do not "refer to 'reality' or to objective positions in space or time but to the utterance, unique each time, that contains them" (Benveniste 1971, 219). The lyric "I" of Mandela's address to the Cape Town Rally is offered and refracted, through the utterance, in relation to a multifaceted "you" present at the time of the address but identified in terms of the echoes of history.

Now if the I–you logic of address is present to the utterance, each time, in Benveniste's terms, it is a present that can be understood only insofar as it destabilizes linear or historical notions of time. Utterances themselves (and the "you" and "I" they necessarily convey) can be infinitely cited, grafted, disseminated—which is to say, uprooted, from a particular moment in time and space, in ways which always leave open the possibility of speaking, and being heard, beyond the here and now. Thus, even though the I–you logic refers to the present moment of each speech event, in order to have any addressive purchase at all (in other words, in order for a "you" *to be called*), the speech event depends on its capacity for temporal and spatial iterability. In Mandela's address, the simultaneous harking back and reaching forward, the evocation of an elsewhere through the present site of address, the instantiation of a multivalent and transhistorical "you"—all of this aporetically constitutes the here and now as a moment of *interruption* in the present. This brings me back to Mandela's reflections on his symbolic role "in court" at the time of the Rivonia trial: "That day, I felt myself to be the embodiment of African nationalism, the inheritor of Africa's difficult but noble past *and* her uncertain future" (Mandela 1994a, 312, my emphasis).

V

I would like to consider further the question of the time of address by referring to Paul Celan's prose writings on poetry.[7] The "poem is not timeless," writes Celan. "True, it lays a claim to the infinite and tries to grasp through time—but *through* it, not above it" (Celan 1986, 34). It is in this sense that the "you" of Mandela's Cape Town address is singular in *each* relation to the "I": Each "you" is situated within a political and historical trajectory but instantiated *as such* in the singular event of the address itself.

Celan speaks of the poem as a movement through time: He uses the expressions *Bewegung, Unterwegssein*, "en route." Further, in this reaching through time, "the poem speaks. It is mindful of its dates, but it speaks" (Celan 1986, 48). What the poem—or, for my purposes here, the address—evinces is an implacable tension between historically bound instances of address and the infinite capacity for future readings. In "The Meridian," Celan puts it this way:

> The poem holds its ground on its own margin. In order to endure, it constantly calls and pulls itself back from an "already-no-more" into a "still-here."

---

7. Derrida's *Schibboleth: Pour Paul Celan* and Christopher Fynsk's *Language and Relation . . . That There Is Language* both offer brilliant accounts of Celan's prose writings. Derrida's text constitutes a meditation on the concept of the date in Celan; Fynsk, taking the cue from Celan, discusses the temporally inflected relation to the other instantiated through language. My discussion here is indebted to both these works.

This "still here" can only mean speaking. Not just language as such, but responding and—not just verbally—"corresponding" to something.

In other words: language actualized, set free under the sign of a radical individuation which, however, remains as aware of the limits drawn by language as of the possibilities it opens.

Celan 1986, 49, emphasis in the original

In its iterability, the text enacts what Christopher Fynsk calls "*a movement* of self-situation" (Fynsk 1996, 141), a self-situation that is effected in the approach, the relation opened to the time of the other. That is to say, the lyric "I" is reconstituted—differently—each time it is read by the "you" that the discourse engages. In the Cape Town Rally speech, in the speech event itself, *and* in the communicated message, Mandela gives himself over to the time of the "you" he addresses, in a gesture that is "simultaneously a recollection and a reaching forward" (Fynsk 1996, 149).

Let us recall Benveniste's insights about "I" and "you": namely, that these pronominal forms "do not refer to 'reality' or to objective positions in space or time but to the utterance, unique each time, that contains them" (Benveniste 1971, 219). The addressee, the anticipated "you" that comes into being in each "reading" of the text across time and space, cannot possibly be contained within the intentional grasp of the "I." "You" are always incipient in, and coincide with, the site and the time of the address, and it is you who recall to yourself an "I" uprooted from the time and the place of writing. But in order for "you" and "I" to be instantiated, to effect the relation in language that shares the time of the other, we need to recognize that the text is an address in the first place. This, in turn, presupposes a shared language. At the very least, it is this shared language that is asserted in the anticipation of a response. It was the context of the initial hearings of the Rivonia Trial that first insisted that Mandela's words could call the apartheid government to account, even in the teeth of the opposing legal proceedings still taking place. The "language shared" in this instance, I am suggesting, was not contained by the apartheid laws and could not be suppressed by those laws even *in court*.

Each event of address is an instantiation of and a giving of an "I" to a "you" who hears. In that the text of the address is infinitely iterable, the "I" can reach through time and space to an elsewhere that interrupts the presence of the utterance. Mandela's speech act at the Rivonia Trial is one striking example of this interruption, where the rule of apartheid law is already seen to have been short-lived—paradoxically in the very instant of staging its institutional force. "In court," Mandela symbolically addresses and appeals to a "you" beyond the range of an apartheid hearing. In this symbolic interruption of the presence of the law, the "you" of Mandela's speech makes an appeal that is greater than one that could be addressed to those *in office* in the courtroom in Rivonia, South Africa, at the initial hearings in 1962, and greater than the appeal that could be made later in his statement from the dock in 1964. Mandela's gesture of a giving over of an "I" to a "you" as coparticipants in the interlocutionary event brings with it an altered and more subtle sense of the sites of legal, political, and ethical responsibilities. Ten years after the first democratic elections, on April 14, 2004, Mandela yet again draws our attention to the intricate dynamics of responsibility subtending the I–you logic of the speech event. When Mandela cast his vote, he was asked, in a live television broadcast, whom he had voted for, and he replied, "*I voted for you.*" "For you"—in all its multivalency, which is to say, on your behalf, in your best interests, in your stead—and importantly, *for you*, in the sense that you are the one to whom I entrust legal and political responsibilities to come.

PART II

Crossing the Line

Justice and the Art of Transition

I

In conversation with Angela Breidbach, South African artist and filmmaker William Kentridge speaks about his early interest in art: "I come from a very logical and rational family. My father is a lawyer. I had to establish myself in the world as not just being his son, his child. I had to find a way of arriving at knowledge that was not subject to cross-examination, not subject to legal reasoning" (Kentridge and Breidbach 2006, 70). Kentridge explains that his drawing "was a way of trying to find knowledge or find opinions that came through a completely different route." In the end, he continues, "there was some meaning. It wasn't as if I dreamed it up with nothing, no thoughts, but they had to come through different ways, other ways entirely to those of legal reasoning" (Kentridge and Breidbach 2006, 70). Kentridge presents art and legal reasoning as working toward forms of knowledge in entirely different ways, yet the creative process of making a drawing, for Kentridge, involves a movement on the part of the artist that is partly "projection" and partly "reception" of an emergent image—it has to do with "what you recognize as the drawing proceeds" (Kentridge and Breidbach 2006, 70).

This act of projection, reception—and hence of recognition—also applies to the event of viewing a drawing, and it is within a cultural context of the visual arts and language that I discuss "drawing the line" (and "crossing the line") in all its ambiguity in this chapter. Drawing a line in the literal sense, as a graphic artist would, is a gesture that may not be subject to legal reasoning (to use Kentridge's phrasing); yet in conversation with Breidbach, Kentridge is careful to distinguish between, on the one hand, the a priori forms of knowledge associated with the law and other academic discourses and, on the other hand, the responsiveness in creative practices, in being able to see "not what you know, but what you recognize" (Kentridge and Breidbach 2006, 62). In the drawing's *address* to those who may view it, the artwork depends on and anticipates a ground of recognition. "There is no art except for and by others," writes Paul Sartre, and still, "The writer neither foresees nor conjectures; he *projects*" (Sartre 1978, 28–29). The creative work (even while the artist does not have determinate knowledge of a future audience in the act of creation) sets perimeters to a potential field of response. With this in mind, the literal act of drawing a line can be understood as beginning to approach the metaphorical meaning of the phrase "to draw the line": that is, "to fix a limit or boundary" (*OED*).[1] The art of drawing the line, then, appears to involve a delicate interplay between uncertainty and recognition, a projection into an unknown yet anticipated field of response that the lines themselves (if unwittingly) set.

The discussions in this chapter play out in the interstitial zones of art and justice, justice and the law, law and language, language and art. What role could the arts play in a transitional time of an appeal for political and legal transformation? These are my central preoccupations in this chapter, where I explore the ethical implications of various attempts to imagine, cross, and redraw existing lines in South Africa's postapartheid cultural, political, and legal landscapes. In reconfiguring the lines that trace out patterns of meaning and perception (so the argument in this chapter goes), the arts play an active role in the time of establishing a new legal constitution, the instan-

---

1. Heidegger, on Nietzsche, writes: "Art is not only subject to rules, must not only obey laws, but is in itself legislation. Only as legislation is it truly art. What is inexhaustible, what is to be created, is the law. Art that dissolves style in sheer ebullition of feelings misses the mark, in that its discovery of law is essentially disturbed; such discovery can become actual in art only when the law drapes itself in freedom of form, in order in that way to come openly into play" (Heidegger 1991, 130–31).

tiation of which is itself an "aesthetic act"—in the sense that it creates a template of what can be seen and heard and recognized as significant within its jurisdiction. In the course of the discussion I refer particularly to the work of contemporary South African language-artist Willem Boshoff and to the architecture and design of the new Constitutional Court building in Johannesburg.[2]

My argument is structured by what I see as a convergence of two of Derrida's essays, written nearly thirty years apart: "Force and Signification" (first published in French in 1963) and "Force of Law: The 'Mystical Foundation of Authority'" (1990; complete—and rather different—English version, 2001).[3] Underwriting the present chapter—and, in fact, the argument of the book as a whole—is the thought that the idiom of the arts constitutes lines of force and fracture that inaugurate new meanings, precipitating at each turn the possibility of a future "we."

II

Derrida read the first part of "Force of Law" at a colloquium, "Deconstruction and the Possibility of Justice," held at the Cardozo Law School in 1989. Here are the opening sentences of Derrida's address: "C'est pour moi un devoir, je dois *m'adresser* à vous en anglais. This is for me a duty, I must *address* myself to you in English" (Derrida 2002, 231). This "question of language and idiom," far from being a playful diversion from the more serious business of justice and the law, Derrida tells us, "will doubtless be at the heart of what I propose for discussion tonight" (Derrida 2002, 233). The issue of the language spoken at the event of the Cardozo conference is inextricably bound up in its theme. English is the language of the majority, but, "through hospitality, it grants speech to the stranger or foreigner." This is a law "of which it is hard to say whether it is a rule of decorum, politeness, the law of the strongest [*la loi du plus fort*], or the equitable law [*loi*] of democracy." Further, Derrida goes on to say, "I must be capable, up to a certain point, of understanding the contract and the conditions of the law [*loi*]—that is to say, of at least minimally appropriating to myself your language" (Derrida 2002, 232). Derrida's address itself, then, runs along the lines of contract law, and through his response to the request that he address the problem, in

---

2. Most of Boshoff's artworks can be viewed on his website: www.willemboshoff.com. For an insightful reading of Boshoff's oeuvre, see Ivan Vladislavić's 2005 study.

3. References throughout are to this later English version, published in *Acts of Religion* (2002).

English, of "deconstruction and the possibility of justice," the entire speech event brings into force an exacting geometry:

> Tonight, I have agreed by contract to "address," in English, a problem, that is to say, to go straight toward it and straight toward you, thematically and without detour, in addressing myself to you in your language. In between the law or right [*droit*], the rectitude of address, direction and straightforwardness [*droiture*], one should find a direct line of communication and find oneself on the right track.
>
> Derrida 2002, 243–44

But deconstruction has the reputation of being indirect, oblique, of taking the detour, of never quite arriving, and Derrida's primary philosophical medium is French, not English. By the time of his address, an act of translation, a linguistic detour, has already taken place. The theme of justice that Derrida is asked to speak about is also not as straightforward as the interlocutionary geometry demands—and it too is caught up in the "anguishing gravity of this problem of language" (Derrida 2002, 245). At a primary level (there are other levels, more of which later), "the violence of an injustice has begun when all the members [*partenaires*] of a community do not share, through and through, the same idiom" (Derrida, 2002, 246). It is thus that the question of idiom—in the sense not only of a national language but also of nuanced and local inflections—exposes the potential injustices of the linguistic contractual law as its vectors cut across from addressor to addressee, over fault lines in the political terrain. Even an oblique line, as Derrida points out in a different essay, runs the risk of insensitivity to the nuances of a dialogic exchange:

> What one would have to criticize in the oblique, today, is without doubt the geometrical figure, the compromise still made with the primitiveness of the plane, the line, the angle, the diagonal, and thus of the right angle between the vertical and the horizontal. The oblique remains the choice of a strategy that is still crude, obliged to ward off what is most urgent, a geometric calculus for diverting as quickly as possible both the frontal approach and the straight line: presumed to be the shortest path from the one to another. Even in its rhetorical form and in the figure of figure that is called *oratio obliqua*, this displacement still appears too direct, linear, in short, economic, in complicity with the diagonal arc.
>
> Derrida 1995b, 13–14

The question of language in relation to the law, of a vernacular or local idiom in relation to the possibility of justice and political and legal transformation, could hardly be more urgent in South Africa, a country with eleven official languages: Afrikaans, English, isiNdebele, Sesotho, Sesotho sa Leboa, Setswana, Siswati, Tshivenda, isiXhosa, Xitsonga, isiZulu. There are other "unofficial" languages too (Sign language, for example), and still others that are no longer spoken or that are on the brink of extinction: San, Khoisan, Khoehoen, Nama, Griqua . . . Language issues in South Africa have been at the core of some of the most brutal staging of apartheid's institutional force. The 1976 Soweto uprising, for example, which would lead to the deaths of hundreds of students, was a protest against the Bantu Education Department's ruling that Afrikaans should hold equal status with English as a medium of instruction in African schools. It is therefore unsurprising that questions about language recur as a central preoccupation in the work of several South African artists and writers.

A concern with the operations of language, and an interest in its material aspect (both visual and tactile), is central to the work of Willem Boshoff, a leading contemporary South African conceptual artist. Given the context of South Africa's infamous language policy under apartheid, and its current recognition of eleven official languages, Boshoff's work has political and ethical ramifications, as I hope to demonstrate in much of the discussion to follow in this chapter.

Boshoff's art defies ready categorization; it bears family resemblances to conceptual art, to sculpture, and to concrete poetry. Taken together, his works play out a series of implacable tensions—tensions between system and anarchy, sense and non(-)sense, concept and percept. An enquiry into the material and performative aspects of language informs Boshoff's work in a philosophically radical way, to the extent that the uncertain play between what is *seen* and what is *read* in each encounter with a Boshoff piece seems to reenact a primal awareness of inchoate meaning as it surfaces in writing and runs along the purposive lines of graphic inscription. Boshoff is preoccupied with the very earliest *meaningful* marks. A mark, scratch, inscription, or line can be understood as being meaningful—and the appreciation of something's being meaningful or not sets the perimeter to the work's "responsive range."[4] It draws the line between those who are included or

---

4. This is Peter Fitzpatrick's phrase. See his 2004 essay, "Juris-fiction: Literature and the Law of the Law," 224. The notion of "reponsive range" is a leading concept in chapter 2, "Redrawing the Lines."

excluded from that mark's address, and this has momentous sociopolitical implications. Boshoff, through his artworks, explores the effects of the way in which meaning-bearing signs mark out those readers or viewers who are able to respond to them. Writing calls readers at circumscribed sociopolitical sites, and Boshoff, in his language artworks, draws attention to those different places within the field of address that the artwork instantiates in relation to its viewers. Many of Boshoff's works are three-dimensional dictionaries: sequences of words in wood, sand, or stone, with definitions or translations that prescribe the limits to the meanings of the words but in a way that also serves as a disconcerting reminder of the linguistic boundaries that actively divide speakers within the *polis*.

One such work is a huge mural, *Abamfusa Lawula—The Purple Shall Govern* (1997, 3,660 mm x 2,440 mm, printed text on paper, masonite and wood). Printed along the length of the wall in large, bold letters are the words of the rhythmic protest chants performed with such energy and urgency during the apartheid years. Between the lines, in a much smaller script, one can read the English translations of the songs. Viewers who know an indigenous African language can read the work from a distance, but those who do not will find themselves up against the wall, forced to read between the lines to gain some understanding of the writing that was always on the wall in the apartheid era. *Abamfusa Lawula* thus actively positions its addressees; sites of response are determined by different lengths in the linguistic lines of address that the work throws out to those variously responsive to its call. The work dramatizes the political and legal distances that "not-speaking-your-language" effects. Of course, under apartheid, protest songs were banned by law and would not have been seen in writing, let alone in translation. *Abamfusa Lawula*, in positioning its viewers apart, constitutes a theatrical reenactment of *apartheid*—in unambiguously spatial terms. In a physical way it draws attention to the enforced legal segregation and political distance between people *as* they fall under the jurisdiction of apartheid law.

III

"In what language does the fundamental outline of that thinking speak that prefigures a crossing of the line?" Martin Heidegger asks in his essay "Über die Linie" ("Concerning 'the Line,'" later translated as "On the Question of Being"). Heidegger's essay, in its turn, is a response to Ernst Jünger's text "Über die Linie" ("Across the Line"). Heidegger's essay is written within a highly specialized philosophical context. Starting out with Jünger's presentation of the line as a "zero meridian" and a "zero point" (Heidegger 1998, 291), Heidegger furthers his own exploration of the relation between beings and Being; in crossing the zero meridian from one zone to the next, what language would one speak? What moment of transition with regard to a language of metaphysics? "As meridian," writes Heidegger in response to Jünger,

> the zero line has its zone. The realm of consummate nihilism constitutes the border between two world eras. The line that designates this realm is the critical line. By this line will be decided whether the movement of nihilism comes to an end in a nihilistic nothing, or whether it is the transition to the realm of a "new turning of being." . . . The movement of nihilism must thus of its own accord be disposed toward different possibilities and in keeping with its essence be ambiguous.
>
> Heidegger 1998, 292

Clearly the tenor of Heidegger's discussion is best appreciated within the context of a history of Western metaphysical thinking, but for the purposes of this chapter, I note that the essay raises valuable questions that I will formulate in terms relevant to my discussion.[5] Any thought of crossing the line, for Heidegger, must attempt something other than *ratio*, or reason. The "judiciary of *ratio*" is "not at all a legitimate judge. It unthinkingly thrusts everything that is inappropriate *to it* into the alleged mire of the irrational, a mire that, moreover, it itself first delimits. Reason and representational activity are only *one* kind of thinking and are by no means self-determined" (Heidegger 1998, 293).[6] It is easy to become trapped in a binary conceptual field of rational/irrational—"one denies any possibility that thinking might be brought before a call that maintains itself outside of the alternative of rational or irrational," but, Heidegger continues, "such a thinking could nonetheless be prepared by the tentative steps attempted in the manner of historical elucidation, reflection, and discussion" (Heidegger 1998, 294), and

---

5. It is necessary to consult Heidegger's entire essay to track the extent of my interpretative translation of this text for the purposes of my chapter.

6. I am reminded here of Elizabeth Costello's plea in J. M. Coetzee's *The Lives of Animals*: "And that, you see, is my dilemma this afternoon," she says, "Both reason and seven decades of life experience tell me that reason is neither the being of the universe nor the being of God. On the contrary, reason looks to me suspiciously like the being of human thought; worse than that, like the being of one tendency in human thought. Reason is the being of a certain spectrum of human thinking. And if this is so, if that is what I believe, then why should I bow to reason this afternoon and content myself with embroidering on the discourse of the old philosophers?" (Coetzee 1999b, 23).

"would not crossing the line then necessarily have to become a transformation of our saying and demand a transformed relation to the essence of language?" (Heidegger 1998, 306).

Crossing the line, then, means speaking in ways that have not been articulated before, in ways that may not be subject to standard legal reasoning but *nevertheless* speaking with a sensitivity to history. In attempting to think this crossing of the line, I turn to Derrida's use of the word "force" as it appears in two of his essays, "Force and Signification" and "Force of Law." In its multivalency, "force" exposes Derrida's conception of the aporetic relation between justice and the law, and between what he terms the founding and the preserving violence of the law. The titular prominence given to "force" in both "Force and Signification" and "Force of Law" invites me to bring about a convergence of questions of law and of signification—which in this chapter I associate with literary signification and signification in the visual arts. The operative space of South Africa's transition to democracy, I argue, is at this point of convergence (of law and signification).

First, it is necessary to consider the way in which "force" exposes an aporetic relation between justice and the law. On the one hand, for Derrida, "force" is not exterior to the law, and neither is justice: Force is "essentially implied in the very concept of *justice as law*, of justice as it becomes law, of the law as law" (Derrida 2002, 233). But this is not to say that justice is absolutely *subsumed* within the law: On the other hand, Derrida is insistent that he "reserve the possibility of a justice, indeed of a law [*loi*] that not only exceeds or contradicts law but also, perhaps, has no relation to law" (Derrida 2002, 233). Thus, "law is the element of calculation, and it is just that there be law, but justice is incalculable, it demands that one calculate with the incalculable" (Derrida 2002, 244).

As I have already begun to suggest, justice demands that the participants speak a mutually shared language, but this question of language in itself circles back on the aporia of justice and the law, on the force that justice as law demands:

> To address oneself to the other in the language of the other is both the condition of all possible justice, it seems, but, in all rigor, it appears not only impossible (since I cannot speak the language of the other except to the extent that I appropriate it and assimilate it according to the law [*loi*] of an implicit third) but even excluded by justice as law, inasmuch

as justice as law seems to imply an element of universality, the appeal to a third party who suspends the unilaterality or singularity of the idioms.

Derrida 2002, 245

It seems to me that the potential for legal and political transformation arises in this linguistic force field between justice and the law, where the singular idioms surface in what is universally readable, even in the very attempt to meet the singular idiom of the other. The transition to a new social order demands that one engage the possibility of stepping beyond the limits of one's own given discourse, which, in itself, involves a measure of violence. The effects of this step beyond may not be predictable or calculable, but at the same time, it needs to be readable by those toward whom a reconciliatory gesture is made, or from whom it is sought. This fiat of giving oneself over to the discourse of the other is prior to any subsumptive "theme" or "message" that might be communicated, so that (as Derrida points out in *On Cosmopolitanism and Forgiveness*, and which I have already cited in section IV of chapter 2): "Even if I say 'I do not forgive you' to someone who asks my forgiveness, *but whom I understand and who understands me*, then a process of reconciliation has begun; the third has intervened" (Derrida 2001, 49, my emphasis). This "process of reconciliation" is not safely situated within the bounds of a received grammar; it requires a crossing of the line, a breach with the *directive* geometry of the law, which opens onto questions of justice, and an ethics of address and response: "And so we have already, in the fact that I speak the language of the other and break with mine, in the fact that I give myself up to the other, a singular mixture of force, *justesse* and justice" (Derrida 2002, 244).

This "break" with one's own idiom is something that the poet Paul Celan understands as being integral to the creation of and response to a work of art; art's encounters thus have an ethical resonance. In his essay "The Meridian,"[7] first presented as a speech on the occasion of receiving the Georg Büchner Prize in 1960, Celan writes that the one "whose eyes and mind are occupied with art . . . forgets about himself. Art makes for distance from the I. Art requires that we travel a certain space in a certain direction, on a certain road" (Celan 1986, 44). But this is not to say that art *follows* a clearly marked path to a predetermined destination: "Perhaps poetry, like art, moves with the

---

7. I mention Celan's essay very briefly, and in a different context, in the closing section of chapter 2.

oblivious self into the uncanny and strange to free itself. Though where? in which place? how? as what? This would mean art is the distance poetry must cover. . . . *La poésie, elle aussi, brûle nos étapes*" (Celan 1986, 44–45, emphasis in the original). All of which is to say that art *breaks* the path, it is "language actualized, set free under the sign of a radical individuation which, however, remains as aware of the limits drawn by language *as of the possibilities it opens*" (Celan 1986, 49, my emphasis). The "place" of art, and the "direction" in which it travels, cannot be mathematically determined by a set of a priori spatial and temporal coordinates:

> The poem is lonely. It is lonely and *en route*. Its author stays with it.
> Does this very fact not place the poem already here, at its inception, in the encounter, *in the mystery of encounter*?
>
> Celan 1986, 49, emphasis in the original

My discussion is gradually bringing about a convergence of two lines of force: the force of law, and the force of art. I do not wish to make a crude claim that law and art operate in exactly the same way, but the movement of convergence is toward this point: Both the force of law and the force of art reach out for the *creation* of a new semantic articulation. In speaking about transitional justice in South Africa, I find myself at this chiasmatic intersection, which is not exclusively in the realm of law or in that of the political.[8] Both law (especially constitutional law) and the politics of transformation raise the possibility of a reconstituted future community within the fields of affect that they instantiate.[9] And this instantiation of new fields of affect is surely one source of motivation for art.

What is at stake in the act of creating meaning in the arts? For Celan (as we have seen), the place of art is in the mystery of an encounter that breaks rather than follows new paths of meaning. In other words, art is a risk, the meaning of which is not guaranteed in advance. In ways that are strikingly reminiscent of the passages I have cited from Celan above, Derrida in his

---

8. The question of reconciliation in relation to the fields of law and politics is cause for debate in contemporary legal theory. See, for instance, the collection of essays edited by Scott Veitch, *Law and the Politics of Reconciliation*.

9. South Africa's Truth and Reconciliation Commission has attracted a great deal of scholarly attention, not least in relation to questions of the role of narrative in a newly emergent social order. Apart from several books written from within the discipline of critical legal studies, there is a range of other modes of engagement with the TRC—see most especially Antjie Krog's *Country of my Skull* (1998) and *There Was This Goat* (2009); Fiona Ross's *Bearing Witness: Women and the Truth and Reconciliation Commission in South Africa* (2003); and Mark Sanders's *Ambiguities of Witnessing: Law and Literature in the Time of a Truth Commission* (2007).

early essay "Force and Signification" speaks about the literary meaning and its directedness toward an uncertain future: "It is because writing is *inaugural*, in the fresh sense of the word, that it is dangerous and anguishing. It does not know where it is going, no knowledge can keep it from the essential precipitation toward the meaning that it constitutes and that is, primarily, its future" (Derrida 1978a).

Yet in its precipitation toward a future meaning, toward potential sites of reception, a work of art is primarily an *address*, even if that address is inflected by risk and uncertainty, by temporal and spatial drift. And of course, this vexed question of "address" is precisely what sets "Force of Law" into philosophical orbit—"if, at least, I want to make myself heard and understood, it is necessary [*il faut*] that I speak your language" (Derrida 2002, 232). This, then, is another level at which the question of justice/injustice has to do with language and the contractual law of meaningful address: All possible future meanings cannot be exhaustively calculated in the moment of the utterance (all possible future meanings are incalculable, as justice is incalculable), yet it is necessary to *project* one's utterance—to address it—along a trajectory that will become readable (that is, along the ruled lines of a language, which are the laws with which one calculates). So, then, what is at stake in literary creation—and perhaps even more so in the visual arts—is an aporetic vibration of the calculable and the incalculable, where something can be *recognized as new*. And perhaps it is in this recognition of the new in the utterance of the other that a process of transitional justice might begin. If this is so, then the constitution of a new legal order has primarily to do with the problem of *speaking a newly readable language*.

In the idea of the paradoxical *re*-cognition of a language that is readable *from now on*, I am reminded of Derrida's deconstruction of the relation between the founding and the preserving violence of the law. In the second part of "Force of Law," Derrida responds intimately to Walter Benjamin's *Zur Kritik der Gewalt*. One of the distinctions that Derrida draws (following Benjamin), and deconstructs, is that between the founding violence of the law (*die rechtsetzende Gewalt*) and the preserving violence of the law (*die rechtserhaltende Gewalt*). *Gewalt* can be translated as "violence" but also as "'legitimate force,' authorized violence, legal power, as when one speaks of *Staatsgewalt*, state power" (Derrida 2002, 262). This complex account of force provides the cue for the rest of my discussion. Force inaugurates a field of potential addressees; it precipitates the possibility that something *beyond* the given boundary of the readable may one day also be read as meaningful.

Force thus evokes cognate conceptions of creation and *constitution*, in both the colloquial and the legal senses of this last term. The beating of a precipitous path that crosses previously existing boundary lines toward a new (site of) readability is as much a preoccupation of the arts as it is of law's effort to render justice within the climate of an urgent political plea for transformation and reconciliation.

This brings me back to the term *constitution*. The event of founding a law, or a state, does not fall within the jurisdiction of the existing law. The inaugural moment of constitution is to be "before a law still nonexisting, a law still ahead, still having to and yet to come [*une loi encore devant et devant venir*]" (Derrida 2002, 270). Now it is in these terms that Derrida speaks about literary signification: Let us recall, writing is inaugural; in *breaking* the path, it "does not know where it is going, no knowledge can keep it from the essential precipitation toward the meaning that it *constitutes* and that is, primarily, its future" (Derrida 1978, 11). It is in these terms, too, that Andrew Schaap, following Hannah Arendt, speaks of political reconciliation. The "act of constitution" Schaap sees as the first step in a sequence of reconciliation, an act that

> entails both beginning and promising. On the one hand, it requires that we conceive the present as a point of origin, which might appear *in retrospect* as the moment in which a "people" first appeared on the political scene. On the other hand, it requires that former enemies promise "never again" in order to condition the possibility of community in the future.
>
> Schaap 2007, 10, my emphasis

Schaap thus uses the word "constitution" to refer not only "to issues of jurisdiction and state organisation" but to the "performative constitution of a 'we' through collective action and the constitution of a space for a reconciliatory politics in which the appearance of this 'we' is an ever-present possibility" (Schaap 2007, 10). The process of political reconciliation, for Schaap, is future-directed, but his use of the phrase "in retrospect" in the passage I have just cited demands careful attention.[10] The concept of retrospection, as Derrida argues in his nuanced way, exposes the aporia between the founding

---

10. Thoughout his essay Schaap relies on a somewhat too tidy distinction between "the certainty of law," associated with the restoration of a "universal moral community," and "the risk of politics," associated with the contingency of a future political community (see especially the introductory and concluding paragraphs, pages 9 and 29).

and the preserving violence of the law. An act of constitution—a founding violence—"interrupts the established law to found another. This moment of suspense, . . . this founding or revolutionary moment of law is, in law, an instance of nonlaw [*dans le droit une instance de nondroit*]" (Derrida 2002, 269). But in order to found something that will last, this originary instance of "nonlaw" has to be readable in the future, with a retrospective gaze, as the legitimate origin of the new order. This retrospective assertion of the legitimacy of an act, which *in its time* was an instance of nonlaw, is the preserving violence of the law.

It is significant, for the purposes of the present discussion, that Derrida speaks about these founding and preserving forces in terms that conflate a discourse of law and politics, on the one hand, with a discourse of creative writing and literary interpretation on the other. In his discussion of the American Declaration of Independence, for instance, Derrida speaks of "fabulous retroactivity": The signatories of the declaration, "the people," are *invented* by a signature rather than the other way round (Derrida 1986, 10). In "Force of Law," the act of founding a state (a political event of nonlaw) inaugurates, in what will become a retrospective interpretation, a new way of *reading* the event: "There is something of the general strike, and thus of the revolutionary situation, in every reading that founds something new and that remains unreadable in regard to established canons and norms of reading—that is to say the present state of reading or of what figures the State (with a capital *S*), in the state of possible reading" (Derrida 2002, 271).

Andrew Schaap uses this logic to apply it specifically to the initiation of a process of political reconciliation: "Political reconciliation is initiated not by the acknowledgement of wrongdoing in terms of an already established set of shared norms but by the act of constitution: the constitution of a space for politics makes possible a future collective remembrance" (Schaap 2007, 15).[11] In this view, the initiation of a process of reconciliation entails all the risk, creative ingenuity, and technical consideration one usually associates with the making of a work of art: The process of reconciliation begins with the invention and the projection into the future of an event that will become a past worth remembering.

---

11. The paradoxical logic and the political implications of acts of constitution give rise to rigorous debate in contemporary legal theory. See, for example, Emilios Christodoulidis (2007), "Against Substitution: The Constitutional Thinking of Dissensus," and Hans Lindahl (2007), "Constituent Power and Reflexive Identity: Towards an Ontology of Collective Selfhood."

It is precisely this logic that informs the architecture and overall design of South Africa's new Constitutional Court in Hillbrow, Johannesburg, which is built on the site of the Old Fort, the high-security prison where Nelson Mandela was held, among many other political prisoners.[12] In his speech of April 8, 1998, announcing the winners of the architectural competition for the new Court, Mandela speaks of the way in which the building's artistic conception transforms a reading of what has taken place at that site. Certain events from the past *now* become the history of the constituted future, and the physical act of constructing the building itself lays the foundational stone of the constitution in both a literal and a metaphoric sense:

> The Court's physical foundations will rise from the horrific memories of torture and suffering which [were] perpetrated in the dark corners, cells and corridors of the Old Fort prison. Rising from the ashes of that ghastly era, this new institution will shine forth as a reminder for the future generation of our prevailing confidence and optimism that South Africa will never return to that abyss and indeed is a better place for all.
>
> Mandela in Segal 2006, 84

In fact, in many accounts of the building and of daily life at Constitutional Hill, the creation of the artworks and museum spaces, the foundation of the Constitution, and the founding of a polis are all understood to happen *in the same gesture and in the same space*.[13] "Like the Constitution," writes Albie Sachs, Constitutional Court judge,

> the Court belongs to and serves the whole nation. We want the eyes, hands and hearts of all our artists famous and unknown, to be involved. We do not want to acquire loose art and place it in the building but rather ensure that the art is integrated into the very fabric of the building. We want this to be a national project. We want to include people

---

12. For a history of the prison and the building of the new Constitutional Court, see Lauren Segal (compiler, lead writer, and editor), *Number Four: The Making of Constitutional Hill* (2006).

13. The name of the precinct was cause for debate. Albie Sachs: "I proposed that the whole area be called 'Freedom Hill' and that it be dedicated to freedom. Chief Justice Arthur Chaskalson responded with 'Constitution Hill.' I was a little dubious; I thought that was giving a kind of a legal slant to the place. But I'm very pleased that he made that suggestion" (Segal 2006, 74). This anecdote perhaps adds point to Andrew Schaap's argument: "Law frustrates political reconciliation by representing community as the given end of politics rather than a contingent historical possibility that conditions the possibility of politics in the present. The tendency of a legal constitution to undercut the ethical constitution of a 'we' in this way was demonstrated, for instance, in the constitutional politics of South Africa" (Schaap 2007, 26).

who don't even know they are artists. We want people who do beautiful doors, crafts and mosaics.

Sachs in Segal 2006, 108

In ways that remind me of Paul Celan's reflections on poetry and of Derrida's analysis of the founding and the preserving violence of the law, Sachs comments that the architectural design of the building "opened up the whole hill. The site wasn't the end of the journey. It was a place of thoroughfare and *encounter*—ongoing, mobile, fluid, moving—for people coming past. And connecting Hillbrow with Parktown with Braamfontein: the three totally different Johannesburgs" (Sachs in Segal 2006, 89, my emphasis). Paul Celan concludes his speech "The Meridian" with the following remarks,

> I find something which consoles me a bit for having walked this impossible road in your presence, this road of the impossible.
> I find the connective which, like the poem, leads to *encounters*.
> I find something as immaterial as language, yet earthly, terrestrial, in the shape of a circle which, via both poles, rejoins itself and on the way serenely crosses even the tropics: I find . . . a *meridian*.
> With you and Georg Büchner and the State of Hesse, I believe I have just touched it again.
> Celan 1986, 54–55, my emphasis on "encounters"

Another line, then! It is the notion of "encounter" (the word that Sachs also uses) that I wish to consider in the next section. But to conclude this section, on the question of lines, at least this much should be clear: The lines I have been speaking about in this chapter are not simply the visible outlines of discrete objects in the world—it is in a more abstract sense that I have referred to lines of address, to lines that mark legal, political, and linguistic limits, to lines that project signification beyond normative boundary lines, opening up new ways of reading.

IV

Derrida's "Force and Signification" offers a detailed and provocative reading of Jean Rousset's structuralist work *Forme et Signification: Essais sur les structures littéraires de Corneille à Claudel*. A structuralist approach, especially as it is evinced by Rousset, writes Derrida, practices a certain literary geometry; it grants an absolute privilege to spatial models, mathematical functions, lines, and forms.... But, in fact, time itself is always reduced. To a *dimension* in the best of cases. It is only the element in which a form or a curve can be displayed. It is always in league with a line or design, always extended in space, level. It calls for measurement.

Derrida 1978, 16

Rousset, in Derrida's reading, is preoccupied with the lines that trace out the internal thematic structures and patterns of the work. Of Célidée and her lover in *La galerie du Palais*, for example, Rousset writes: "Initial accord, separation, median reunification that fails, second separation symmetrical to the first, final conjunction. The destination is a return to the point of departure after a circuit in the form of a crossed ring" (Rousset, cited in Derrida 1978, 17). To delineate the thematic patterns in this way is to presuppose the structural boundary of that literary work in advance. It is to disregard the lines of address that the writing sends out to potential readers; it is to consider the work as self-contained *representation* rather than as historically inflected *appeal*. I use this last word in the sense of "language addressed *to*, or likely to influence, some particular principle, faculty, class, etc." (*OED*). It is in the understanding of an artwork as an appeal that it becomes possible to speak about art's *encounters*. By way of the references I have made to Celan thus far, these encounters can be understood as encounters between the artwork and the viewer/reader or, perhaps in a more abstract way, as encounters between the artist and the reader. But what interests me within the context of a political climate of transitional justice is the encounter that an artwork effects *between its readers*. Many of Willem Boshoff's works (some of which, incidentally, have a strong presence at the new Constitutional Court) are at once poignant and adventurous in this regard. The shift in emphasis, from an interaction with the work itself to the interactions that the work causes between its viewers, deepens the ethical and political engagements of Boshoff's art, especially since these works are so relentlessly preoccupied with the question of a readable language.

The Blind Alphabet ABC (1991–2000), for example, consists of 338 exquisitely carved wooden sculptures, each one representing a word that designates a shape, form, or texture. Each carving is housed in a steel mesh cage with an aluminum lid. The word, its derivation, and examples of its use are written on the lid. The only trouble—but also the work's raison d'être—is that the writing on the lid is in Braille. In front of the installation, a sighted person cannot see the sculptures clearly through the steel mesh and will need to ask someone who is blind, someone who can read Braille, for guidance. An understanding of this work demands a conversation with a person you might not ordinarily find yourself talking to; you have to cross your usual linguistic limit in order for the work to become readable. In the process, a social balance of power so readily taken for granted is inverted: It is the blind person who becomes the seer. The artwork thus demands a collaborative reading between the artwork's viewers, where difference from the linguistic norm is valued rather than elided. The artwork thus draws attention to an awareness of difference *that provokes dialogue*, and this is the remarkable consequence of much of Boshoff's work.[14] His installations have the potential to become sites of dialogic interaction where the viewer/reader is forced to cross a line—in this case, between the world of the sighted and the world of the blind. An artwork such as *The Blind Alphabet* exposes the fragility of supposedly infrangible barriers and opens the possibility that at least some lines can be redrawn.

Like *The Blind Alphabet*, Boshoff's *The Writing in the Sand* (2000) is a work that is striking not in some "theme" or image that it *represents* but in the encounters that it potentially effects between its readers. *The Writing in the Sand* consists of a list of words and definitions stenciled onto the floor in black and white sand. The words all end in "–ology" or "–ism"—for instance, "pogonology," "concettism," and "carphology." The headwords are written in English, but the definitions are written in South Africa's other official indigenous languages. As an English speaker, one is obliged to defer to the expertise of speakers of these other languages in order to understand what is written. Once again, a shift in the balance of power is brought about, as the English speaker is unseated from his or her usual linguistic position of the one who knows. Now the *content* of the work is far from being politically committed in a thematically representational way. In fact, the words and their definitions are breezy, to say the least. Pogonology is the study of beards, "concettism" means the art of appearing intelligent without actually saying much, and "carphology" is an inordinate fondness for fondling one's pajamas . . . well, that is what Boshoff says![15] But the point is this: The importance of the work lies in the encounters it potentially brings about rather than in some subsumptive theme that it might represent. A work such as

---

14. See Vladislavić 2005, 61.
15. See the artist's notes at www.willemboshoff.com.

this one is a reminder of Adorno's observation that "there is no straightforward relationship" between the "appeal and the thematic content of the work" (Adorno 1977, 190). Further, it seems to me, *The Writing in the Sand* has the potential to initiate the kind of political reconciliation discussed in much of contemporary legal theory where reconciliation is not primarily considered to be the restoration of a predetermined community that relies on the myth of a communal past. Instead, in this view of the politics of reconciliation, community is a "contingent historical possibility" (Schaap 2007, 26) and readers (I use this word in the broadest possible sense) are aware that being attuned to difference (rather than riding roughshod over it) can recalibrate the sociopolitical settings at which new kinds of dialogue might now take place. But those readers are aware also that their very differences render notions of "reconciliation" and "community" extremely vulnerable.[16] With a further poignant twist, Boshoff's work leads us to realize that an unthinking preoccupation with "speaking the same language" runs the risk of hastening the extinction of minor and indigenous languages and cultures. The work is made of sand, so easily disturbed or blown away, and, of course, once each exhibition is over, *The Writing in the Sand* will be swept up, gone. Unless existing relations of power are challenged, the desire to speak the same language—in both a literal and a metaphorical sense—is certainly tantamount to what Stewart Motha calls "reconciliation as domination" (Motha 2007, 69).

But, for the time being, as viewers stand and talk before *The Writing in the Sand*, they themselves *perform* the protest raised by the artist against linguistic and hence cultural exclusions, against prejudicial social hierarchies, against the extinction of indigenous languages, in ways that actively transcend the barriers that occasioned the artwork in the first place.

The Writing in the Sand has been exhibited three times—at the seventh Havana Biennale in Cuba (2000), at Den Frie Udstillings Bygning in Copenhagen (2001), and at Rand Afrikaans University (2001).[17] On the one hand, one might be skeptical about a work like *The Writing in the Sand*: Just how many Xitsonga or siSwati speakers, one might be tempted to ask, have actually seen it and enlightened their fellow English-speaking art lovers? But

---

16. My indirect allusion here is to Schaap reading Christodoulidis—see Schaap 2007, 16. Schaap's reference is to Christodoulidis 2000, 198.

17. In January 2005, Rand Afrikaans University merged with Vista University and with the Witwatersrand Technical College. The new institution is now known as the University of Johannesburg.

I think that to ask this question is somewhat to miss an important point. "Committed art in the proper sense," writes Adorno, "is not intended to generate ameliorative measures, legislative acts or practical institutions—like earlier propagandist plays against syphilis, duels, abortion laws or borstals—but to work at the level of fundamental attitudes" (Adorno 1977, 180).

Each event of art's being *read* attentively, in a way that does not necessarily depend on the work's internal representative delineations, goes some way toward operating at the level of "fundamental attitudes" on the part of those readers. An artwork sends out lines of force into the sociopolitical field beyond the limits of that work's own physical or representational quiddity. These lines have the potential (but no guarantee) to reconnect, along different routes, previously closed or isolated circuits of meaning. In speaking about art lines in this way, I am interested in the abstract patterns of space that *surround* the art object. This is certainly not to dispense with the importance of the materiality of the work and the sensory perception of it; it is precisely *on the basis* of the material that the abstract spatial patterns can delineate art's force field at all. I think of an act of art not only as the act of creating and placing some physical thing in the world but as a gesture that *displaces* the space around it.

It is with these ideas in mind that I read Derrida's "Force and Signification"—an essay that offers a sustained critique of structuralist literary discourse. Implausible as it may seem initially, this essay has important bearing on questions of reconciliation and, more specifically, on what I would like to call an aesthetics of reconciliation. Structuralism, says Derrida, "will be interpreted, perhaps, as a relaxation, if not a lapse, of the attention given to *force*, which is the tension of force itself. *Form* fascinates when one no longer has the force to understand force from within itself. That is, to create" (Derrida 1978a, 4–5).

If we understand the artwork as initiating possible encounters that break open new paths of meaning between the work and its readers and between the readers themselves, then it is easy to see why a classical structural analysis of the kind that Rousset conducts falls short of paying attention to art's force field. It is in this context, perhaps, that it is easier to understand Derrida's interesting claim that "there is no *space* of the work, if by space we mean *presence* and *synopsis*" (Derrida 1978, 14). In its lapse in the attention given to force, a structuralist reading is conducted in *purely* spatial terms, running the risk of overlooking a history, more difficult to conceive: the history of the meaning of the work itself, of its *operation*. This history of the meaning of the work is not only its *past*, the eve or the sleep in which it precedes itself in an author's intentions, but is also the impossibility of its ever being *present*, of its ever being summarized by some absolute simultaneity or instantaneousness.

Derrida 1978a, 14

Force is associated with notions of creation, constitution—which applies both to the founding/preserving violence of the law and to the force of signification in an artwork. It is in very similar terms that Derrida speaks about "the history of the meaning of the work" (in the passage just cited) and the history of the law. Here is a passage from "Force of Law"—to be read alongside the passage from "Force and Signification." The moment of founding a law, as we have seen, is an instance of "nonlaw"—but, Derrida continues,

> it is also the whole history of law. *This moment always takes place and never takes place in a presence.* It is the moment in which the foundation of law remains suspended in the void or over the abyss, suspended by a pure performative act that would not have to answer to or before anyone. The supposed subject of this pure performative would no longer be before the law [*devant la loi*], or rather he would be before a law [*loi*] still undetermined . . . a law still ahead, still having to and yet to come [*une loi encore devant et devant venir*].
>
> Derrida 2002, 269–70

The most striking example of this "history of law"—which will also have become the "history of the meaning" of one of Boshoff's artworks—is the statement Nelson Mandela delivered from the dock at the Rivonia Trial in 1964.[18] Mandela voiced a powerful *political* protest; it was an instance of operating beyond the limit of apartheid law but in ways that would nevertheless redirect the lines of judgement and defence and reconfigure Mandela's responsive range. He was not making a statement *to the judge* in his official capacity, and he was not simply speaking *in* an apartheid court. Mandela's was an ethical appeal for justice, addressed to the conscience of his fellow human beings. "By representing myself," says Mandela in his autobiography, *Long Walk to Freedom*, "I would use my trial as a showcase for the

---

18. I speak in more detail about Mandela's Rivonia Trial statement in chapter 2, "Redrawing the Lines."

ANC's moral opposition to racism. I would not attempt to defend myself so much as put the state itself on trial" (Mandela 1994a, 304). Of course, in the court of apartheid law, Mandela had no illusions—that he would be pronounced guilty was a given, but already, at the initial hearings of the trial in 1962, he insisted: "I have no doubt that posterity will pronounce that I was innocent and that the criminals that should have been brought before this court are the members of the government" (Mandela 1994a, 319). The effect of Mandela's speeches during the Rivonia Trial was this: His words crossed law's line and inaugurated his addressees *beyond* apartheid's field of affect. "Right from the start," says Mandela, "we had made it clear that we intended to use the trial not as a test of the law, but as a platform for our beliefs" (Mandela 1994a, 346). Further, Mandela tells us, "We had agreed not to plead in the traditional manner, but to use the moment to show our disdain for the proceedings" (Mandela 1994a, 341). Mandela's decision to make a statement from the dock, instead of giving testimony and going through cross-examination, was taken explicitly so that he would "open the defence with a statement of our *politics* and ideals," even in the knowledge that what he said in the statement wouldn't carry "the same *legal* weight as ordinary testimony" (Mandela 1994a, 347, my emphasis). Mandela's speeches had the extraordinary power, let us say *force*, to recalibrate the sociopolitical—and, ultimately, the legal—setting in which those words would be heard. Retrospectively, his statement from the dock would be regarded as an originary moment in the founding of South Africa's democracy.

One excerpt from Mandela's statement has been cited in several different contexts: "I have cherished the ideal of a democratic and free society in which all persons live together in harmony and with equal opportunities. It is an ideal which I hope to live for and to achieve. But if needs be, it is an ideal for which I am prepared to die" (Mandela 1994a, 354; 1994b, 217).

Mandela repeated this part of his Rivonia Trial statement in Cape Town when he addressed the crowds when he was released from prison in 1990; the speech is cited in *Long Walk to Freedom*, which was published in the same year as the first democratic elections in South Africa, and the words "It is an ideal which I hope to live for and to achieve. But if needs be, it is an ideal for which I am prepared to die" are engraved on a massive panel in the new Constitutional Court. In each instance, the mode in which the words are said shifts the ground of their reception—at the Rivonia Trial the ground shifts from law to politics. At the Cape Town Rally speech, Mandela reconstitutes his subject position, in relation to his addressees, as political leader, no longer state prisoner. In his autobiography the words inscribe their addressees as interested readers of a past worth remembering as historical narrative, and in the Constitutional Court they address the readers as inheritors of the democratic state that Mandela's voiced aspirations founded.

A structural analysis, writes Derrida, is a "reflection of the accomplished, the constituted, the *constructed*. Historical, eschatological, and crepuscular by its very situation" (Derrida 1978a, 5). It is an analysis that divests a field of its operative forces, oblivious to the ways in which the process of signification *performs* its field of affect. An attentiveness to the responsive range of the work (whether this work is a law, a constitution, an artwork) can tell us much about the history of that work's *operation*, which is a discussion altogether different from a structural analysis of a supposedly sealed-in content.

The words of Mandela's statement from the dock at the Rivonia Trial make a reappearance, nearly thirty years later, in two etchings by Willem Boshoff, *Neves I* and *Neves II* (2003, ink on paper, 52 cm x 64 cm). The letters are minute—"micrographic," as Boshoff would say—and because this is an etching, the letters are reversed. From a distance, the etchings look like a scribble pattern; but on closer inspection, the large sweeping lines that form the overlapping word "neves," twice on each etching, in a casual copper-plate style, can be seen to be made up of tiny, spidery mirror writing. With patience, a word here and there, or a phrase from Mandela's Rivonia Trial statement, can be made out, but the script is barely legible at all. The word "neves," Boshoff tells us in the exhibition catalogue, *Licked*, is used by prisoners to refer to "a really long prison stretch—seven years at least . . . and longer" (Willem Boshoff 2003[19]). He sees his work as "a vague mirror, held up to acknowledge, in a *small* way, a *great* man's *perplexing* life" (Boshoff 2003).[20] *Now* the addressees of these words are in an art gallery; the speech and its first speaker take on near-legendary status as they inspire the cultural manifestations of a postapartheid society. In looking at the history of the meaning of this work, in terms not simply of the express content of Mandela's speech but of the modes of its saying,[21] the focus is as much on the configurations of the perceptual field as it is on the work itself. It is with

---

19. There are no page numbers in the catalogue.
20. I am reminded of Derrida's essay, "The Laws of Reflection: Nelson Mandela, in Admiration," in *For Nelson Mandela* (1987).
21. I am echoing a sentence on page 7 of the introduction, by Emilios Christodoulidis and Scott Veitch, to *Law and the Politics of Reconciliation*.

this in mind that one can begin to discuss the implications of the *operation* of the work and to move away from the staid calculations of a supposedly self-contained structure. In each dramatic event of a work's perception, the *force* of signification erupts, and "what is at stake, first of all, is an adventure of vision, a conversion of the way of putting questions to any object posed before us, to historical objects—[one's] own—in particular" (Derrida 1978a, 3).

v

In his essay on the paintings of Cézanne, Merleau-Ponty writes that "the world is a mass without gaps, a system of colors across which the receding perspective, the outlines, angles, and curves are inscribed like lines of force; the spatial structure vibrates as it is formed" (Merleau-Ponty 1964, 15). These lines of force are contingent, kinetic, and not necessarily coterminous with *objectively* discrete objects in the world. Further, they do not presuppose clearly defined areas to be marked off and colored in afterward; the lines are projected by the mass of colors in the world, as they become more intense, and press outward. The art of reconciliation (in all the multivalency of this phrase) has to do with a decision of where and when to draw these lines; lines that reconfigure the margins of exposure of one to the other.

4

Intersections:
Ethics and Aesthetics

I

At the traffic-light intersection, where one crosses over the M3 from Newlands Avenue into Rhodes Drive in Cape Town, the wait for the lights to change from red to green takes an eternity, not least in summer, *with* two children, but *without* airconditioning in our Golf Chico, when temperatures in Cape Town sometimes rise above 40 degrees Celsius. As the lights turn red, street hawkers prance out into the traffic, touting an extravagant range of wares: *The Big Issue*, peanuts, hands-free cellphone sets, plastic refuse bags, grapes, peaches, *The Cape Times*, avocado pears, sunglasses, arum lilies, oranges, children's parasols, strawberries, vuvuzelas, caps, corroded metal sculptures, naartjies, handbags, *Funny Money* (a little pamphlet with printed jokes), peppermints, South African flags, Christmas decorations, windscreen shades, life-sized chickens fashioned out of lurid-colored plastic, net covers to keep the flies off your comestibles, and lampshades, Baobob trees, and animal keyrings made of beads and wire . . . in addition to multimedia artworks depicting scenes of township life.

The sales patter itself can be just as colorful: "Grapes without pips, good for your lips"; "sweet like honey, value for your money" (strawberries); "nice and firm without a worm" (peaches). But it is the discussion I had on the day I bought a painting that, in retrospect, became the inspiration for bringing these essays together in this book under the theme of an aesthetics of transitional justice. My predicament in choosing one of the pictures was more complicated than I would have imagined. I pulled over and got out of the car to have a better look. "This is a good picture," I said to one of the vendors (three were now vieing for my attention with deafening enthusiasm). "It has a balanced composition." A split second of nonplussed silence made me change tack: "I mean, I like this one; it has a dog!" This met with the riposte while my own words were still in my mouth: "Well, what about *this* one? This one has *two* dogs, *looking in different directions!*" Clearly no ordinary rules of aesthetics would apply here.

The pictures depict vibrant shantytown streets, invariably with Table Mountain and an extravagantly orange sky in the background. ("The ladies like the sunsets!" one vendor explained). Little figures—children, bicycles, women hanging out the laundry—are painted in an almost stickman style; the shacks and other buildings are made of tin cutouts set in relief and nailed to the board, with the writing on the tins (soda cans, insect repellent, deodorant, furniture polish, tins from air fresheners . . .) often featured prominently on the roofs and walls of the shacks. "Glade Secrets," says one, belying its shantytown setting. "On the Coke Side of Life," says another. At the level of the scenes represented in the pictures, judgment with recourse to usual Western aesthetic norms (perspective, composition, balance, line, color . . .) seem violently inappropriate: The flamboyant foregrounding of power lines and TV aerials (a welcome sign of electricity), or the outlandish size of the letters MTN (a leading cellphone-service provider), which dwarf even Table Mountain, would be cause for negative judgment on the part of the ignorant and mean-spirited rather than on the part of the man of discerning aesthetic judgement. Here I am thinking of the term "aesthetics" in its originary meaning—"the science of the conditions of sensuous perception" (*OED*).

But quite apart from this, the purchasing of *any* item at the traffic lights in South Africa does not fit well with the rules and protocols of a straightforward business transaction.[1] I cross the intersection at least twice every day, and unsurprisingly, at nearly all of these crossings I sincerely do not want three kilograms of grapes, or a pink beaded Pegasus, or a life-sized chicken fashioned out of eye-achingly bright plastic, or a wire Baobab tree that we would have difficulty wrestling through the window of the Golf Chico. But to say "No!" seems to be a refusal of so much more than the undesirable item for sale. To refuse the offer of a newspaper, or of *Funny Money* or a value pack of purple coat hangers, will almost certainly lead to the next level of exchange between the vendor and me: "Please support me"; "any small change?"; "have you got any money for me to buy coffee?" (this, one freezing morning as I was crossing the intersection the other way, taking a sip from my own thermal mug in the car).[2] One late afternoon: "You are my first customer—I need money for my taxi ride home." At each crossing you run the risk of hearing an appeal: "My child is sick: I need medicine," and yet again,

---

1. The vendors of *The Big Issue* have a different ethos, though. See volume 192, the South African fifteenth-anniversary edition, which includes essays by four long-standing vendors in Cape Town. One of these is by Mzwe Themba Tinzi, the vendor of *The Big Issue* at the intersection I cross every day. Themba has been a vendor for ten years, and he plays in the Homeless soccer team, which participated in the Homeless World Cup in Melbourne in 2008. "I don't want people to feel sorry for me," writes Tinzi. "I love my job and the reason I am still selling *The Big Issue* after 10 years is because it has opened so many doors for me. Dreams that I hadn't thought possible have become true for me, and I still have more dreams" (Tinzi 2012, 22). Graeme Clark has been selling *The Big Issue* in Pinelands, Cape Town, for almost fifteen years. He writes: "We are not beggars, we are salespeople. We can take care of our families with dignity instead of depending on handouts" (Clark 2012, 20). Nevertheless, Tinzi ends his article: "Everyone supporting vendors should know that they are doing so much for us. Your help goes beyond that R18 [eighteen South African Rands]. You give us confidence and show that people still care" (Tinzi 2012, 22).

2. Marion Charles, in Zoë Wicomb's novel *Playing in the Light*, encounters parking attendants every day where she works. She thinks to herself: "You can't go anywhere nowadays without a flock of unsavoury people crowding around you, making demands, trying to make you feel guilty for being white and hardworking, earning your living; and of course there's no getting around it: hundreds of rands it costs per month, being blackmailed by the likes of these every time you park your car. And then the impudence of watching as you get out, watching as you lock the door, willing you to feel uncomfortable about your own belongings" (Wicomb 2006, 28). Ivan Vladislavić's *The Exploded View* describes a traffic intersection in Johannesburg: "Vendors moved between cars, proffering coathangers, rubbish bags, sock puppets, baseball caps, trays of naartjies, hands-free kits for cellphones. A balsa-wood schooner, swept up in a black boy's hands, came sailing through the Highveld air. From a distance there was an illusion of intricacy and craft; from close up it was shoddily made, stuck together with staples and glue. A slave ship, mass-produced, he supposed, by children in a sweatshop somewhere in Hong Kong or Karachi or Doornfontein. And how about this: a man with a sign around his neck—Keep South Africa Beautiful: Give Me Your Litter—holding out a waste-paper basket in one hand and cupping the other for a tip. He thought of handing something over—the cab was a mess—or rewarding him for sheer cheek with a few coins from the parking-meter stock in a compartment on the console. Thought again, as the lights changed and he jerked forward with the lane, keeping one eye on the wing mirror to make sure no one lifted anything off the back. Should have laced that cover properly, even though it was late when he dropped Josiah and the temps off in Tembisa" (Vladislavić 2004, 162–63).

Any small change please support me shoes bread taxi medicine . . .
Today, today, this time, only this time!

Where do you draw the line? If you are unswervingly resolute in your refusals, the vendor will say, hopefully: "Maybe next time?" And you are obliged to reply, "OK, maybe next time. . . ." Tomorrow the exchange will happen all over again, and the next day, and the next. Perhaps for once the lights will be green.

There is no undoing of this appeal. The vendor and I, less than a meter apart in the middle of the traffic intersection, inhabit worlds apart—economically, socially, professionally. As the lights turn green, Yvonne Mokgoro's gentle voice echoes in my thoughts: "The deprivation of the Other demeans You."[3]

II

The French philosopher Emmanuel Levinas is preoccupied with the ethical relation of self to other. His writing hinges on a diction of the third person, of "il" (he), "l'autre" (the other), and "autrui" (the other person, others, or—as it is most frequently translated—the Other). But with Yvonne Mokgoro's words in mind ("the deprivation of the Other demeans You"), this chapter is attentive to the role that the *second* person can be seen to play in Levinas's ethical philosophy. My daily crossings at the traffic lights insist on the kind of infinite and ineluctable responsibility that Levinas writes about.[4] Yet in order to receive this call to responsibility, it is necessary that I accept the role of addressee. That is to say, a responsiveness to the appeal of the Other demands that I step down from the position of "I," to become the second person, the "you" of the address.

Part of the inquiry in this chapter demands a careful examination of Levinas's distinction between what he terms the "Saying" and the "Said." Taking

---

3. "The Utility of Ubuntu in South Africa," talk, University of Cape Town, July 30, 2008. Justice Yvonne Mokgoro served as a judge of the Constitutional Court from 1994 to 2009.

4. At the same time, I am reminded of Derrida's discussions of responsibility and irresponsibility in *The Gift of Death*: "I can respond only to the one (or to the One), that is, to the other, by sacrificing the other. I am responsible to any one (that is to say to any other) only by failing in my responsibilities to all the others, to the ethical or political generality. And I can never justify this sacrifice, I must always hold my peace about it. Whether I want to or not, I can never justify the fact that I prefer or sacrifice any one (any other) to the other" (Derrida 1995a, 70). See Hillis Miller's sprightly and thought-provoking essay "Derrida's Ethics of Irresponsibilization; or, How to Get Irresponsible, in Two Easy Lessons" (in Miller 2009, 191–221).

off from this distinction, and with reference to the opening scene of the chapter, my discussion finds itself at an intersection of ethics and aesthetics in Levinas's work.

To think of the event of the Saying as a moment of "I" ceding ground to become the "you" of the Other opens onto one of my leading arguments, namely, that an encounter with a work of art can also be considered an ethical event of the Saying.

This may sound surprising within the context of a reading of Levinas's philosophy: Whereas for the Ludwig Wittgenstein of the *Tractatus* "Ethik und Aesthetik sind Eins" ("Ethics and aesthetics are one" [Wittgenstein 1922, § 6.421]), for Levinas ethics and aesthetics often seem at odds with one another. The notorious argument in Levinas's most explicit essay on aesthetics, "Reality and its Shadow" (first published in *Le Temps Moderne* in 1948), is that art, in its immobilizing of time, constitutes an irresponsible evasion of the world. But in this chapter I read "Reality and Its Shadow" alongside a very different essay, "Paul Celan: From Being to the Other," to come to a more nuanced appreciation of the relation between ethics and aesthetics in Levinas's philosophy: A Levinasian ethical encounter can be understood to be instantiated in each reader's or a viewer's moment of "becoming-you"— that is, in the responsiveness to an appeal sent out in a situation of address.

An argument for the role of the second person in Levinas's philosophy demands, first of all, attentiveness to some rather intricate linguistic distinctions, with special reference to the grammar of pronouns, or to what J. M. Coetzee has productively termed "the deep semantics of person, as carried by the pronoun" (Coetzee 1992, 197). When we deal with pronominal forms such as "I," "you," and "he," the question that most readily arises is, To whom do these pronouns refer? That is to say, which referents are in question? In this chapter, though, the question becomes one of *how* these terms refer: The philosophical grammar of "I," "you," and "he" will be shown to shed unexpected light on Levinasian ethics.

III

Pronominal forms are what Roman Jakobson (following Otto Jespersen) calls "shifters": The referent in each instance of use is different, instantiated by the context of the utterance. But Jakobson goes on to make a further subtle distinction: a distinction between the *speech* event, with addresser and addressee, and the *narrated* event—the "content" of the speech event

(Jakobson 1990, 390).⁵ It is through this distinction that the different grammatical operations of "I" and "you," on the one hand, and "he" or "she," on the other hand, become clear. "I" and "you" refer to the addresser and the addressee of the *speech* event (see Jakobson 1990, 388), but "he" refers to a participant in the *narrated* event. Whereas "you" is always instantiated as present to my utterance, I can refer to "him" in his absence. The linguist Emile Benveniste states the matter clearly with respect to "I" and "you": "*I* is 'the individual who utters the present instance of discourse containing the linguistic instance *I*.'" Similarly, "*you* [is] the 'individual spoken to in the present instance of discourse containing the linguistic instance *you*.'" (Benveniste 1971, 218).⁶ In his chapter "Subjectivity in Language," Benveniste takes the matter even further:

> Then, what does *I* refer to? To something very peculiar which is exclusively linguistic: *I* refers to the act of individual discourse in which it is pronounced, and by this it designates the speaker. It is a term that cannot be identified except in what we have called elsewhere an instance of discourse and that has only a momentary reference. The reality to which it refers is the reality of the discourse.
>
> Benveniste 1971, 226

The implications of Benveniste's claims here are several: In order for the "I" and the "you" of the speech event to be actualized, a certain presence of the addressee to the discourse is required. Differently put, an address to you requires your presence to the discourse in order for that address to take effect.⁷ In that the utterance is "unique each time," "you" cannot be definitively limited, in an a priori way, by the intention or by the epistemological ambit of the "I." You, whom my address anticipates, can be activated at an infinite number of different sites and future instances of address—you are at once anonymous, singular, and infinite. Again following Benveniste, the signs "I" and "you" are "always available and become 'full' as soon as a speaker introduces them into each instance of his discourse" (Benveniste 1971, 219). To reiterate, but now with a slightly different emphasis: These

---

5. I first raised Jakobson's distinction in section II of chapter 2, "Redrawing the Lines."
6. For a related discussion of Benveniste within the context of an ethics of address, see section V of chapter 2. Benveniste is an invaluable source of reference in my discussions of linguistic and narrative techniques in the writing of J. M. Coetzee. See especially chapter 1 ("Not I") and chapter 2 ("You") of *J. M. Coetzee: Countervoices* (Clarkson 2009).
7. I take the terms "address," "utterance," and "speech event" to apply to written texts as much as to spoken dialogue; the logic of the address is not limited to speech in its narrow, literal sense.

signs "cannot exist as potentialities; they exist only insofar as they are actualized in the instance of discourse" (Benveniste 1971, 220).

But "you" signals a curious type of embodiment: You, the referent, are simultaneously embodied and suspended in this sign.[8] My address ineluctably anticipates a "you," but the moment I ask the question "Who are you?" and try to refer to you by name, you shift your grammatical position and occupy the place of a third person. In your name, or as a third person, you need not be present to my utterance, to my *speech* event, but "*you*," the second person, are obliged to be in the presence of this very discourse. Shifting over to the grammatical position of the third person, sometimes at the site of a proper name, "you" would become a referent in a *narrated* event.[9] To stay "you" without becoming a person specified by name, you have to remain infinitely beyond my epistemological reach, anonymous, *at the same time* that you are singularly instantiated, in each instance, in the "presence" of my discourse.

IV

The discussion thus far considers the situation of address from the perspective of "I," the speaker, addressing a "you." And surely, the way in which I have been speaking about "you" reminds you of Martin Buber's seminal work *I and Thou* (more of which later), and perhaps also of Emmanuel Levinas's evocation of what he calls the Other in the interlocutionary event of the Saying: "Our relation with the other (*autrui*) certainly consists in wanting to comprehend him, but this relation overflows comprehension" (Levinas 1996a, 6). Levinas again: "The relation with the other (*autrui*) is not therefore ontology. This tie to the other (*autrui*) . . . does not reduce itself to the representation of the Other (*autrui*) but rather to his invocation, where invocation is not preceded by comprehension" (Levinas 1996a, 7).

Like "you," of whom I spoke earlier, Levinas's Other exceeds my cognitive grasp and is not reducible to thematization within an epistemological

---

8. For a moving and provocative account of "I" and "you" in the sonnet sequence of Dutch poet Gerrit Achterberg, see J. M. Coetzee, "*Achterberg's 'Ballade van de Gasfitter': The Mystery of I and You.*" The sentence to which this endnote is tagged echoes Coetzee: "The notion of identity [that Achterberg's poem] embodies is a suspended one" (Coetzee 1977, 288). Natalie Pollard's *Speaking to You* offers a rigorous, entertaining, and incisive account of "you" in contemporary British poetry.

9. The question of proper names in Levinas demands a separate paper of its own. For an illuminating account of proper names in Derrida and Levinas, see Christian Moraru, "*'We Embraced Each Other by Our Names': Levinas, Derrida, and the Ethics of Naming*" (2000).

compass—which is to say, in Levinas's terms, that the Other is not reducible to the Same. Further, Levinas alerts us to the implications of trying to stabilize and contain the referents of pronominal signs within the horizon of an attempt to know:

> If the question "who?" tends to discover the situation of the subject, that is, the place of a person in a conjuncture, a conjunction of beings and things—or if it consists in asking, as Plato puts it in the *Phaedrus* . . . "who is it?" "from what land does he come?"—then the question "who?" asks about being. Such a "who?" amounts to a "what?," to "what about him?"
>
> Levinas 1981, 27

In the passage I have just cited, the voice of Martin Buber reverberates, except that Buber uses the term "You," where Levinas insists on the term "Other"—here is Martin Buber: "I do not find the human being to whom I say You in any Sometime and Somewhere. I can place him there and have to do this again and again, but immediately he becomes a He or a She, an It, and no longer remains my You" (Buber 1970, 59).

Later on, Buber returns to this idea: "Only as things cease to be our You and become our It do they become subject to coordination. The You knows no system of coordinates" (Buber 1970, 81). It is specifically in this context that Levinas cites Buber approvingly: "The relation to the other man is irreducible to the knowledge of an object," says Levinas in an interview with François Poirié. "This is certainly a terrain of reflection where Buber has been before me. . . . The interpersonal relation is distinguished from the object relation in a very convincing and brilliant way, and with much finesse" (Levinas 2001, 72).

A face-to-face encounter with the Other, the Saying in Levinas, is a performative interlocutionary event that is to be carefully distinguished from the constative communication that Levinas locates in the Said.[10] In other words, Levinas's Saying can be loosely linked to Jakobson's "speech event," and the Said to the "narrated event." It is a logic of this sort that Levinas attempts to articulate in *Totality and Infinity*. The Saying is the irrecuperable event of the address; the Said is the retrospective assimilation of that event:

---

10. The distinction between constative and performative uses of language is made in J. L. Austin's groundbreaking series of lectures, published as *How to Do Things With Words*. I speak in more detail about Austin's distinction in section I of chapter 2, "Redrawing the Lines."

> The relation proceeding from me to the other [in the Saying] cannot be included within a network of relations visible to a third party. If this bond between me and the other could be entirely apprehended from the outside it would suppress, under the gaze that encompassed it, the very multiplicity bound with this bond. . . . I have access to the alterity of the Other from the society I maintain with him, and not by quitting this relation in order to reflect on its terms.
>
> Levinas 1979, 121

Yet the distinction between the Saying and the Said is one of vertiginous subtlety, as we learn from the Levinas of *Otherwise than Being*. The Saying is "antecedent to the verbal signs it conjugates, to the linguistic systems and the semantic glimmerings, a foreword preceding languages, it is the proximity of one to the other, the commitment of an approach, the one for the other, the very signifyingness of signification" (Levinas 1981, 5).

If the Saying precedes and is antecedent to verbal signs, in its invocation of an addressee, it is nevertheless an *interlocutionary* event, a "foreword," an orientation of addresser to addressee. This is clearer in the original French text: "Avant-propos des langues" (Levinas 1974, 6) could be translated as "foreword of languages" rather than as "foreword *preceding* languages" (as in the English publication). Elsewhere Levinas writes in ways that emphasize the linguistic underpinnings of an encounter with the other: "To be in relation with the other (*autrui*) face to face is to be unable to kill. It is also the situation of discourse" (Levinas 1996a, 9), and "I think that the first language is the *response*" (Levinas, 1988, 174, my emphasis). It is the performative fact of the speech event itself, rather than its subsumptive content, that takes priority: "Should language be thought uniquely as the communication of an idea or as information, and not also—*and perhaps above all*—as the fact of encountering the other as other, that is to say, already as a response to him?" (Levinas 2001, 47, emphasis in the original).

In yet another interview, Levinas states the matter deftly, and with even greater clarity: "Language is above all the fact of being addressed . . . which means the saying much more than the said" (Levinas 1988, 170). Thus the Saying, even while it is associated with the ethical in Levinas, is also always a *linguistic* event. Language is the common denominator of the Said *and* the Saying: "Language as *saying* is an ethical openness to the other, as that which is *said*—reduced to a fixed or sychronized presence—it is an ontological closure to the other" (Levinas 1986, 29).

By now at least this much should be clear: Levinas locates his face-to-face encounter in the Saying, in what Jakobson might call the speech event. Further, Levinas insists on the priority of the *performative force* of the Saying before any communicated content or discursive theme. A subjective assimilation of thematized concepts, for Levinas, is part of the Said—or, to put it in Jakobson's terms, part of the narrated event.

But here is the difficulty: In section III of this chapter, following Benveniste and Jakobson, I aligned the performative *speech* event with the pronominal forms "I" and "you," and the constative *narrated* event with the third person pronouns "he," "she," or "it." Now Levinas's Saying seems to fulfill the conditions of a *speech* event, and yet he speaks of the face-to-face encounter as a relation to a third person, "il" (he), rather than staging an encounter between a first person, "I," and a second person, "you." This can catch one unawares, since, as I have already intimated, it is you and me rather than him who are necessarily and singularly instantiated, each time—through the logical grammar of the address or invocation. Why, then, does Levinas relentlessly speak of the third person, when the performative instantiation of a singular and infinite "you" and "I" in each instance of discourse is arguably more congruent with his account of the Saying? The reasons are as wide-ranging as they are subtle.

v

Most importantly (if also somewhat ironically), Levinas explicitly refutes the diction of the second person when distancing himself from the philosophy of Buber.[11] Levinas repeatedly voices his opposition to Buber on the grounds that the latter's "I–Thou" relation is one of reciprocity, that the relation is self-sufficient and intimate to the extent that it excludes any social responsibility to the rest of the world (see, for example, references to Buber in *Totality and Infinity*, 68–69; 213; 265). Certainly, there is much in Buber to support such a reading: "Relation is reciprocity," he says (Buber 1970, 58), and "When one says You, the I of the word-pair I-You is said, too" (Buber 1970, 54). Further, in Buber, the relation to "you" seems to affirm the "I:" "I require a You to become; becoming I, I say You" (Buber 1970, 62). It is through this affirmation of the subjec-

---

11. For a rigorous discussion of Levinas's relation to Martin Buber, see Robert Bernasconi's 1988 essay "'Failure of Communication' as a Surplus: Dialogue and Lack of Dialogue between Buber and Levinas."

tive, conscious I that the "you" in Buber is read as a "theme" by Levinas (Levinas 1981, 12–13).

The relation to the Other in Levinas, if anything, has the opposite effect—it amounts to a desubstantiation of the I, even a substitution of the one for the other. The "il," or "illeity," as Levinas would have it, "indicates a way of concerning me without entering into conjunction with me" (Levinas 1981, 12). The tacit implication here is that Buber's I–thou relation *is* one of conjunction.

Nevertheless, Levinas's relation to Buber is by no means straightforward; and Levinas's take on reciprocity, for example, might have been different, had he read the afterword to *I and Thou* that Buber wrote in 1957.[12] As he elucidates there, his "reciprocity" does not entail psychological mutuality. "Reciprocity" subtends relations "outside of the tamed circle" (Buber 1970, 172); we can say "You" (in Buber's sense) not only to humans and to other animals but also to plants and even to the inanimate world. It is a relation that "reaches from the stones to the stars"—it is a "reciprocity that has nothing except being" (Buber 1970, 173).[13]

To return more specifically to the question of pronouns, though, it seems to me that Levinas's preoccupation with describing an ethical relation, perhaps at the expense of considering the logical performative operation of the second person *linguistically*, together with his wish to distance himself from Buber's I–thou relation, accounts (at least in part) for his preference for the vocabulary of the third person rather than for that of the first or the second person. More generally, Levinas seems to assume an easy distinction between proper names and personal pronouns, without his taking heed of the implications of the different subject positions that can be occupied in the first, second, and third persons through pronouns *and* through proper names. Yet once we remind ourselves of the *grammar* subtending any situation of address, we may well come to a more nuanced appreciation of the *ethics* of address and interlocutionary exchange—not least in the philosophy of Emmanuel Levinas and, more specifically still, in the relation of Levinas's philosophy to that of Martin Buber.

---

12. Bernasconi, pointing out that Levinas did not read the postscript, speculates that if he had, Levinas "might not have gone on to ask whether Buber had been aware of 'the logical originality of the relation'" (Bernasconi 1988, 111).

13. Levinas would argue, though, that what he terms an ethical relation extends beyond this horizon of being; it is a relation to alterity, the "otherwise than being."

VI

In this section I return to the opening scene of the chapter—the intersection of the M3 and Newlands Avenue in Cape Town. Drawing on the discussions in sections II through V (and with reference to Jean-François Lyotard's *The Differend*), this section argues that the ethical relation in Levinas demands a moment of *I-becoming-you*; that is to say, a stepping down of "I," who holds the position of command as speaker, to the responsive position of "you," the addressee. The *I-becoming-you* cedes the ground of speaker to the other in the moment of responsiveness to the other's appeal.

This is the experience at the traffic lights: The vendor makes an appeal—and I become the "you" of his address. In this instant of responsiveness before responding (to respond is to take up the position of "I," the speaker), you are the vendor's hostage, unable to speak: *As you*, you are the listener recognizing and receiving an ineluctable call to respond. Lyotard, in his "transcription" of Levinas's aphoristic "The messenger is the message," writes:

> An addressor appears whose addressee I am, and about whom I know nothing, except that he or she situates me upon the addressee instance. The violence of the revelation is in the ego's expulsion from the addressor instance, from which it managed its work of enjoyment, power, and cognition. It is the scandal of an I displaced onto the you instance. The I turned you tries to repossess itself through the understanding of what dispossesses it.
>
> Lyotard 1988, 110

Lyotard emphasizes the ethical drama played out in every instant of address: "This is what the I's displacement onto the *you* instance marks: You ought to" (Lyotard 1988, 110). What is interesting in Lyotard's reading of Levinas is the rigorous appreciation of the ethical consequences of linguistic and cultural grammars, where "I," the speaker, is hierarchically in a position of dominance and command. Further, in the instant of *becoming you* in response to an appeal—"Such is the universe of the ethical phrase: an I stripped of the illusion of being the addressor of phrases, grabbed hold of upon the addressee instance, incomprehensibly. The obligation is immediate, prior to any intellection, it resides in the 'welcoming of the stranger,' in the address to me" (Lyotard 1988, 111).

Levinas speaks of the other as "destitute"—in ways that resonate on metaphorical and literal levels in countless exchanges at traffic-light intersections every day in South Africa. Lyotard's commentary on Levinas has a particular poignancy when considered in this distinctively local context: "The other arises in my field of perception with the trappings of absolute poverty, without attributes, the other has no place, no time, no essense [sic], the other is nothing but his or her request and my obligation" (Lyotard 1988, 111). Where Levinas's discourse sometimes comes across as rather abstract, Lyotard's reading offers a way of appreciating Levinasian ethics in ways that can be meaningfully recognized in everyday situations: "The ethical realm is not a realm," writes Lyotard, "it is a mode of the *I/you* situation which happens unforeseeably as the scrambling of the phrase universe in which *I* is *I*" (Lyotard 1988, 112). To be in a position of responsiveness is to be able to recognize that an appeal is being made to *you*; it is to become addressable in an act of transformation as "I" becomes "you."[14]

It is at this juncture that I would like to suggest that this act of responsiveness—an I-*becoming-you*—is what is demanded of the reader, viewer, or listener by the work of art. "The work of art is a value because it is an appeal," writes Sartre in his seminal text *What Is Literature?* (Sartre 1978, 34). The passage leading up to this statement is reminiscent of Levinas's account of the Saying, and (as we shall see in the following section) it also provides the opening onto a discussion that offers a way of aligning ethical and aesthetic preoccupations in Levinas. For Sartre, the appeal "resounds at the basis of each painting, each statue, each book" (Sartre 1978, 34), and one's response to a work of art is intimately tied to the question of freedom—in the specific sense that Sartre accords to this term. In conversation with the writings of Kant, Sartre elaborates (I cite at some length the argument leading up to the statement that "art is a value because it is an appeal"):

---

14. Thanks to Louis Blond for his focusing of the encounter in the phrase "becoming addressable." See Judith Butler's extended discussion of the ethics of address in chapter 5 of *Precarious Life*: "The structure of address is important for understanding how moral authority is introduced and sustained if we accept not just that we address others when we speak, but that in some way we come to exist, as it were in the moment of being addressed, and something about our existence proves precarious when that address fails. More emphatically, however, what binds us morally has to do with how we are addressed by others in ways that we cannot avert or avoid; this impingement by the other's address constitutes us first and foremost against our will or, perhaps put more appropriately, prior to the formation of our will. So if we think that moral authority is about finding one's will and standing by it, stamping one's name upon one's will, it may be that we miss the very mode by which moral demands are relayed. That is, we miss the situation of being addressed, the demand that comes from elsewhere, sometimes a nameless elsewhere, by which our obligations are articulated and pressed upon us" (Butler 2004, 130).

> Kant believes that the work of art first exists as fact and that it is then seen. Whereas, it exists only if one *looks* at it and if it is first pure appeal, pure exigence to exist. It is not an instrument whose existence is manifest and whose end is undetermined. It presents itself as a task to be discharged; from the very beginning it places itself on the level of the categorical imperative. You are perfectly free to leave that book on the table. But if you open it, you assume responsibility for it. For freedom is not experienced by its enjoying its free subjective functioning, but in a creative act required by an imperative. This absolute end, this imperative which is transcendent yet acquiesced in, which freedom adopts as its own, is what we call a value. The work of art is a value because it is an appeal.
>
> Sartre 1978, 34

For Sartre, then, as for Levinas and Lyotard, the recognition *that an appeal is being made*, even before the specific details of that appeal are delineated and understood, occasions an ethical encounter in which I become you, the addressee, at once free and responsible. This double injunction, in the Sartrean sense, is no light matter: "What the writer requires of the reader is not the application of an abstract freedom but the gift of his whole person," Sartre writes (Sartre 1978, 36). Differently put, the recognition of the appeal made by the other, or by a work of art, demands an act of I becoming you. This is provocative in its leading us to think of the event of reading a literary text as an event of the Saying. In the dynamic potential of the literary text to instantiate an "I-becoming-you" *each time* it is read, and in ways that cannot be exhaustively predicted or epistemologically saturated in advance, the artwork effects an open yet responsive encounter with the Other.

VII

For Levinas (as we have seen), language itself can be an instance of the Said ("reduced to a fixed identity or synchronized presence—it is an ontological closure to the other") *or* it can be an instance of the Saying—"an ethical openness to the other" (Levinas 1986, 29). The point I wish to develop now is this: A reading of "Reality and Its Shadow" alongside the essay "Paul Celan: From Being to the Other" invites the application of Levinas's dual understanding of language to the domain of an encounter with a literary work, or a work of art. That is to say, in Levinas's own terms, an encounter with a work of cultural production can be regarded as either an instance of the Said or an ethical event of the Saying. Even more directly: There is an argument to be made for the *convergence* of ethics and aesthetics in Levinas, and this in the teeth of the essay "Reality and Its Shadow," which has (justifiably) given rise to a long-standing view that Levinas's aesthetic understanding cannot be reconciled with his ethics.

In "Reality and Its Shadow" (first published in *Les Temps Modernes* in 1948), Levinas reads the artwork as "a stoppage of time"; "every artwork is in the end a statue," he says (Levinas 1989a, 137). He goes on to elaborate:

> Within the life, or rather the death, of a statue, an instant endures infinitely: . . . the Mona Lisa will smile eternally. . . . An eternally suspended future floats around the congealed position of a statue like a future forever to come. The imminence of the future lasts before an instant stripped of the essential characteristic of the present, its evanescence.
>
> Levinas 1989a, 138

The essay reiterates the notion that art freezes time: Time is "immobilized" (139), "suspended" (138), "congealed" (138). The artist "transform[s] time into images" (139) and effects "petrification" (140), "fixity" (139), "death" (138). The characters represented lead "a lifeless life, a derisory life which is not master of itself, a caricature of life" (138). The "power of freedom congeals into impotence" (139). Characters are "shut up, prisoners" (139), and this is not because the artist or writer "*represents* being crushed by fate—beings enter their fate *because they are represented*" (139, my emphasis). Of course, given his emphasis that the effect of the artwork is to arrest time, Levinas is committed to the view that art (within the context of his own understanding of ethics) constitutes an irresponsible relation to the Other: The ethical relation *cedes* the time of the Other without assimilating or synchronizing alterity within the present structures of the Same.[15] Further, given this disengagement from real time, from "a world of initiative and responsibility," Levinas sees in the artwork "a dimension of evasion" (141) and "irresponsibility" (142): "The poet exiles himself from the city. From this point of view, the value of the beautiful is relative. There is something wicked and egoist and cowardly in artistic enjoyment. There are times when one can be ashamed of it, as of feasting during the plague" (Levinas 1989a, 142).

---

15. I discuss the question of time in Levinas in the next chapter.

Much of the discussion in "Reality and Its Shadow" has to do with the artist's relation to the characters represented within the artwork—which is to say that the conversation takes place at the level of the thematizing mechanisms of the Said. But in his essay on the poetry of Paul Celan (first published in 1975), Levinas turns his attention to the logic of literary address itself before exploring any subsumptive content. Here the accent falls on the relations between writer, text, and reader rather than on the characters represented within the work, and in this context it is possible to see the literary work as instantiating an event of the Saying, which is not reducible to the Said. Levinas (via Celan) foregrounds the dynamic positionings of addresser and addressee (loosely, the poet and the reader) in relation to the *event* of reading/writing the poem. Studying Levinas's essay with Benveniste in mind, we are now in a position to understand the interlocutors of the Saying as being "present" to a discourse, the utterance—in this case, the literary text. Nevertheless, within this grammar of address, Levinas still uses the *vocabulary* of a third-person "Other," even though (thanks to Benveniste and Lyotard) we have come to appreciate that, in the ethical event of the saying, we are dealing with a *dynamic* of intersubjective positionings, where "I" becomes "you"—that is to say, the one who hears the call from the Other becomes the addressee, and the Other, in turn, emerges as speaker, the "I." Read this way, key concepts in Levinas, such as the notion of "passivity" or "substitution," come into clearer ethical focus: Passivity is not simply apathy but is perhaps best understood as an acceptance of the role of addressee—of "you," the one responsive to the other, but in that moment before taking up the active and dominant position of speaker responding through "I." Similarly, from your position as you, your "I" is ceded to the Other, who now takes up the role as speaker while you are responsive to that call.

Levinas's essay on Celan constitutes a meditation on a comment Celan once made in a letter: "I cannot see any basic difference between a handshake and a poem" (Celan 1986, 26). In his essay, Levinas speaks about the event of the poem in exactly the same terms that elsewhere in his writings he uses to speak about the Saying. He speaks of the poem as a "saying" a "fact of speaking to the other [that] precedes all thematization" (Levinas 1996b, 44). Further, poems are "important by their interpellation rather than by their message; important by their attention!" (Levinas 1996b, 43). It is here that we see most clearly Levinas's account of the aporetic nature of the embodiment of the addressee. Thus, following Celan, he writes that

> the poem is situated precisely at that pre-syntactic and . . . pre-logical level, but a level also pre-disclosing: at the moment of pure touching, pure contact, grasping, squeezing—which is, perhaps, a way of giving. . . . A language of proximity for proximity's sake, older than that of "the truth of being"— . . . the first of the languages, response preceding the question, responsibility for the neighbor, by its *for the other*, the whole marvel of giving.
>
> Levinas 1996b, 41

If, on the one hand, you, the addressee, are a tangible physical presence to the poem, the poem itself constitutes a movement toward a null-site, a *utopia*, with all the etymological history of *utopia* (from the Greek "not" + "place") in force. Thus, despite a sensory, physical contact between reader and text, the question "where?" evaporates. Like Buber's "Thou" (which Celan, incidentally, explicitly evokes), the movement of the poem, as an infinitely reiterable invocation of an unknowable "you," is not subject to a system of coordinates of latitude and longitude. Neither is it restricted to one moment in history. This is because "you" and "I" function in precisely the same way as do other deictics, such as "now" and "here": "Now" can happen on any *date*; "here" can be any *place*. If "you" and "I" are present to this *utterance*, then you and I, too, are not anchored to a time or a place outside of this very situation of address. You are in a certain way "freed and vacant," as Levinas puts it (1996b, 41); "you" are constituted precisely in your diachronous relation to the lyric "I," in ways that render the questions "who?" and "where?" completely off the mark. In the intricate language of Celan's essay "The Meridian," the poem is simultaneously a response to and an invocation of *you*, the sign that is infinitely open to being "filled" in a unique way each time.

This is a far cry from the immobilizing of time that Levinas attributes to artwork in general in "Reality and Its Shadow." Through his response to the writings of Celan, Levinas perceives the poem as a movement toward a "utopia"—in the sense, too, that it cannot be synchronized or assimilated within a static instant in time or space. This null-site of the literary text is thus ineluctably an instantiation of you and I—but with no reference to the map or the clock or the sovereign self. It is a null-site "outside all enrootedness and all dwelling." Such is the meridian movement of the lyric "I": "It is as if in going toward the other I met myself and implanted myself in a land, henceforth native, and I were stripped of all the weight of my identity. A native land owing nothing to enrootedness, nothing to first occupation; a native land owing nothing to birth" (Levinas 1996b, 44–45).

Further, the event of the poem, far from stabilizing the historical identity of the poet, projects a lyric "I" infinitely into new situations of address, into new I–you relations. Each lyric utterance is thus a "singular de-substantiation of the *I*" (Levinas 1996b, 43) as much as it is an *in*stantiation of that I. It is in this desubstantiation of the I that responsibility (in Levinas's understanding of the term as a self-substitution) is mobilized: "The responsibility for the other is the locus in which is situated the null-site of subjectivity, where the privilege of the question 'Where?' no longer holds" (Levinas 1981, 10).

If the discussion seems to have shifted, almost imperceptibly, from "he" to "you" and "I" in a movement of desubstantiation and substitution, then perhaps it is worth recalling the epigraph that Levinas uses for chapter 4 of *Otherwise than Being*. The chapter is called "Substitution," and the epigraph is a quotation from Paul Celan:

Ich bin du, wenn
    ich ich bin.
I am you, when
    I am I.
Celan in Levinas 1981, 99

VIII

Part of the difficulty in reading Levinas is not so much in coming to terms with a neologistic diction—it is not that one has to come to grips with a new *vocabulary*.[16] Instead, reading Levinas demands the developing of a canniness of a new semantic field in which Levinas puts familiar words into sophisticated philosophical play—words such as "saying," "said," "same," "other," "passivity," and "responsibility."

In this chapter I have spoken about the instance of the Saying in Levinas as the demand for "I" to become "You." This demand, I have suggested, provides a way of thinking through to a possible intersection of ethics and aesthetics in Levinas. Art's appeal (which constitutes its value, in Sartre's sense) instantiates the reader or viewer as addressee, as "you."

---

16. Derrida, by contrast, often opens new paths of thought by way of neologism—deconstruction, grammatology, signifier, différance, destinerrance, countersignature—or by way of the conceptually pivotal use of an untranslated Greek or Latin word; *aporia* is perhaps the best known among these.

By way of concluding this chapter, and as a way of broaching a discussion that finds fuller expression in chapter 7 ("Who Are We?") and in the conclusion of this book, I would like to consider briefly the African saying "*Umuntu ngamuntu ngabantu.*" The saying is most frequently translated along the lines of "A person is a person through other people" or "A person is a person because of other people." But in a talk presented at the University of Cape Town in July 2008, Yvonne Mokgoro, former justice of South Africa's Constitutional Court, offers a different translation: "*I am because you are.*" This translation carries layered meaning: An "I" comes into being thanks to my acknowledgment of the being of the Other whom I address.[17] But we might also read Mokgoro's translation this way: In my willingness to become "you"—that is, to become addressable, responsive to an *appeal*—I recognize the existence of the Other, and in my responsiveness I come into being as one with a sense of shared humanity myself. Thi realization, in turn, casts Celan's words in a slightly different light: "I am you, when I am I."

In Nguni languages, the root –*ntu* (in words like *ubuntu*) is variously translated as "humanity," "humaneness," and "personhood"; it is the essence of individuated yet related being. African philosopher V. Y. Mudimbe puts it this way in his groundbreaking text *The Invention of Africa*:

> In sum, the *ntu* is somehow a sign of universal similitude. Its presence in beings brings them to life and attests to both their individual value and to the measure of their integration in the dialectic of vital energy. *Ntu* is both a uniting and a differentiating vital norm which explains the powers of vital inequality in terms of difference between beings. It is a sign that God, father of all beings . . . has put a stamp on the universe, thus making it transparent in a hierarchy of sympathy.
>
> Mudimbe 1988, 148[18]

The willingness of "I" to become "you" is surely one way of attesting to one's individual value and to the measure of one's integration in a dialectic of vital energy. In another presentation (this time at the University of Pretoria in August 2011), Yvonne Mokgoro voiced an appeal: "Let's not leave *ubuntu* to the courts." Our responses to the vendors at the traffic lights may be one way of beginning to put this into practice.

---

17. Recall Martin Buber's dictum here—"When one says You, the I of the word-pair I-You is said, too" (Buber 1970, 54).

18. See Mudimbe's *The Invention of Africa* (1988), 147–50, for an extended discussion of the root -*ntu*. I return to the concept of *ubuntu* in chapter 7 and in the conclusion.

5

Poets, Philosophers, and Other Animals

I

"On the list of the nation's priorities," says Lucy Lurie of J. M. Coetzee's novel *Disgrace*, "animals come nowhere" (Coetzee 1999a, 73). Certainly the Constitution of South Africa makes no specific mention of animals other than human—unsurprisingly so, given the context of this new constitution, that is to say, the radical change in human politics and the national transition from the rule of apartheid law to democracy. Perhaps there is also something to be made of the view held by another one of Coetzee's characters, the philosopher Professor Thomas O'Hearne, in *The Lives of Animals*. O'Hearne points out to Elizabeth Costello that his "first reservation about the animal rights movement . . . is that by failing to recognize its historical nature, it runs the risk of becoming, like the human-rights movement, yet another Western crusade against the practices of the rest of the world, claiming universality for what are simply its own standards (Coetzee 1999b, 60).

An attention to the plight of animals, in a context where human political affairs are arguably more important, runs the risk in South Africa of being yet another instance of the imposition of Western colonial thinking. This chapter takes up the gauntlet thrown down by Lucy Lurie: It is concerned with other animals, at the same time recognizing that the nation's priorities lie elsewhere. This in itself is yet another instance of an "aesthetic act"—to return to Rancière's term—that resonates with the explicit purpose of animal-rights activist Michelè Pickover in her book *Animal Rights in South Africa*. "The aim of this book," writes Pickover, "is to give voice to the voiceless, to make the invisible visible, and to be a catalyst to reveal all our dormant feelings" (Pickover 2005, 2). This chapter also contributes to one of the larger ambitions of my book—namely, its exploration of the boundary between literature and philosophy and a questioning of the certainty with which the line between these disciplines is often drawn. I would go so far as to say that for the most part the questions and discussions in this book are generated in the interstitial zones between literature, philosophy, and the visual arts.

But to begin with a question of animals: Where do we draw the line (the question of the ambit of "we" gains critical urgency in the chapters to follow)—not only between human and nonhuman animals but in relation to practices, deemed humane or otherwise, regarding other animals? Further: What do scientists, philosophers and poets respectively have to contribute toward serious thinking about animals other than human?

Scientists and philosophers mark the coming into being of the human in ways that resonate with their respective disciplines: Scientists speak of a DNA profile; the philosophers are interested in the capacity for rational argument. One marker of human identity (but one that is not discussed in scientific or even philosophical enquiry) is the specifically human capacity for deliberate artistic expression—"We like to distinguish ourselves from other animals by saying we're a rational species," says Roger Rosenblatt. "That is sort of a commonly shared joke. But a narrative species? That, one can prove" (Rosenblatt 2011, 20).

Picking up on references to Plato's *Republic* in the introduction, and also in section IV of chapter 1, this chapter raises questions about the philosophers and the poets in relation to animal ethics. If philosophical reasoning is traditionally associated with the human, one rationale for banishing the poets from the ideal state in Plato's *Republic* is that the literary arts appeal to characteristics conventionally associated with an animal side of human nature, that is, desire, sensation, affect. The poet "wakens and encourages and strengthens the lower elements in the mind to the detriment of reason" (Plato 2003, § 605b) and encourages the "unreasoning part" of the mind (§ 605c); in short, "pleasure and pain become your rulers instead of law and the rational principles commonly accepted as best" (§ 607a). Yet in the admission that an unreasoning part of the mind is also constitutive of human experience, do the visual and literary arts not also participate in an active, positive, and more holistic expression of what it is to be "human"? If "what we feel for other people must infect what we feel for ourselves" (Plato 2003, § 606b), could literature in its appeal to the sympathetic imagination (rather than philosophy with its reasoned arguments) have a better chance of affecting the way humans think about others, and about other animals? These are the leading questions of this chapter.

As a way of exploring these questions, this chapter leads up to a discussion of a contemporary philosophical dialogue: "The Death of the Animal: A Dialogue on Perfectionism," by Paola Cavalieri. The dialogue is published in the book *The Death of the Animal*, which includes contributions by eminent contemporary philosophers in two roundtable discussions that follow from Cavalieri's dialogue. Matthew Calarco, Harlan Miller, and Cary Wolfe participate; Peter Singer has written the foreword. The philosophers represented in the book come from both analytic and Continental traditions of philosophy, responding directly to Cavalieri's dialogue, in which the interlocuters—Alexandra Warnock and Theo Glucksman—represent analytic and Continental approaches respectively in their discussion of perfectionism.

But part of what makes the dialogue such a valuable site of discussion for this chapter is that the discussions include three contributions by Nobel Prize–winner and South African–born writer John M. Coetzee.[1] Coetzee is best known as a novelist—he is the first writer to have won the Booker Prize twice (for *Life & Times of Michael K* and for *Disgrace*), yet apart from his novels and three fictional autobiographies, Coetzee has published five books of nonfiction—works that include interviews, critical essays, and literary reviews. Novels such as *Elizabeth Costello* and *Diary of a Bad Year* incorporate extensive literary-philosophical reflections of the sort we would more readily expect to find in a collection of critical essays than in a novel. The relation

---

1. On the covers of all his published works, the author's name is written "J. M. Coetzee." This is the first time I have seen the writer presented as "John M. Coetzee."

between philosophical and literary discourses constitutes a sustained line of inquiry throughout Coetzee's writing, not least when it comes to questions of the sympathetic imagination and of human encounters with other animals.

Before discussing *The Death of the Animal* and the philosophers and the poets in sections III and IV of this chapter, I turn to the scientists and the question of "speciesism" in section II. I offer a reading of two of Darwin's groundbreaking works, *On the Origin of Species by Way of Natural Selection* and *The Descent of Man*, and with oblique reference to the previous chapter (chapter 4, "Intersections: Ethics and Aesthetics") I carry through thoughts of Levinas's ethical philosophy. Reading Darwin with Levinas in mind, so the argument in the present chapter goes, opens up a different appreciation of the nineteenth-century naturalist's contribution to thinking about human relations to other animals. This leads into debates about perfectionism as they are raised in Paola Cavalieri's dialogue, and I go on to discuss them in sections III and IV.

II

In this section I focus on the conclusion of Darwin's *On the Origin of Species* and draw attention to passages from *The Descent of Man*, all the while keeping an eye on Levinasian ethics. This strategy in itself is open to discussion, since Levinas, on more than one occasion, explicitly sets his own ethical concerns as being at odds with Darwin's theory of evolution. Nevertheless, reading Darwin while thinking about Levinas leads us to notice a remarkable, self-conscious awareness in Darwin of an aporetic logic at work in his taxonomic epistemology. This, in turn, leads us to question assumptions we may have had about a presumed Darwinian speciesism. In both Darwin and Levinas, the discussion in this section argues, the effect of time undercuts the attempt to stabilize ontological "essences" within the compass of the known. The matter becomes interesting with the recollection that it is the breakup of essence that for Levinas is the starting point of ethics (Levinas 1981, 14).

Levinas makes reference to Darwin several times in his writings and interviews in ways that pitch his own ethical philosophy decisively against evolutionary biologism. The "relation to the face," argues Levinas, challenges what Spinoza calls the *conatus essendi*, the natural "right to existence" (Levinas 1986, 24). Spinoza goes so far as to say that the will to self-preservation is the foundation of ethics. Proposition 18 in part 4 of Spinoza's *Ethics* states:

> As virtue is nothing else but action in accordance with the laws of one's own nature . . . , and as no one endeavours to preserve his own being, except in accordance with the laws of his own nature, it follows, *first*, that the foundation of virtue is the endeavour [*conatum*] to preserve one's own being; *secondly*, that virtue is to be desired for its own sake, and that there is nothing more excellent or more useful to us, for the sake of which we should desire it.
>
> Spinoza 1891, 201

In the same paragraph, Spinoza makes the claim that "virtue is nothing else but action in accordance with the laws of one's own nature" (Spinoza 1891, 201), but Levinas takes the opposite line: "The ethical I is a being who *asks* if he has a right to be!" (my emphasis)—to the extent that "my duty to respond to the other suspends my natural right to self-survival, *le droit vitale*" (Levinas 1986, 24). This "first truth of ontology—the struggle to *be*" is, in Levinas's view, refused by ethics: "Ethics is, therefore, *against nature* because it forbids the murderousness of my natural will to put my own existence first" (Levinas 1986, 24). In the same interview, Levinas speaks of ethics as the "conversion," the "reversal," and the "opposite" of nature (24–25).

Thus Levinas (not surprisingly) speaks of ethics as being wholly at odds with any notion of "survival of the fittest." The struggle for existence, as Levinas sees it, is determined by a primary drive for self-preservation, which could hardly be further removed from his own philosophy of ethics as an absolutely non-egocentric self-substituting responsibility for the Other.

But views along the lines of Spinoza's proposition are regaining some philosophical currency, and, together with recent developments in the fields of evolutionary psychology and neurobiology, the relation between "nature" and "ethics" is perhaps more vexed than Levinas allows. I am thinking, for example, of E. O. Wilson's "biology of ethics"—a line of enquiry that "combines the findings of biology with those of the social sciences," and in which the mind is "more precisely explained as an epiphenomenon of the neuronal machinery of the brain. That machinery is in turn the product of genetic evolution by natural selection" (Wilson 1978, 195). Antonio Damasio examines the neurobiological apparatus and cognitive configurations that predispose humans toward ethical behavior within a social context. He speculates on the evolutionary origins:

> The construction we call ethics in humans may have begun as part of an overall program of bioregulation. The embryo of ethical behaviors would have been another step in a progression that includes all the non-conscious, automated mechanisms that provide metabolic regulation; drives and motivations; emotions of diverse kinds; and feelings. Most importantly, the situations that evoke these emotions and feelings call for solutions that include cooperation. It is not difficult to imagine the emergence of justice and honor out of the practices of cooperation.
>
> Damasio 2004, 162

With particular reference to the *Origin of Species*, Darwin's theory of evolution has been read as positive impetus for an ethics that extends the field of responsibility beyond that of an anthropocentric Christian humanism. In his reflections on Darwin, poet and novelist Thomas Hardy writes at the turn of the twentieth century that it is the *ethical* implication of Darwin's work that is the most far-reaching: If humans are related to other animals through a common ancestor, then our ethical obligations should extend to those creatures too. Hardy sees this as a logical consequence of Darwin's theories—a "*necessity of rightness*" (Hardy 1984, 377).² If questions of ethics are indeed generated by Darwin, then it still remains to be asked, specifically, on what ground such an ethics could be seen to take root. Further, could there be any point of contact at all between Darwin and Levinas in the teeth of the opposition that the latter sets up, namely, that of nature *versus* ethics?

That ethical obligations arise with regard to creatures other than humans Levinas is not in disagreement: "The ethical extends to all living beings," he says in an interview (Levinas 1988, 172). But the argument that *biological kinship* to other animals should underwrite these ethical obligations is not one that Levinas holds. Biological kinship as a way of grounding ethics, for Levinas, would come dangerously close to a totalizing ontology, to a reduction of the Other to the Same of the ego's comprehensive range: "The

---

2. Darwin's influence on Hardy's fiction has been discussed in interesting ways by a number of literary critics. See especially "Finding a Scale for the Human: Plot and Writing in Hardy's Novels," chapter 8 of Gillian Beer's *Darwin's Plots*; Phillip Mallett's "Noticing Things: Hardy and the Nature of 'Nature'"; Sophie Gilmartin's "Geology, Genealogy, and Church Restoration in Hardy's Writing"; and Hillis Miller's "'Wessex Heights': The Persistence of the Past in Hardy's Poetry."

individuals would appear as participants in the totality," writes Levinas in a slightly different context (one to which I shall return later). "The Other would amount to a second copy of the I—both included in the same concept" (Levinas 1979, 121). Approaching the Other by way of a generic name is thus the opposite of what Levinas terms the "ethical": Ethics, in Levinas's specialized use of the word, entails an infinite deference to the absolute *alterity* of the other. Let us examine this relation between Darwin and Levinas more closely. (The extended example to follow is one of vertiginous intricacy.) Darwin in his conclusion to *On the Origin of Species* writes:

> The terms used by naturalists of affinity, relationship, community of type, paternity, morphology . . . will cease to be metaphorical, and will have a plain signification. When we no longer look at an organic being as a savage looks at a ship, as at something wholly beyond his comprehension; when we regard every production of nature as one which has had a history; . . . how far more interesting, I speak from experience, will the study of natural history become!
>
> Darwin 2009, 423

For Levinas, however, it is the *metaphoricity* of the filial bond, the irreducibility of kinship to the empirical field of biology, that opens up the possibility for ethics:

> The father-son relationship, for example, should not be thought of only in biological terms. The father-son relationship can exist between beings who, biologically, are not father and son. Paternity and filiality, the feeling that the other is not simply someone I've met, but that he is, in a certain sense, my prolongation, my ego, that his possibilities are mine—the idea of responsibility for the other can go that far.
>
> Levinas 1988, 179–80

Now *on the one hand* these two citations seem completely at odds. Darwin appeals to an empiricist ontology firmly situated within an epistemological and historical ambit, which assures the kinship of all living beings. This is the basis of Hardy's appeal for an ethical reading of Darwin: "The most far-reaching consequence of the establishment of the common origin of all species is ethical," he writes (Hardy 1984, 376). For Levinas, ethics precedes "any liaison contracted. . . . Here there is a relation of kinship outside of all biology, 'against all logic.' It is not because the neighbour would be recognized as the same genus as me that he concerns me. He is precisely *other*" (Levinas 1981, 87). Moreover, the appropriation of the Other to the Same within an epistemological and historical horizon is precisely what preempts an ethical relation to alterity: "History as a relationship between men ignores a position of the I before the other in which the other remains transcendent with respect to me. . . . When man truly approaches the Other he is uprooted from history" (Levinas 1979, 52).

And yet, on the other hand, *both* Darwin and Levinas assert filial ties that extend further in time and in space than we might at first have thought. Each of these thinkers does so in ways that begin to challenge ready assumptions about the ability to isolate or to privilege *presence*, either temporally or spatially, in a neatly defined instance. This challenge to the sovereignty of the present, as we shall see, amounts to a challenge to the sovereignty of the "I." And this challenge underpins Levinas's ethical philosophy in crucial ways.

Firstly, I return more carefully to the term "history" as it is used in Darwin and Levinas in the passages cited earlier. Darwin makes an appeal to regard "*every production of nature* as one which has had a history"—where, of course, "every production of nature" is not restricted to the human realm; in Darwin, "productions of nature" include other animals, plants, geological phenomena, and, importantly, the fossils of extinct species. "History," in Darwin's sense, thus exceeds the political, to the extent that it is questionable whether the span of time at stake here can be contained by human ratiocinative measure at all. This excession of time, in relation to human scales and measurements, is stressed several times in the conclusion of *On the Origin of Species*. For example, Darwin speaks of "ancient and utterly unknown epochs in the world's history" (Darwin 2009, 405); of a "lapse of time . . . so great as to be utterly inappreciable by the human intellect" (Darwin 2009, 405). Later in the conclusion, Darwin elaborates: "The whole history of the world, as at present known, although of a length quite incomprehensible by us, will hereafter be recognised as a mere fragment of time, compared with the ages which have elapsed since the first creature, the progenitor of innumerable extinct and living descendants, was created" (Darwin 2009, 425).

For Darwin, then, "history" is not restricted to human politics—but Levinas, drawing on a more conventional understanding of the term, explicitly glosses "history" as a "*relationship between men*" (my emphasis). Thus the question hinges not so much on Darwin's and Levinas's mutually exclusive applications of history (in relation to the ethical); instead, the question hinges on different, and in each case, quite specific uses of the *term* "history." This sheds an entirely different light on key passages in Darwin and Levinas. Let us reexamine the citation from *Totality and Infinity* where Levinas writes that "history as a relationship between men ignores a position of the I before the other in which the other remains transcendent with respect to me.... When man truly approaches the Other he is uprooted from history" (Levinas 1979, 52).

On a cursory reading, this appears to be very different from Darwin's *recourse* to history as a way of approaching the other. But, as we have also seen, history in Darwin is not restricted to a human history, and far from ignoring the "transcendence" of the other, it is this history—in the sense of a reach of time that extends far beyond anthropocentric scales—that *elevates* the other in Darwin's eyes: "When I view all beings not as special creations, but as the lineal descendants of some few beings which lived long before the first bed of the Silurian system was deposited, they seem to me to become ennobled" (Darwin 2009, 426).

I am reminded here of Levinas's metaphor of the "height" of the Other with respect to me, in that I am unable to bring the Other completely down to the level of my epistemological frame: The "Other (*l'Autre*) thus presents itself as human Other (*Autrui*); it shows a face and opens the dimension of *height*, that is to say, it *infinitely* overflows the bounds of knowledge" (Levinas 1996c, 12, Levinas's emphasis).

Further, and more specifically, each existent, for Darwin, cannot be isolated or sealed off within an absolute full presence to itself: All beings are "lineal descendants," which is to say that each one bears within it traces of the past. And that past, as we have seen in Darwin, is "utterly unknown" (405), "quite incomprehensible" (425), "utterly unappreciable by the human intellect" (405). Each existent in Darwin, then, instantiates a singular yet transmissive relation to time that cannot, by definition, be subsumed within a unitary present.[3] "*To be*" (as Derrida puts it deftly in *Specters of Marx*),

> means ... to inherit. All the questions on the subject of being or of what is to be (or not to be) are questions of inheritance.... That we *are* heirs does not mean that we *have* or that we *receive* this or that, some

---

3. Hardy uses "transmissive," but in a different, if related way: "It was a typical summer evening in June, the atmosphere being in such delicate equilibrium and so transmissive that inanimate objects seemed endowed with two or three senses, if not five" (Hardy 2000, 108).

inheritance that enriches us one day with this or that, but that the *being* of what we are *is* first of all inheritance, whether we like it or know it or not.

Derrida 1994, 54

Affinities, contiguities, or kinships with other creatures are thus most importantly traced through reference to an absent and irrecuperable past. Any connectedness to other creatures, for Darwin, is certainly not situated within a simple co-presence: "The real affinities of all organic beings are *due to inheritance* or community of descent," Darwin is at pains to elucidate in *On the Origin of Species* (Darwin 2009, 417, my emphasis). Further, this primordial transmissive movement of existence *through time* is reiterated, rather than brought to a halt or *arrested* in a scientific nomenclature. Darwin himself is acutely aware of this: "Our classifications will come to be, as far as they can be so made, *genealogies*" (Darwin 2009, 423–24, my emphasis). Genealogies insist on paths of inheritance, on networks of relations that cut across time.

A biological taxonomic system, with its intention to classify and to assimilate the diversity of existence into one totalizing epistemological framework, would yet again seem at a far remove from a Levinasian ethics premised on the absolute alterity or singularity of an Other that cannot be contained within any horizon of the knowable. Yet by now at least this much should be clear: Darwin insists on the irreducibility of what he terms "history" to our comprehensive range. Further, it is a relation to this very history that underwrites biological taxonomic systems "*as far as they can be so made*" (Darwin 2009, 424, my emphasis). The caveat here is Darwin's own, and in countless other instances he insists on the *im*possibility of defining and appropriating the universe—living and extinct—within a named order. Thus, Darwin acknowledges, "we shall have to treat species in the same manner as those naturalists treat genera, who admit that genera are merely artificial combinations made for convenience" (Darwin 2009, 423).

The implications are more radical than one might at first suppose: The inability to name something adequately, in turn, raises questions about what is to be named. Given that each existent sounds the echoes of a past too distant to be imagined—that affinities between creatures, and hence, their identities, are subtended in an irreducible *diachrony*—self-contained "essences" can no longer be assured, let alone presumed. Immediately following the passage about "genera" and "species" being "artificial combinations made for convenience," Darwin continues: "This may not be a cheering prospect; but we shall at least be freed from the vain search for the undiscovered and undiscoverable essence of the term species" (Darwin 2009, 423). Thanks to the effects of a temporality that can no longer be understood as a neatly uncontaminated succession of past, present, and future, the "essence" of "species" is unknown, and never can be known.

Darwin insists on the impossibility of encompassing within an epistemology the diversity of existence by means of a nomenclature—thanks to infinite and continuous evolutionary variations through time. The concluding sentence of *On the Origin of Species* stresses this: "Endless forms most beautiful and most wonderful have been, and *are being*, evolved" (Darwin 2009, 427, my emphasis). The naming of species is thus an act of radical undecidability, fraught with "inextricable doubts" (Darwin 2009, 408), where "*no line of demarcation can be drawn between species*, commonly supposed to have been produced by special acts of creation, and varieties which are acknowledged to have been produced by secondary laws" (Darwin 2009, 410, my emphasis). A little further on Darwin puts this slightly differently: "No one can draw any clear distinction between *individual differences* and slight varieties" (409, my emphasis). That is to say, it is questionable, in Darwin's view, whether difference (alterity, let us say), can be adequately accounted for within the categorical circumference of "species" at all—and the impossibility of defining a species in the first place is something that cedes (rather than overrides within a generalizing "essence") the singularity of each existent.

Levinas takes a further step—epistemological inadequation is a prerequisite for an ethical encounter (I include the brief passage already cited earlier):

> In order that multiplicity be maintained, the relation proceeding from me to the Other . . . must be stronger than the formal signification of conjunction, to which every relation risks being degraded. This greater force is concretely affirmed in the fact that the relation proceeding from me to the other cannot be included within a network of relations visible to a third party. If this bond between me and the other could be entirely apprehended from the outside it would suppress, under the gaze that encompassed it, the very multiplicity bound with this bond. The individu-

als would appear as participants in the totality: the Other would amount to a second copy of the I—both included in the same concept.

Levinas 1979, 120–21

In *Totality and Infinity*, diachrony is played out as an asymmetrical confrontation between the limits of my epistemological frame of reference and the infinite demand of the "face" that "exceed[s] *the idea of the other in me*" (Levinas 1979, 50). In *Otherwise than Being*, diachrony is the very rupture of the supposedly present, controlling I in this way: The ethical call is *anterior* to any moment of knowing, so that my "response" to it does not constitute a stable, subjective position that I can intentionally assume. In response to this call, the self is "doubled" back on a time that is beyond being, where ontological questions of the sort "who?" and "where?" no longer pertain. This is the context of the following discussion of diachrony in *Otherwise than Being*: "Recurrence becomes identity in breaking up the limits of identity" (Levinas 1981, 114) and "I am a self in the identifying recurrence in which I find myself cast back to the hither side of my point of departure! This self is out of phase with itself, forgetful of itself" (Levinas 1981, 115).

Now for Darwin, it is the necessary *inheritance* of existence that dictates that singularity is never taken up entirely within an absolute presence. If, for the nineteenth-century naturalist, the "essences" of species are "undiscovered" and "undiscoverable," it is worth remembering in the context outlined above that Levinas asserts that "the breakup of essence is ethics" (Levinas 1981, 14). This is not to confuse Darwin's empirical assertion with Levinas's definition of ethics, but severing the tie to philosophical essentialism on the part of each of these thinkers means that their respective claims are not necessarily mutually exclusive.

The discussion thus far is taking us to this realization: A chiasmatic intersection between Darwin and Levinas is surely in evidence when it comes to the question of time and the encounter with the other. For Darwin, each being is a "descendent"—which is to say that every individual may be regarded as primordially reaching through time, and it is the encounter with the diachronous time of other selves that Levinas terms "ethics." The point is argued in "Time and the Other" and stressed repeatedly elsewhere in Levinas's writings. For example:

Diachrony is the refusal of conjunction, the non-totalizable, and in this sense, infinite.

Levinas 1981, 11

> The non-simultaneous and nonpresent are my primary rapport with the other in time. Time means that the other is forever beyond me, irreducible to the synchrony of the same.
>
> Levinas 1986, 21
>
> Time fashions man's relation to the other, and to the absolutely other or God, as a diachronic relation irreducible to correlation.
>
> Levinas 1986, 23

It is interesting to note in passing that the term "diachrony" is used in geology to designate "the *transgression*, across time planes or biozones, by a rock *unit* whose age differs from place to place" (Bates and Jackson 1980, 171, my emphasis), which is to say that the boundaries of the rock unit and the limits of the time zones are irreducibly out of phase. Each diachronous unit is thus not uniformly self-identical. "Diachrony" is crucial to Levinas's notion of the "otherwise than being," which cannot be assimilated within the binary opposition of being and nonbeing, presence and absence. "Diachronic thought" for Levinas is not merely an empirical phenomenon but becomes an ethical imperative if one is not going to reduce the Other to the Same: "Simultaneity is already to reduce being's *other* to *being* and *not being*. We must stay with the extreme situation of a diachronic thought" (Levinas 1981, 7).

In Darwin, as I have mentioned, diachrony takes effect through inheritance. Further, his assertion of the undiscoverable essence of species, the assertion that it is impossible to draw, on the one hand, an unwavering line between *individual* differences and variations and, on the other hand, the variations that call for the naming of a different species had, in 1859, the following startling implication for *Homo sapiens*: There is no *essential* difference between man and other nonhuman animals. The traditional marker of man's capacity for reason, and the sovereignty of that rationality in the universe, was now open to question. Thus chapter 3 of *The Descent of Man* sets out "to shew that there is no *fundamental* difference between man and the higher mammals in their mental faculties" (Darwin 1901, 99). Darwin's argument is extended to include complex emotions, memory, imagination, and altruistic behavior. *That* there is no definitive difference between man and the higher animals is linked again to the idea of a diachronic inheritance that gives rise to, as much as it challenges, taxonomic patterns. Differently put, the notion of transgenerational and transtemporal inheritance, and the genealogical pattern supervenient on it, brings into focus the aporia of "identity," or "essence": Any identity or essence is marked, through the genealogical pattern, as a non self-presence that is the echo of another time. This dynamic interplay between identity and difference, read through the logic of time and genealogical lines of descent, is the subject of chapter 6 of *The Descent of Man*—"On the Affinities and Genealogy of Man"—yet elsewhere too the kinetic interchange of similarity and difference, routed through inheritance, is never far from the surface of Darwin's writing, as even a tiny sample demonstrates. The following few examples have to do with man's mental faculties and his capacity for ethical behavior:

> The mental faculties of man and the lower animals do not differ in kind, although immensely in degree. A difference in degree, however great, does not justify us in placing man in a distinct kingdom, as will perhaps be best illustrated by comparing the mental powers of two insects, namely, a coccus or scale-insect and an ant, which undoubtedly belong to the same class.
>
> Darwin 1901, 226

> Of all the differences between man and the lower animals, the moral sense or conscience is by far the most important.
>
> Darwin 1901, 148

> Any animal whatever, endowed with well-marked social instincts, the parental and filial affections being here included, would inevitably acquire a moral sense or conscience, as soon as its intellectual powers had become as well, or nearly as well developed, as in man.
>
> Darwin 1901, 149–50

> The moral sense follows, firstly, from the enduring and ever-present nature of the social instincts.
>
> Darwin 1901, 933

> It is not improbable that after long practice virtuous tendencies may be inherited.
>
> Darwin 1901, 935

One striking feature of the above passages is Darwin's recourse to what today we would term evolutionary psychology as a way of explaining the origins of distinctively human ethical behavior. Does the field of evolutionary psychology have anything helpful to offer in the attempt to draw the line between humans and other animals? Again, Levinas explicitly distances himself from this possibility. In an interview with Tamra Wright, Peter Hughes, and Alison Ainley, Levinas responds to a question about ethical obligations to animals other than human:

> The widespread thesis that the ethical is biological amounts to saying that, ultimately, the human is only the last stage of the evolution of the animal. I would say, on the contrary, that in relation to the animal, the human is a new phenomenon. . . . I do not know at what moment the human appears, but what I want to emphasize is that the human breaks with pure being, which is always a persistence in being. This is my principal thesis. A being is something that is attached to being, to its own being. That is Darwin's idea. The being of animals is a struggle for life. A struggle for life without ethics. It is a question of might. . . . However, with the appearance of the human—and this is my entire philosophy—there is something more important than my life, and that is the life of the other. That is unreasonable. Man is an unreasonable animal.
>
> Levinas 1988, 172

In his assertion that "in relation to the animal, the human is a new phenomenon" (Levinas 1988, 172), he dismisses any bearing that evolution might have on his thinking: Ontogenetic and evolutionary considerations thus fall outside his project. But to read Levinas against his own grain for just a moment, he is not entirely at odds with a Darwinian view that I have sketched out thus far. For Darwin (we recall), "of all the differences between man and the lower animals, the moral sense or conscience is by far the most important" (Darwin 1901, 148). Although Darwin cites numerous examples of animals engaging in what *we* might term altruistic behavior, he is also wary that such actions could be seen to fall in the domain of the instinctive rather than the ethical. Yet again, Darwin points out, "it appears scarcely possible to draw any clear line of distinction of this kind" (Darwin 1901, 169)—and as for Levinas, "I do not know at what moment the human appears" (Levinas 1988, 172).

But ultimately, both overtly and implicitly, Levinas conducts his ethical enquiry along completely different lines from Darwin: He explicitly distances his preoccupations from those of evolutionary psychology, and if the social instincts in Darwin can be understood to lead to altruism, Levinas would argue that this is an altruism that serves the interests of one's own kind and therefore still falls within an economy of reward for the Same.

Yet another striking feature of the passages cited above from Darwin's *Descent of Man* is that the opposition between distinctiveness and affinity, identity and otherness is kept in perpetual suspense, thanks to the ineluctable effects of time. The implication of emphasizing the mutability of species is that it insists on each being *as a relation to the past*. The very notion of "presence" in its traditional sense is thus unhinged, sometimes to disconcerting effect, as Darwin realized when he first encountered the Fuegians in his travels on the *Beagle*.

Certainly, the Fuegians are constructed by the nineteenth-century English naturalist as the non-Western Other of colonialism, and yet, as the following passage attests, even this meeting disrupts any complacent notion of one's being fully present to one's own time. There is a sense in which the Fuegian makes an ethical demand. In the *present* event of the encounter with the Other, Darwin felt he was face to face with his own *ancestors*, which rather shocked his decent Victorian sensibilities, to the extent of destabilizing his conception of himself: "The astonishment which I felt on first seeing a party of Fuegians on a wild and broken shore will never be forgotten by me, for the reflection at once rushed into my mind—such were our ancestors. These men were absolutely naked and bedaubed with paint, their long hair was tangled" (Darwin 1901, 946).

The passage becomes increasingly politically incorrect as Darwin's narrative unfolds, but the point is this: If it is certain that the Fuegians would not feel any affinity with nineteenth-century English society, and vice versa, it is precisely Darwin's realization of his inalienable proximity to this Other, who embodies nothing less than his own ancestry, that unseats his sense of subjective sovereignty. Much as he would prefer to be descended from a "heroic little monkey," Darwin writes rather ruefully, "there can be hardly any doubt that we are descended from barbarians" (Darwin 1901, 946). Despite man's "exalted powers," the concluding sentence of *The Descent of Man* reminds us, "man still bears in his bodily frame the *indelible* stamp of his lowly origin" (Darwin, 1901, 947, my emphasis). Yet as we have seen elsewhere in Darwin's writings, this "indelible" trace of an illimitable lineal descent, startling as the revelation is, confers nobility on each existent.

To read Darwin through the lens of Levinas's philosophy certainly opens the way for an understanding of nineteenth-century natural science that is less deterministic than we might at first have assumed: Such a reading reveals striking congruities in Darwin and Levinas on questions of time and of essences, and hence on the challenge this poses to any presumed epistemological closure, to any presumed sovereignty or autonomy of the present, or of the self.

III

In E. M. Forster's novel *A Passage to India* (1924), two devoted missionaries hold a discussion with their charges about the kingdom of heaven:

> In our Father's house are many mansions, they taught, and there alone will the incompatible multitudes of mankind be welcomed and soothed. Not one shall be turned away by the servants on that veranda, be he black or white, not one shall be kept standing who approaches with a loving heart. And why should the divine hospitality cease here? Consider, with all reverence, the monkeys. May there not be a mansion for the monkeys also? Old Mr Graysford said No, but young Mr Sorley, who was advanced, said Yes; he saw no reason why monkeys should not have their collateral share of bliss, and he had sympathetic discussions about them with his Hindu friends. And the jackals? Jackals were indeed less to Mr Sorley's mind, but he admitted that the mercy of God, being infinite, may well embrace all mammals. And the wasps? He became uneasy during the descent to wasps, and was apt to change the conversation. And oranges, cactuses, crystals and mud? And the bacteria inside Mr Sorley? No, no, this is going too far. We must exclude someone from our gathering, or we shall be left with nothing.
>
> Forster 1982, 58

It is a conundrum of a related kind that Paola Cavalieri's characters face in the philosophical dialogue *The Death of the Animal*. "What do you mean by perfectionism?" Theo Glucksman asks his interlocutor, Alexandra Warnock, who, as part of her response, explains the concept of moral status:

> One's moral status is one's place in the moral community: how much does one count? To what degree are one's interests protected? As you can see, questions of moral status lie at the very core of ethics. And, to put it very simply, perfectionists hold that there is a hierarchy in moral status. They maintain that conscious beings, and their interests, deserve

different consideration according to their level of possession of certain characteristics.

Cavalieri 2009, 3

The title of Cavalieri's dialogue, *The Death of the Animal*, is perhaps a riff on Roland Barthes's seminal essay "The Death of the Author." "The birth of the reader must be at the cost of the death of the Author," writes Barthes (Barthes 2001, 1470). The verbal echo in Cavalieri's title tempts us with the thought that "the birth of the human must be at the cost of the death of the Animal"—in Cavalieri's dialogue, though, the philosophical implications are more nuanced. Barthes's provocative statement arises out of a specific literary-historical context: "Classical criticism has never paid any attention to the reader; for it, the writer is the only person in literature" (Barthes 2001, 1469). Barthes hopes to effect a shift in a long-held focus in literary-critical enquiry, but in Cavalieri's dialogue the stakes in the presumed categorization of "human" and "animal" are philosophically high. The category "the animal," as Alexandra Warnock points out, "is the metaphysical ground for and the existence condition of perfectionism. The notion of animality is the pole that sheds its negative light on whoever is to be derogated" (Cavalieri 2009, 4); that is to say, to be anything other than "human" is to be *less than* human. One of the foundational myths of Western civilization is that moral status is acknowledged for humans but not for other animals, to the extent of forgetting that humans, too, are animals. Being human, attaining moral status, is to be something other than animal; by implication, the birth of the "human" necessitates the death of the "animal."

But what would mark the birth of the human? Like the two missionaries in Forster's novel, Cavalieri's characters confront the difficulty of where to draw the line, to make the cut. Is empirical science of any help in this question? For Thomas Hardy, the recognition of biological proximity between humans and other animals is reason enough to grant moral status to all living creatures, but the idea of using empirical data as a way of grounding ethics is itself a matter that demands further discussion.

Jonathan Marks writes about this specifically in his book with the thought-provoking title "What It Means to Be 98% Chimpanzee." Modern genetics tells us that we share over 98 percent of our genes with chimpanzees (Marks 2002, 4)—and this number has been used by activists as hard supporting evidence in many appeals for changes in human relations to other animals. But the procedure of using a percentage as a way of comparing genetic codes and hence grounding an ethical imperative is, as Marks points out, far more complicated than we may have thought:

> The universe of genetic similarities is quite different from our preconceptions of what similarities *mean*. For example, the very structure of DNA compels it to be no more than 75% different, no matter how diverse the species being compared are. Yet the fact that our DNA is more than 25% similar to a dandelion's does not imply that we are over one-quarter dandelion.
>
> Marks 2002, 5, my emphasis

Still, on the issue of percentage—DNA strands, when compared, can be seen to be different in a number of ways: A section of one strand can be substituted by a different one in another strand, or it might be omitted entirely. These are known as DNA-base substitutions and DNA-base deletions respectively. What a number such as 98 percent does is to mask these different differences; it treats base substitutions and base deletions "as if they were biochemically identical and quantitatively equivalent" (Marks 2002, 26). The further consequence is that different ways of comparing genetic strands can yield different results: On some scores, we are 99.44 percent chimpanzee (Marks 2002, 27). It is clear, then, that even the most precise numbers require acts of interpretation. Further (still following Marks), what does this number *mean*, and specifically for the purposes of this chapter, what do numbers have to tell us about ethical obligations? Surely nothing. Marks puts it this way: "Sameness/otherness is a philosophical paradox that is resolved by argument, not by data" (Marks 2002, 22). Even further still, as Alexandra Warnock (one of the characters in Cavalieri's dialogue) points out: "'Data' tend to be interpreted under the influence of implicit metaphysical premises, which keep shaping their interpretation by an obstinate policing of the human/animal boundary" (Cavalieri 2009, 4). So here is a twist, then: The numbers in themselves do not *mean* anything, particularly when it comes to a question of ethical obligation, but at the same time these numbers seem to be inextricably snared in a priori metaphysical assumptions about the "human" and the "animal," which, in turn, color our interpretations of the numbers in the first place. Derrida broaches a related issue in conversation with Jean-Luc Nancy: "What I am proposing here should allow us to take into account scientific knowledge about the complexity of 'animal languages,' genetic coding, all forms of marking within which so-called human language, as original as it might be, does not allow us to 'cut' once and for all where we would in general like to cut" (Derrida 1991, 116–17).[4] What gradually becomes clearer in the pursuit of empirical data that would enable us to draw the line, once and for all, between the "human" and the "animal" is that science itself puts the very existence of those categories into question in the first place. Of the common categorical premise "human" versus "animal," Matthew Calarco observes in his response to Cavalieri's dialogue, "not only does this approach gloss over the enormous differences that exist among animals themselves, it also offers a false characterization of the (nonessential) differences between human beings and animals (there is no single, insuperable dividing line)" (Calarco in Cavalieri 2009, 82).

Now if science fails to draw the line, what are the implications for ethics when it comes to a human–animal divide? Peter Singer, in his foreword to Cavalieri's dialogue, deftly presents the problem of perfectionism as leading to a logical and ethical solecism: "Perfectionism justifies the superiority of humans over animals, but within our own species, moral equality must prevail. How can that be defensible?" (Singer in Cavalieri 2009, ix). This is a leading question in Cavalieri's dialogue, taking us to a further insight: The whole enterprise of wanting to draw the line in the first place may not be the best way of entering into an ethical conversation. Put slightly differently: A definition of "moral status" is questionable as a sound basis for ethical enquiry. This issue is a pivotal one in the dialogue, as it tips the positions held by Alexandra Warnock and Theo Glucksman in terms representing the philosophical freight that each character brings to bear: Alexandra comes from an analytic tradition of philosophy, and Theo comes from a Continental background.

Matthew Calarco draws attention to this in "Toward an Agnostic Animal Ethics," his response to Cavalieri's dialogue. In Calarco's terms, the definition of moral status as an ethical premise can be understood as a characteristic gesture in Western metaphysical thinking. In his version of animal ethics, inspired by Levinas, Calarco writes: "The effort to determine who does and does not belong to the moral community is one of the most problematic foundational gestures in the Western metaphysical tradition and is indicative of its imperialist tendencies" (Calarco in Cavalieri 2009, 77). Calarco goes on to ask what the implications for ethics would be "if we were to aban-

---

4. This passage is cited by Cary Wolfe in his essay "Humanist and Posthumanist Antispeciesism"—a response to Paola Cavalieri's dialogue "*The Death of the Animal*" (Cavalieri 2009, 57).

don the aim of determining the proper limits of moral status altogether" (Calarco in Cavalieri 2009, 77). He continues:

> Is it at all reasonable to conclude that there is a genuinely rational or objective way to determine the limits of moral status? And does not a historical survey of the failures that have attended every such attempt to draw *the* line (or lines) of moral considerability provide enough evidence to persuade common-sense moral discourse that this approach is inherently pernicious, both morally and politically?
>
> Calarco in Cavalieri 2009, 79

Calarco's approach thus differs from one we would more readily associate with analytic philosophy—that is, from an approach that would *start out* by attempting to define "*the* criterion or criteria by which something . . . has moral status." Instead, Calarco casts his version of animal ethics as "a *risk*, a 'fine risk' of the sort Levinas speaks of in *Otherwise Than Being: Or Beyond Essence*" (Calarco in Cavalieri 2009, 84). Certainly in Darwin it is the *absence* of a definitive line between the "human" and the "animal" that clears a site for ethical debate; ethics has to do with making decisions (that is, making the call about where to draw the line) when the existing boundaries are *not* clear, or perhaps not even drawn at all.

In sections II and III of this chapter, the discussions have explored science and philosophical argument as a way of grounding questions of ethics. More specifically, section III has focused on the identification of moral status as a way of determining ethical action. But Cavalieri's dialogue provokes a further question, which gains a distinctive urgency in Coetzee's responses in the roundtable discussions. The question has to do with the role of literature in contemporary ethics: Could literary texts contribute to ethical thinking in ways that the reasoned arguments of philosophy fail to do? Section IV of this chapter brings us back full circle back to Plato's dialogue, the *Republic*—that is, to the "ancient antagonism" between the philosophers and the poets.

IV

Thanks to a reading of Darwin with Levinas in mind, the previous sections have highlighted some of the difficulties in drawing the line between the "human" and the "animal." At a more radical level, though, the discussion has brought us to a point of challenging a philosophical method that *starts out* by defining the categories "human" and "animal"—one that attempts to fix the moral status of a sentient being first as a way of determining the extent of our ethical obligation to it. Neither science nor philosophy in its accepted method of a definition of terms followed by logical argument seems adequate to the task of determining, once and for all, ethical obligations to animals other than human. My discussion of Cavalieri's dialogue thus far has concentrated on its *content*—that is, the ideas relating to perfectionism that Alexandra and Theo speak about. But now I would like to concentrate on the *form* of the dialogue itself, paying particular attention to Coetzee's contributions to the roundtable discussions of Cavalieri's dialogue.

In her response, "Pushing Things Forward," Cavalieri speaks about the emergence of rational ethics in ancient Greece—which assumed the form of the philosophical dialogue. "The art of dialectics," she writes, "whose seed can be traced back to pre-Socratic eras, can plausibly be seen as the root of the appearance of logical thought in a world dominated by magical thinking" (Cavalieri 2009, 93). This sheds light on one of the observations in Plato's *Republic*: "So great is the natural magic of poetry," says Socrates. "Strip it of its poetic coloring, reduce it to plain prose, and I think you know how little it amounts to" (Plato 2003 § 601a–b). But as I pointed out in the introduction to this book, there are at least two ways of reading this observation: (1) poetry amounts to nothing; (2) poetry enables something to be said that *in plain prose* would amount to nothing.[5] Taking Cavalieri's observation on board, philosophical thinking (dialectics) sets itself against the genre of poetry. Poetry appeals to the emotions; in poetry, reason—and hence the truth—clouds over. Certainly, this is the explicit message in Plato's *Republic*: "The dramatic poet produces a . . . bad state of affairs in the mind of the individual, by encouraging the unreasoning part of it, which cannot distinguish greater and less but thinks the same things are now large and now small, and by creating images far removed from the truth" (Plato 2003, § 605b–c).

It is surely this line of thinking that leads Hardy to observe sardonically, "If Galileo had said in verse that the world moved, the Inquisition might have let him alone" (Hardy 1984, 302). The accreted underlying assumption is that "plain prose," the embodiment of reason rather than affect, has access to truths that poetry distorts. Poetry therefore cannot be taken seriously. But if we pursue the second reading—poetry enables something to be said that in prose would amount to nothing—then truth and seriousness can no

---

5. Socrates and his interlocutors are not drawing a distinction between poetry and prose in the same way that we would today. "Poetry" for the ancient Greeks would have included all genres of literary production at the time; in this sense it can be understood loosely in relation to the modern term "fiction."

longer be neatly and entirely disaggregated from poetry and attributed to prose alone.

The genre of Plato's philosophical dialogue gives reasoned argument center stage. The double entendre of this claim is intended: Philosophical reasoning is presented as a way to discover the truth, but at the same time Plato speaks "in character" in the dialogue—each interlocutor speaks in the first person. With a further twist, Plato, through his first-person speakers, classifies poetry (as opposed to narrative) in terms of the extent to which a work uses the formal device of direct, rather than indirect, speech. Direct speech—explicitly associated with "representation"—admittedly "gives most pleasure," especially to "children and nurses and the general public," but Socrates and his friends agree that this form is "unsuitable for our state": Each person should stick to one station in life. The poet, using direct speech, is "someone who has the skill to transform himself into all sorts of characters and represent all sorts of things," but "he and his kind have no place in our city, their presence being forbidden by our code" (Plato 2009, § 397d–e and § 398a). The philosophical dialogue itself thus carries the distinctive (and seductive) traits of "poetry"; each character speaks in the first person, enabling the writer to represent different sides of an argument, different points of view. From our contemporary perspective, Plato's dialogues can be appreciated as having an affiliation with literary genres—not least when these dialogues are set alongside the style and method of contemporary analytic philosophy. (Think of the *Symposium*, say, alongside Bertrand Russell's *The Philosophy of Logical Atomism*.)

It is in the fault line between what is generally accepted as "philosophy" and as "literature" that the writing of J. M. Coetzee plays such a vital role in thinking through contemporary ethical questions, particularly in the first edition of *The Lives of Animals*. Coetzee first presented *The Lives of Animals*—a work of fiction—in the Tanner Lectures at Princeton University in 1997. The Tanner Lectures in Human Value usually take the form of philosophical essays; *The Lives of Animals* tells a story in two parts: "The Philosophers and the Animals" and "The Poets and the Animals." Elizabeth Costello, the protagonist, is an Australian writer invited to give the annual Gates Lecture at Appleton College in the States. Contrary to the expectation that she would speak about her novels, Costello delivers a lecture on animal rights. She also teaches a poetry seminar in the English department (she discusses Rilke's poem "The Panther" and two poems by Ted Hughes, "The Jaguar" and "Second Glance at the Jaguar"), and with the philosopher Thomas O'Hearne she participates in a staged debate that revisits the themes raised in her Gates lecture.

Throughout *The Lives of Animals*, the narrative is interleaved with the reactions of other characters to Costello and her ideas, giving the text the flavor of a philosophical polylogue. Elizabeth's son, John Bernard (assistant professor of physics and astronomy at Appleton College), holds rather strained conversation about his mother with his philosopher-wife, Norma. After her Gates lecture, Costello takes questions from the floor. Her audience is somewhat nonplussed at her answers to questions of clarification about the main substance of her talk—"I was hoping not to have to enunciate principles," Costello says. "If principles are what you want to take away from this talk, I would have to respond, open your heart and listen to what your heart says" (Coetzee 1999b, 37). Members of the faculty engage in animated conversation at the formal dinner after Costello's lecture; staff and students raise questions and hold discussion at the English-department seminar. Throughout, we are privy to John's agonized thoughts as he steers his ageing mother through a minefield of strong-minded, articulate, and opinionated academics. Much of *The Lives of Animals* is written in first-person interlocutionary direct speech—and it is perhaps the sustained and sophisticated use of this literary device that leads philosopher Ian Hacking to assert that Coetzee's *Lives of Animals* "shows a mastery of the dialogue form greater than that of any philosopher in living memory" (Hacking 2008, 141).

As part of the question of human relations to other animals, *The Lives of Animals* raises another philosophical question: To what extent can literature, rather than philosophy, make a serious contribution to ethical thinking and practice? Coetzee's decision to read *The Lives of Animals* in the designated frame of the Tanner Lectures is a radical performative gesture. Responding to Paola Cavalieri's dialogue in *The Death of the Animal*, philosopher Cary Wolfe speaks about

> that oldest of philosophical (or is it literary?) forms that would seem to unsettle the boundary between philosophy and literature in ways whose implications are not to be underestimated. For it is a critical commonplace . . . to ask whether and how, in the dialogue form, we can know how much of the project's success is due to the logical and propositional force of the argument (which is not reducible to the second-order, cosmetic operations of language, or so the story would go), and how much to the linguistic and literary means of persuasion (including those

strange pauses and interludes, in the dialogue and yet not in it, where one fetches some grapes or goes for a swim, and god knows what else transpires between the interlocutors).

Wolfe in Cavalieri 2009, 47

Coetzee's *Lives of Animals* sustains richer characterization and narrative line than Cavalieri's dialogue does, so that the "linguistic and literary means of persuasion"—or should we say, of plausibility—are far more compelling in Coetzee's work of fiction. Coetzee's act of reading a work of fiction rather than presenting a straightforward philosophical discourse in the 1997 Tanner Lectures thus revisits questions first raised by Plato's *Republic* performatively—with all the magic of poetry and staged dialogue on its side. In addition to its exploration of human relations to other animals, Coetzee's work generates sustained literary-critical *and* philosophical interest in questions having to do with the "ancient antagonism" between the philosophers and the poets.[6]

Now further, it is worth taking heed of the *imbrication* of these two questions: Relations between humans and animals; relations between the philosophers and the poets. In outrageously simple terms: Philosophers are safely in the camp of human reason; animals, in the wild terrain of sensation and affect. The poets trouble the boundary. Coetzee's contributions in *The Death of the Animal* speak to this directly: Does Cavalieri's rather staid philosophical dialogue not reiterate the presumed authority of reason, thus affirming the perfectionism that Alexandra and Theodore are purportedly arguing against? Here is an excerpt from one of Coetzee's responses in the roundtable discussions:

> A and T are children of Socrates, not only in the way in which they speak but also in the relationship they have with each other. Whatever may go on between them once they have stepped off the page, on the page they exhibit an amicability of a rather bloodless and certainly sexless nature. They speak fluently, at times eloquently, but never with heat.

---

6. The original publication of *The Lives of Animals* includes responses by Wendy Doniger (professor of history of religions, University of Chicago), Marjory Garber (professor of English, Harvard), Amy Gutmann (founding director, University Center for Human Values, Princeton), Peter Singer (professor, Centre for Human Bioethics, Monash University), and Barbara Smuts (professor of psychology and anthropology, University of Michigan). Coetzee's novels *Disgrace* and *Elizabeth Costello* (which incorporates a slightly different version of *The Lives of Animals*) spark many of the discussions in *Philosophy and Animal Life* (with essays by philosophers Stanley Cavell, Cora Diamond, Ian Hacking, John McDowell and Cary Wolfe). See also Stephen Mulhall's *The Wounded Animal* and the anthology of essays edited by Anton Leist and Peter Singer, *J. M. Coetzee and Ethics*.

> Their inhuman calm, which is of a piece with their unvarying rationality, is accompanied by an inhuman moderation of appetite. . . .
>
> A and T appear to have transcended those passions and appetites we might call animal or, equally well, human. In their calm they are more than inhuman—they become superhuman, godlike.
>
> It is hard not to take the cool rationality they practice—it would seem in all respects—as an affirmation of and advertisement for the life of reason.
>
> Coetzee in Cavalieri 2009, 85

Coetzee's piece is then divided into sections, with the headings "Question," "Answer," "Question," "Answer," "Conclusion," and a final "Question." This passage is from the section "Conclusion": "It is hard not to take this dialogue as an affirmation of a life of reason as a higher life, higher than a life of passion and appetite, but also higher than the life of beings to whom flights of reason are unavailable and perhaps even impossible" (Coetzee in Cavalieri 2009, 86).

Truth in Plato's dialogue is presented as a priori and stable; reasoned argument has the best chance of reaching it. But what happens when you actively wish to change perceptions of what constitutes a truth—a presumed truth such as the sovereignty of humans over other animals? A shift in perception demands what I have termed (following Rancière) an "aesthetic act," and perhaps the poetical world of affect and sensation has a role to play alongside the philosophical strategies of reason and logic. In short, an appeal to the "animal" in you is surely valuable as a way of effecting a change in thinking. Coetzee probes this in his roundtable responses: "Regarding the project of rational ethics," he writes,

> it is worth saying that there are people (among whom I number myself) who believe that our ethical impulses are prerational (I would be tempted to go along with Wordsworth and say that our birth is but a sleep and a forgetting, that what Wordsworth calls our moral being is more deeply founded within us than rationality itself), and that all that rational ethics can achieve is to articulate and give form to ethical impulses.
>
> Coetzee in Cavalieri 2009, 121[7]

---

7. In his contribution entitled "On Appetite, the Right to Life, and Rational Ethics," Coetzee puts it this way: "Regarding rights for nonhuman animals, enshrined in law, as a way of making the world a better place, let me simply put the question: if one actually wishes to bring about such rights, which is

It is in a related context that Coetzee refers to Levinas. The "mute appeal" of the Other is "irrefutable—irrefutable by any means, including rational argument" (Coetzee in Cavalieri 2009, 89). If one task of philosophy is to give "reasoned backing" to an ethical impulse, another important task would be to alert people to the "appeal that might come at any moment in their lives" (Coetzee in Cavalieri 2009, 89).

V

For Sartre, the value of art is in its *appeal*. If an encounter with a work of art is an aesthetic act that enables the possibility of challenging assumptions about perceived truths, then it seems to me (following Coetzee) that one duty of philosophy is to draw attention to art's appeal, which is to say, to take the poets seriously in their potential contribution to human thinking. Yet further (as Cary Wolfe observes), in its exclusive methodological practice of reasoned argument, not least when it comes to the exploration of human relations to other animals, philosophy unwittingly runs the risk of reproducing "a certain picture of the human that may foreclose the very project it says it wants to pursue (namely, to break down the division—or at least the taken-for-granted division—between ethical subjects based upon their species designation)" (Wolfe in Cavalieri 2009, 58). What Wolfe argues for is not an antihumanist or posthumanist position but a "humanist antispeciesism" (Wolfe in Cavalieri 2009, 45–58). Scientists, philosophers, and poets use their respective disciplines to set themselves apart from the "animal" (dividing lines are drawn in terms of genetics, the capacity for reason, the capacity for language), but from the perspective of philosophy, literature *appeals* to what is conventionally associated with the animal. The interlocutors in Plato's dialogue speak of "sex and anger, and the other desires and feelings of pleasure and pain which accompany all our actions"—poetry "waters them when they ought to be left to wither" (Plato 2003, § 606d); it heightens susceptibility to empathetic affect, and "what we feel for other people must infect what we feel for ourselves" (Plato 2003, § 606b). Tolstoy's *What Is Art?* takes this notion further but in a way that emphasizes art's serious ethical potential:

---

likely to be the more efficacious way of arguing for them: in the manner of the academic philosopher or in the manner of the parliamentary politician, that is to say, mixing true reasoning with verbal trickery, selective deployment of evidence, appeals to the emotion, ad hominem attacks, and the denigration and browbeating of opponents?" (Coetzee in Cavalieri 2009, 121).

> *To evoke in oneself a feeling one has once experienced, and having invoked it in oneself, then, by means of lines, colours, sounds, or forms expressed in words, so to transmit that feeling that others may experience the same feeling—this is the activity of art.*
>
> *Art is a human activity, consisting in this, that one man consciously by means of certain external signs, hands on to others the feelings he has lived through, and that others are infected by these feelings and also experience them.*
>
> Tolstoy 1930, 123

Literature has the capacity to call out the animal in man in ways that may be of positive ethical consequence. Art is one way of expressing our humanity, yet in its troubling of a presumed dividing line between the "human" and the "animal," it serves as a reminder that the poets and the philosophers, too, are animals.

PART III

Lines of Force

6

Visible and Invisible:
What Surfaces in Three Johannesburg Novels?

I

When *Welcome to Our Hillbrow* was published in 2001, I asked my friend and the author of the novel, Phaswane Mpe, to sign my copy: "Welcome to our Heaven of fictions!" he wrote, alluding to our earlier joking conversation about the novel's Heaven TV lounge. I was pleased with this inscription. Certainly, "our Heaven of fictions" seemed a more congenial place to be welcomed to than "our Hillbrow" at the turn of the twenty-first century. (Figure 1.)

Hillbrow, an inner-city area of Johannesburg, has undergone momentous social change in the last hundred years or so: The gold claims on this ground were first sold off as residential properties in 1895, and according to *The Standard and Diggers' News* of July 25 of the same year, Hillbrow was set to become "Johannesburg's chief and most fashionable suburb" (cited in Smith 1971, 213). In 1896, the estimated population of Hillbrow was 300 (according to the map on the dust jacket of Smith's *Johannesburg Street Names*); by 1993

Figure 1

Figure 2

Figure 3

Figure 4

Figure 5

Figure 6

Figure 7

Figure 8

Figure 9

Figure 10

it was approximately 30,000 (Morris 1999, 3), and by 2003 the population was estimated to be over 100,000 during the week and possibly over 200,000 during weekends (Mpe 2003, 190). These figures become more striking with the realization that Hillbrow comprises less than one square kilometer. Increasingly today, the population of Hillbrow consists of immigrants from other parts of Africa (Mpe 2003, 188).

Until 1991, when the Group Areas Act of 1950 was scrapped, Hillbrow was the legal preserve of white residents, but by 1970 people classified as Indian and Coloured had started moving into the area, and by mid-1993, approximately 85 percent of Hillbrow's population was black. Thus, as Alan Morris points out, "Hillbrow is one of the very few neighbourhoods in South Africa that, despite the Group Areas Act, moved from being an all-white neighbourhood (in terms of the flat-dwellers) to being predominantly black" (Morris 1999, 3).

As students at Wits in the late nineteen eighties, we used to walk from the university, through Braamfontein, to browse in the record shops and book shops in Hillbrow.[1] We would go to the movies and frequent the Café de Paris and the Café Zürich. Hillbrow today presents a different scene. Abdou-Maliq Simone provides a graphic firsthand account of the Hillbrow of 2004:

> I have always seen violent incidents [in the stretch between Goldreich and Caroline streets]: a single shot to the head, or even an *assengai* [*sic*], a short spear, quickly thrust and removed. Crowds gather, mostly in silence, as calls are made to police officers who are in sight just a few blocks away, stopping cars in the cocaine zone.
>
> The next block is inhabited by homeless squatters, whose cardboard edifices and stolen shopping carts line mounds of burnt ash from fires they use to cook and keep warm. There is an acrid smell and the incessant sounds of whistles and catcalls.
>
> Simone 2004, 414

The more time I spent reading *Welcome to Our Hillbrow*, the more Phaswane's inscription ("Welcome to our Heaven of fictions") began to disturb me. The novel explicitly welcomes the reader to "the world of our Humanity" (Mpe 2001, 113), to "our All" (Mpe 2001, 104), but insistently, a readiness to be welcomed to these places is *predicated on* a willingness to be welcomed to our Hillbrow—that inner-city area of Johannesburg. In his essay

---

1. Wits: the University of the Witwatersrand.

"Our Missing Store of Memories," Mpe discusses a poem by Kwa Ngwenya: Hillbrow is presented as a hiding place for the "forsaken." Mpe writes that "while the poem does not say who the forsaken are, or who has forsaken them, and under what circumstances, it is clear that Hillbrow, in its own way, provides sanctuary, and that people who do not live or stay in Hillbrow bear some responsibility for their fellow human beings, a responsibility that leads them to discover Hillbrow's sanctuary" (Mpe 2003, 192). Increasingly, I felt that only by acknowledging Hillbrow's "sanctuary" in person, allowing myself to be welcomed to the inner city, would I begin to do justice to the novel. "*Welcome to Our Hillbrow*" took on all the resonance of an ethical challenge. I felt that I did not deserve to be welcomed to, or find sanctuary in, our Heaven of fictions without taking Phaswane Mpe at his word and allowing myself to be welcomed to our Hillbrow. It became important to me to retrace, in person, the path of the central character, Refentše, as he walks from the city center through Hillbrow and along Twist Street to Vickers Place in Caroline Street. "You have some fascinating ideas!" Phaswane responded to my suggestion that he take me on a walking tour through Hillbrow. It was not safe for Phaswane and me to do this on our own—Phaswane was anticipating "more than a couple of would-be muggers." But after some elaborate arrangements, and in high spirits, we walked in Refentše's footsteps through Hillbrow on Sunday, March 14, 2004; Phaswane's brother, Tamela, and another friend, Thabiso Mohlele, accompanied us.

We soon got the sensation that, in walking side by side through Hillbrow, we were *animating* a dynamic, holographic urban landscape. "Why are you taking a photo of Hyper Hillbrow?" Phaswane asked when I took a photo of one of the buildings. But I had not been taking a picture of Hyper Hillbrow at all—I was taking a photograph of where the Café de Paris used to be: You can still see the Eiffel towers on the balustrade of the upper level. (Figure 2.)

The art deco detailing on a balcony (Figure 3) . . . Twist Street (Figure 4) . . . an alleyway between Hillbrow and Braamfontein (Figure 5) . . . marimba music broadcast from the top of a building, and Tamela's quiet lovely singing in response (Figures 6, 7, and 8) . . . my thoughts of Rodin's white marble bust of Miss Fairfax in the Jo'burg Art Gallery which backs onto Edith Cavell street, where homeless people were tending to oily fires on the tar . . . Where were we?

"Don't shoot without permission," the street kids yelled out to me, hustling me off the pavement and into the road. "*Ja, ja! Ba-be-las!*" Thabiso called. "You've been sniffing too much glue!" In other places it was just too dangerous, or too painful, to take pictures at all.

There would be blind spots in the photographs.

Sipping ice-cold drinks at The Voice in Smit Street later, we couldn't quite assimilate what we'd done, and today I'm still haunted by the echoes of Thabiso's words when I took the final photograph, with Thabo Mbeki smiling over Phaswane's shoulder from a distance on an election poster: "It doesn't get much better than this." (Figure 9.)

Phaswane Mpe died on 12 December 12, 2004. He was thirty-four. (Figure 10.)

II

In *Phenomenology of Perception*, Merleau-Ponty makes the following observation:

> It may well seem strange that the spontaneous acts through which man has patterned his life should be deposited, like some sediment, outside himself and lead an anonymous existence as things. The civilization in which I play my part exists for me in a self-evident way in the implements with which it provides itself. If it is a question of an unknown or alien civilization, then several manners of being or of living can find their place in the ruins or the broken instruments which I discover, or in the landscape through which I roam. The cultural world is then ambiguous, *but it is already present.*
>
> Merleau-Ponty 1962, 348, my emphasis

It is this complex encounter with the "sediment of things" that confronts the characters in the inaugural narrative scenes of the three contemporary South African novels I discuss in this chapter. Marlene van Niekerk's *Triomf* (1994), Ivan Vladislavić's *The Restless Supermarket* (2001), and Phaswane Mpe's *Welcome to Our Hillbrow* (2001) are all set in the urban landscape of Johannesburg in the mid 1990s—which is to say, around the time of the country's first democratic elections. In each novel, the things encountered in the here and now are from a time and a place, a "civilization" (to use Merleau-Ponty's word), different from the characters' own. Each of these novels depicts a physical urban landscape that bears the traces of an immediate and absent past, yet in the moment of recognizing features in the landscape that register a place that is no longer there ("this used to be . . ."), a spatial configuration is projected onto the plane of a meaningful temporal narrative, and a substrate of the past interrupts the present surface in ways that are psychological as much as they are topographical. The novels articulate this chiasmus of the visible and the invisible, of the spatial and the temporal, drawing attention to the contingency of each cultural and political moment, challenging the reader through a literary presentation of different articulations between the past and the present, of what can be said and what can be thought. In this chapter (with reference to Merleau-Ponty and Rancière), I address the implications of this encounter with residual traces of a different cultural past in the urban landscape that is also presently "home" to the characters, if not to the readers. At the same time, I am interested in the reader's encounter with the novel itself as a cultural object from a different time and a different place. What disturbance to the reader's immediate and supposedly stable "here and now" does the novel effect? What change in the margins of the reader's exposure?

"Literary locutions," writes Rancière,

> draft maps of the visible, trajectories between the visible and the sayable, relationships between modes of being, modes of saying, and modes of doing and making. They define variations of sensible intensities, perceptions and the abilities of bodies. They thereby take hold of unspecified groups of people, they widen gaps, open up space for deviations, modify the speeds, the trajectories, and the ways in which groups of people adhere to a condition, react to situations, recognize their images.
>
> Rancière 2004a, 11

The discussions in this chapter filter these reflections through three "literary locutions" of Johannesburg. To what extent does the novel have the capacity to "widen gaps," to "open up space for deviations" in accepted thinking, and to modify the images a reader may have of the city and his or her relations to others living there? My discussion of the three novels extends into the next chapter, which focuses on questions of community.

The first novel I refer to is Marlene van Niekerk's *Triomf*, originally written in Afrikaans and published in 1994. The Benades, the poor white Afrikaners in the novel, occupy a tenuous cultural zone. As part of the government policy of the National Party to "sanitize" the city of Johannesburg, the black people of Sophiatown were forcibly relocated to the township of

Soweto in 1955.[2] The ground of Sophiatown was cleared for government-subsidized housing for poor whites and renamed "Triomf" (which means "triumph"). The Benades, themselves relocated from the multiracial slum area of Vrededorp (which means literally "Peacetown") and now live on the ruins of the black suburb. Even though the novel is set in 1993–34, it is the memory of the scene of the February 9, 1955, focalized through Mol, a poor white Afrikaans woman, that sets the novel into narrative motion:

> Mol stares at all the stuff Lambert has dug out of the earth [in their own backyard]. It's a helluva heap. Pieces of red brick, bits of smooth drainpipe, thick chunks of old cement, and that blue gravel you see on graves. Small bits of glass and other stuff shine in the muck. Lambert has already taken out most of the shiny things—for his collection, he says. He collects the strangest things.
>
> van Niekerk 1999, 1

Immediately following this passage is a graphic recollection of the scene of the forced removal in 1955:

> A lot of their stuff got left behind. Whole dressers full of crockery. You could hear things breaking to pieces when the bulldozers moved in. Beds and enamel basins and sink baths and all kinds of stuff. All of it just smashed.
>
> That was quite a sight.
>
> van Niekerk 1999, 1

I consider this scene in more detail later in this chapter, but first I turn to Ivan Vladislavić's *The Restless Supermarket*. The novel is set in Hillbrow, inner-city Johannesburg, and published in 2001. For the protagonist—Aubrey Tearle, a white, English-speaking South African—the traces of an uncertain and haunting history of the place have a visible topographic presence:

> One Sunday morning not too long ago, on an overgrown plot in Prospect Road, I saw a body in the weeds, under a shroud of pages from the *Sunday Times*. I saw it from the window of my own flat, where I stood with a carton of long-life milk in my hand, and I could almost smell the pungent scent of the kakiebos crushed by its fall. It lay among the rusted

---

2. For a detailed history of the social geography of Johannnesburg, see Beavon's *Johannesburg: The Making and Shaping of the City*. The forced removals from Sophiatown began on February 9, 1955 (see Beavon 2004, 132). For an account of the urban history of the poor white Afrikaner, see especially pages 106–33.

pipes, blackened bricks and outcrops of old foundations that mark every bit of empty land in this city, as if a reef of disorder lay just below the surface, or a civilization had gone to ruin here before we ever arrived.

What do I mean by "we"? Don't make me laugh.

Vladislavić 2001, 6[3]

The characters in *Triomf* and in *The Restless Supermarket* recognize the tenuousness of their presence in the urban landscape. What is past, in that place, is buried, but the past surfaces in the residual signs of the lives of others that disturb complacent assumptions about the supposed stability of the here and now.

The sense of a dislocated present is poignantly explicit in Phaswane Mpe's novel *Welcome to Our Hillbrow*. Like *The Restless Supermarket*, the novel is set in Hillbrow, and it was also published in 2001. But in Mpe's text, the characters are Sepedi-speaking; they leave the place of their birth—the rural village of Tiragolong in the Northern Province—to seek their fortunes in Johannesburg. The narrator addresses the protagonist, Refentše: "Your first entry into Hillbrow, Refentše, was the culmination of many converging routes. You do not remember where the first route began. But you know all too well that the stories of migrants had a lot to do with its formation" (Mpe 2001, 2).

This passage in Mpe's novel seems to resonate with a leading idea in Merleau-Ponty: "The perceived world . . . is the ensemble of my body's routes and not a multitude of spatio-temporal individuals" (Merleau-Ponty 1968, 247), and images of migrancy, transience, an "elsewhere" that inflects the present, are distinctive features of Mpe's writing. For Merleau-Ponty, as Alphonso Lingis puts it, "the presence of the sensible thing is a presence by allusion" (Lingis 1968, xlix); further, "Being is visible as a theme for variation because the visible itself is not *in* time and *in* space, but not outside of them either" (Lingis 1968, xlv). What is in the present conveys an "immense latent content of the past, the future, and the elsewhere, which it announces and which it conceals" (Merleau-Ponty 1968, 114). Thus, the sensible cannot be defined as a brute sense datum, as an undifferentiated and instantaneous "impact," which, for Merleau-Ponty, "corresponds to nothing in our experience" (Merleau-Ponty 1962, 3). Instead, "what we call a visible is . . . a quality pregnant with a texture, the surface of a depth, a cross section upon a

---

3. Aubrey Tearle's question leads the discussion in chapter 7 of this book.

massive being . . . the total visible is always behind, or after, or between the aspects we see of it" (Merleau-Ponty 1968, 136).

Now conversely, some things in plain view are not visible in the nuanced sense that Merleau-Ponty accords to the term. And further, for something to be visible, it has to have some reference to the invisible. Differently put, individual perspectives and understandings (realms of the invisible) are brought to the world of sensory perception in ways that actively influence what can be *seen*. The invisible world each of us brings to bear constitutes a different visible landscape in each instance, to the extent that it is not possible to delimit a perceptual field in an a priori or totalizing way. In one sense, that is not to deny the world's physical objectivity, but while the visible is dependent on the physical, it is not defined by the visible.

To return to a consideration of Johannesburg and the contingency of the invisible histories underwriting the city in each of the three novels: In *The Restless Supermarket* and *Welcome to Our Hillbrow*, the characters walk through the same streets of the inner city—but in each novel respectively, the characters inhabit different worlds. The protagonist of *The Restless Supermarket*, the white, English-speaking Aubrey Tearle, has been living in Hillbrow for decades. He is a retired proofreader of telephone directories; his haunts are the European cafés in Hillbrow, which, by the 1990s had almost all closed down. In contrast, Refentše, the Sepedi-speaking protagonist of Mpe's *Welcome to Our Hillbrow*, comes to the city for the first time in 1991.

The Café Europa provides a fictional setting for the characters of Ivan Vladislavić's novel, *The Restless Supermarket*, and like the Café de Paris in Hillbrow (which has closed down, and which I photographed on the day I went walking with Phaswane Mpe in 2004), the Café Europa in *The Restless Supermarket* has "cast-iron Tours d'Eiffel in the balcony railing" (Vladislavić 2001, 17). On the day I took the photograph of the building where the Café de Paris used to be, I was standing beside Phaswane Mpe. Each of us looked at the same building yet saw a different place. We confronted the realization that (to use Merleau-Ponty's words again) "if we set ourselves to see as things the intervals between them," there would be "in truth another world" (Merleau-Ponty 1962, 16). Certainly, both Phaswane and I embodied the insight that "there are other landscapes besides my own" (Merleau-Ponty 1968, 141).

A photograph such as the one I took of the Café de Paris / Hyper Hillbrow offers, *for me*, a strangely contemporaneous image of the past and the present. As in Vladislavić's image of the wasteland in Prospect Road that I cited at the outset of this chapter, absences and traces from the past are *registered* in the here and now, thereby investing any supposedly stable present with a contingent temporal drift. Michel de Certeau elaborates:

> "*Here*, there used to be a bakery." "*That's* where old lady Dupuis used to live." It is striking here that the places people live in are like the presences of diverse absences. What can be seen designates what is no longer there: "you *see*, here there used to be . . . ," but it can no longer be seen. Demonstratives indicate the invisible identities of the visible: it is the very definition of a place, in fact, that it is composed by these series of displacements and effects among the fragmented strata that form it and that it plays on these moving layers.
>
> de Certeau 1984, 108

In Vladislavić's *The Restless Supermarket*, these "moving layers" are self-reflexively linguistic as much as they are topographical. Thus Aubrey Tearle reads in the "outcrops of old foundations that mark every bit of empty land in this city . . . a reef of disorder . . . just below the surface, . . . a civilization . . . gone to ruin" (Vladislavić 2001, 6). As he proofreads the telephone directories, patterns on the printed pages give rise to Aubrey Tearle's sociogeographic musings:

> As my eye matured, I began to notice subtler things, submerged reefs beneath the placid surface, patterns that only came into focus when one had squinted until one's eyes watered. I noticed, for example, a preponderance of Baums and Blooms in Cyrildene; and likewise of Pintos and Pinheiros in Rosettenville; and of Le Roux in Linmeyer. Fully eleven per cent of the Van Rensburgs in the book of 1973 had settled in Florida.
>
> Vladislavić 2001, 127–28

Vladislavić's narrative deployment of etymologies, of "corrected" spelling mistakes in the "Proofreader's Derby" section of *The Restless Supermarket*, and of Aubrey Tearle's reading of the migratory patterns of surnames in the telephone directories, deserve a separate essay of its own. But for the moment, the point is this: What is invisible or past, *in* the here and now, informs one's perception of the present in important ways.[4] But if

---

4. In his essay "Street Addresses, Johannesburg," Vladislavić refers to photographs taken by the French artist Sophie Calle. Calle speaks about this photographic project: "I visited the places from which symbols of the former East Germany have been effaced. I asked passers-by to describe the objects that

the invisible past (that "foreign country," to use Hartley's phrase),[5] disturbingly interrupts the topographic present in *The Restless Supermarket*, the past has no presence *in* the Hillbrow of Phaswane Mpe's novel. Mpe's *Welcome to Our Hillbrow* tells a story that poses a challenge to generally accepted notions of "home," of what constitutes a "community" as the protagonist, Refentše, moves from the rural village, Tiragalong, to the Hillbrow of 1991. Refentše's personal history and memories originate elsewhere: He is new to Hillbrow, and the place is new to him. *Hillbrow*, for Refentše, is devoid of a history and of an identifiable set of shared values or beliefs. It is as if Hillbrow springs into existence as he alights from the taxi that brings him to the center of town. Mpe's novel is thus set into narrative motion by an event that interrupts social continuities, an event that immediately raises questions about the extent and limit of the individual's social allegiances. Any sense of a shared past in this place is something that can only emerge only in the future. This reminds me of Derrida's meditation on the date: "The date is a future anterior. It gives the time one assigns to anniversaries to come" (La date est un futur antérieur. Elle donne le temps qu'on assigne aux anniversaires à venir) (Derrida 1986b, 48).

It is in this context, of a void past in the present place, that the "Our" of the novel's title is disturbing. "Our Hillbrow" calls up expectations of a community in historical and propertied relation to a specific place, but the narrative to follow systematically undercuts expectations of a stable and locatable community premised on a shared set of inherited beliefs and recognized obligations. Few of the inhabitants of Hillbrow are native to the neighborhood—the buildings and the people themselves are in a radical state of flux, which Mpe mirrors in pages of unpunctuated prose:

> places collapsing while others got renovated . . . Quirinalle Hotel changing names . . . Chelsea Hotel closing down robbery moving flowing from Hillbrow into its neighbours . . . *Mail & Guardian* and David Philip Publishers and others changing offices moving out . . . others . . . coming in to build and occupy . . . and *Makwerekwere* drifting into and out of Hillbrow and Berea having spilt into Berea from Hillbrow . . .

once filled these empty spaces. I photographed the absence and replaced the missing monuments with their memories" (Calle cited in Vladislavić 1998, E11).

5. The prologue to L. P. Hartley's novel *The Go-Between* opens with this striking sentence: "The past is a foreign country: they do things differently there" (Hartley 1984).

the streets of Hillbrow and Berea and Braamfontein overflowing with *Makwerekwere* come to pursue green pastures.

Mpe 2001, 25–26[6]

Mpe's Hillbrow is always already a site of transit and transience; there is not yet a still point to mark for future reference, and the physical world is devoid of what Merleau-Ponty would call a "latency," a "depth." This brings me back to the photograph, and to the question of the past. Merleau-Ponty writes:

> This table bears traces of my past life, for I have carved my initials on it and spilt ink on it. But these traces in themselves do not refer to the past. They are present; and, in so far as I find in them traces of some "previous" event, it is because I derive my sense of the past from elsewhere, because I carry this particular significance within myself.
>
> Merleau-Ponty 1962, 413

It is in this sense that the body activates what is invisible in the physical present, that it brings to bear what is absent or elsewhere. Thus, as Merleau-Ponty puts it (citing Cézanne): "The landscape thinks itself in me, and I am its consciousness" (Merleau-Ponty 1964, 17). Further, once this "body–world relationship is recognized, there is a ramification of my body and a ramification of the world" (Merleau-Ponty 1968, 136n2).

It is when Mpe writes that "Tiragolong [the far-off rural village] was in Hillbrow" (Mpe 2001, 49) that "another landscape" is instituted, that the field *in Hillbrow* is open for an "intercorporeity." "Where are we to put the limit between the body and the world, since the world is flesh?" asks Merleau-Ponty. He goes on to say: "The superficial pellicle of the visible is only for my vision and for my body. But the depth beneath this surface contains my body and hence contains my vision. My body as a visible thing is contained within the full spectacle" (Merleau-Ponty 1968, 138).

In Ivan Vladislavić's novel *The Restless Supermarket*, the taking of what is absent, distant, and invisible and relating it to the shifting, physical present instantiates a dialogic nexus among the characters. Aubrey Tearle, the protagonist, comments on a mural of Alibia, an imaginary city painted on a wall of the Café Europa in Hillbrow:

---

6. *Makwerekwere*: a pejorative term for a black person who is not South African.

A Slav would feel just as at home there as a Dutchman. It was a perfect alibi, *a generous elsewhere* in which the immigrant might find the landmarks he had left behind. I had seen pointed out St Peter's and St Paul's, the Aegean and the Baltic. A receptionist at the German Consulate had shown us a bridge over the Neckar, and once an engineer from Mostar . . . had pinpointed the very house in which he had been born.

Vladislavić 2001, 19

At a party in the Café Europa at the end of the novel, Alibia is up for discussion again: "I can check it's only Cape Town," says Floyd to Aubrey Tearle, "Look. Here's Khayelitsha" (Vladislavić 2001, 253). With multilayered irony, Vladislavić has Aubrey Tearle announce himself to be a "true Johannesburger" because he was "born within sight of the Hillbrow Tower," but the Hillbrow Tower had not yet been built: "Had it been standing at the time of my birth, I would have seen it from my crib" (Vladislavić 2001, 19 and 20). Its landmark significance is thus situated in a future anterior and is allocated on the basis of an elsewhere Tearle has never visited: It is, for him, "our very own Bow Bells" (Vladislavić 2001, 20). Even in its strident presence on the Johannnesburg skyline—it stands up "like the attachment for a vacuum cleaner"—it exists as a "touching contrast" (Vladislavić 2001, 17) to the Eiffel Towers on the cast-iron balcony of the Café Europa, where Aubrey Tearle finds conviviality. But the Café de Paris, for Vladislavić, "endures as no more than a fiction of the remembered city" (Vladislavić 1998, 310).

I return now to the opening chapter of Marlene van Niekerk's novel, *Triomf*, with its depiction of the forced removal of black residents from Sophiatown in 1955. The white Afrikaner protagonist, Mol, registers:

> A lot of their stuff got left behind. Whole dressers full of crockery. You could hear things breaking to pieces when the bulldozers moved in. Beds and enamel basins and sink baths and all kinds of stuff. All of it just smashed.
>
> That was quite a sight.
>
> van Niekerk 1999, 1

The passage works in complex ways. Van Niekerk's characters stage a shocking racism, but interrupting the linguistic surface of a dehumanizing discourse is Mol's empathetic acknowledgment, amid the broken shards of crockery and glass, of a domestic world shared. The litany of beds, baths, and basins bespeaks a lifeworld related to her own. The *significance* of these percepts, to return to Merleau-Ponty, "far from resulting from an association, is in fact presupposed in all association" (Merleau-Ponty 1962, 15). Further: "In the cultural object, I feel the close presence of others beneath a veil of anonymity. *Someone* uses the pipe for smoking, the spoon for eating, the bell for summoning, and it is through the perception of a human act and another person that the perception of a cultural world could be verified" (Merleau-Ponty 1962, 348).

Merleau-Ponty's *The Visible and the Invisible* speaks of "the sensible thing" as "the place where the invisible is captured in the visible," since "in the midst of the sensuous experience there is an intuition of an essence, a sense, a signification" (Lingis, xli). Thus the invisible lives of others are activated in van Niekerk's character Mol, through her relation to cultural objects in a ruined urban landscape. She understands that what she encounters are the broken pieces of a home life once lived in the place she occupies now. *That* the sedimentary patternings of things are part of Mol's phenomenal world, rather than of a purely unreflective physical world, plants a thought seed for political change. At the very least, Mol acknowledges that other human lives have been disrupted and destroyed, making her own domestic existence possible in that place.

III

In this section the discussion returns in some detail to Phaswane Mpe's *Welcome to Our Hillbrow*. The idea of walking with Phaswane through the streets of Hillbrow was at least in part inspired by Sarah Nuttall's essay "City Forms and Writing the 'Now' in South Africa." The abstract announces Nuttall's project: "This essay considers ways of theorizing the now, or the contemporary, in South Africa. It seeks a method of reading that offers unexpected and defamiliarizing routes through the cultural archive" (Nuttall 2003, 1). The essay is inspiring in two ways—in its thinking through of literary representations of the city of Johannesburg, but also in that it led me to question: Is *theorizing* enough? What would happen to abstract notions of "the contemporary," "the now," the "routes through the cultural archive" if I took Mpe at his word, walking through streets just a stone's throw away from the Wiser Institute at Wits, where Nuttall's paper was first presented in August 2003? Could literary and cultural theory be linked to the *act* of walking through Hillbrow in a meaningful way—and, taking a step back— what would be the point of wanting to do this in the first place? In a sense, these are the kinds of questions posed by Rancière in *The Flesh of Words*. "In the beginning was the Word," writes Rancière, beginning his book by citing the opening sentence from the Gospel of St. John. Rancière continues: "It is not the beginning that is difficult, the affirmation of the Word that is God and the assertion of his incarnation. It is the end" (Rancière 2004a, 1). What would be the *end* of the word—its purpose, its destination, its future, if I took Phaswane Mpe at his? The walk with Phaswane opened interstitial zones for both of us: past and present, self and other, visible and invisible. In these zones, could we discover ways of making sense of our Hillbrow? And what is that, *to make sense of* a physical world?

Mpe's novel is explicitly written in the second person, addressed by an anonymous narrator to Refentše, who is already dead and spends much of his time in Heaven's TV lounge. Yet in its relentless address to *you*, the narrative has the disorientating effect of addressing the reader rather than Refentše. In the process of reading, it becomes increasingly difficult to place oneself in the position of a third party, simply overhearing a narrator's address to a fictional character in a novel. You are performatively engaged in the implied community signaled by the "our" of the novel's title; the question of social answerability extends to *you* as much as it does to any of the fictional characters. Through this engagement of the reader at the site of the utterance, the text reconfigures what "here" is and who "we" are. Walking through Hillbrow with Phaswane was a way of activating the novel's "here" and "now," making these words flesh. Merleau-Ponty writes:

> With the first vision, the first contact, the first pleasure, there is initiation, that is, not the positing of a content, but the opening of a dimension that can never again be closed, the establishment of a level in terms of which every other experience will henceforth be situated. The idea is this level, this dimension. It is therefore not a *de facto* invisible, like an object hidden behind another, and not an absolute invisible, which would have nothing to do with the visible. Rather it is the invisible *of* this world, that which inhabits this world, sustains it, and renders it visible, its own and interior possibility, the Being of this being.
>
> Merleau-Ponty 1968, 151

Walking through Hillbrow with Phaswane was to experience "the opening of a dimension that can never again be closed." Primarily this led to different *perceptions* of the urban landscape in Hillbrow. By virtue of the invisible worlds each of us brought to bear (that is, our memories, personal histories, values, cultural capital, expectations, assumptions, fears, prejudices, hopes . . .) as we talked and walked through the streets, our Hillbrow presented itself differently.

At the same time, we gained an appreciation, too, of what a novel—a cultural object in the world—had caused us to do, to see, to hear, to think, and to say. In *The Flesh of Words*, Rancière writes about the "quality" or "status" of the literary text with reference to Plato's *Republic*. For Rancière this "quality" has little to do with the genre in question (poetry or narrative prose); instead,

> it depends on the encounter between a way of speaking—a way of posing or eliding the "I" of the poet—and a way of representing, or not representing, people "as they should be," in the double sense of the expression: people who are as it is fitting they should be, and who are represented as it is fitting to represent them. The enduring lesson of Platonic conceptualization is this: there is no pure poetics. Poetry is an art of composing fables that represent characters and act upon characters. It thus belongs to a political experience of the physical: to the relationship between the *nomoi* of the city—the laws that reign there, but also the songs that are sung—and the *ethos* of the citizens—their character, but also their humor. Poetics is from the beginning political. It is so by the conjunction between a certain type of individual that should or should not be imitated and a certain place of utterance that is or is not suitable to what must be the *tone* of the city.
>
> Rancière 2004a, 11

On a thematic level, that is, in the world conjured up in the pages of the book, Mpe's novel is radical: Its sympathetic yet disturbingly graphic presentation of characters living with AIDS, its provocative questioning of traditional beliefs and practices, and its frank speaking about xenophobia directed against black people from other countries in Africa are risky topics for a South African novel published in 2001. A reader's understanding of the *tone* of the city of Johannesburg is surely altered in an encounter with *Welcome to Our Hillbrow*. In *Drawing the Line against AIDS*—the catalogue for the forty-fifth Venice Biennale held in 1993—the curators write that "there are, of course, many kinds of lines; but none of them can prevent or cure AIDS" (Cheim et al 1993[7]). Their reflection on the exhibition continues:

---

7. There are no page numbers in this exhibition catalogue.

"What sort of lines are being drawn here? There is the line we ask ourselves and you to draw—to draw a line against the blindness, racism, and searing indifference that, all too frequently, still greets this devastation" (Cheim et al 1993). On a thematic level, these are central preoccupations in *Welcome to Our Hillbrow*.

Yet further, on a performative level, Mpe's novel has a radical impact too, not least because of the effects of the second-person address, and a quotation from W. E. B. Du Bois that serves as an epigraph: "Reader, be assured, this narrative is no fiction." The introduction to the catalogue continues: "The other line that is being drawn here is obviously the line that the artists have charted in their fervent quest to bring visible shape and meaning to the mercurial flux of our consciousness. Lines that, if we're willing, let us know ourselves better; lines that may even help us to locate our dignity" (Cheim et al. 1993). A key phrase for me here, in relation to Mpe's novel, is "*if we're willing*"—a willingness to accept the role of addressee, to become *you*, allows Mpe's work to introduce "lines of fracture" in a given social calibration; it opens the possibility for "reconfigurations of the shared sensible order" (Rancière 2004b, 39–40).

Each of these novels discussed in this chapter can be considered to be part of a sedimentary patterning along the shoreline of a South African society in transition. With each reading (or refusal to read) comes the *presupposition* of a shared human, cultural act, the response to a call from the place of an addressee. If the protagonist of Vladislavić's *Restless Supermarket* views Johannesburg's urban landscape with a jaundiced eye—"This endless cycle of building and demolition, this ceaseless production of rubble" (Vladislavić 2001, 161)—it is worth considering the invisible forces each of us brings to bear in making sense of these landscapes. Reading a novel that attempts to do just that presupposes, and does not simply result from, the perception of a world shared.

7

Who Are We?

I

My starting point is an observation that David Schalkwyk makes about linguistic "shifters" in his *Speech and Performance in Shakespeare's Sonnets and Plays*: Linguistic shifters—words such as "I," "we," "you," "here," and "now"—pick out their referents through deixis rather than through the "rigid designation" of a proper name.[1] A text (I use the word in its broadest possible sense here) that makes use of shifters rather than proper names, Schalkwyk suggests, can do so "because of its original rootedness in space, time, event and social purview." Further, an instance where shifters are used

---

I presented the initial version of this paper at the Critical Legal Conference in Johannesburg in 2003. Thank you sincerely to Peter Fitzpatrick: His generous invitation to present my work to a Critical Legal Theory audience opened new fields of enquiry for me.

1. The term "rigid designation" is used by Saul Kripke in his *Naming and Necessity*—a series of lectures first presented in 1971. Arguing against the "theory of descriptions" made famous by Bertrand Russell, Kripke provides an alternative "causal theory" of reference: A rigid designator designates the same referent in every possible world, regardless of the contingent descriptions we might use to identify that referent in the first place (see especially page 48).

without question, or without recourse to further explanation, "means that [the text] assumes a contemporary, shared knowledge of its physical, historical and human referents" (Schalkwyk 2002, 24). But what has come to interest me in several contemporary South African novels, especially the Johannesburg novels that I introduced in the previous chapter, is the way in which the referential field of linguistic shifters is relentlessly questioned and qualified, to the extent that a "shared social purview" is not something that can simply be taken for granted. This is particularly striking in uses of the shifter "we"—a word that invites expectations of communal endeavor, of some notion of community. In the previous chapter I broached a discussion of the ways in which three postapartheid novels draw the reader into an unsettling attentiveness to the historical freight and personal constructedness of what is supposedly and simply "here" and "now."

This chapter takes the discussion further: At the level of constative, representational content, the novels are a testament to "lines of fracture" in the prevailing ideology of the state and also in traditional communal beliefs and values; hence the persistence of the challenge to the parameters of "we" in each novel's *themes*.[2] But at the level of performative event [3]—that is to say, in each instance of the text's being read—the novel inaugurates a new community; it reconfigures a "community" of readers. A dynamic tension thus arises: The novels assert a sense of loss, but this assertion of loss can find expression only in an event that moves beyond it. This is not to say that an expression of the dissolution of community within the novels themselves finds a cozy resolution the moment these books are read. But if, following Rancière, "figures of community are aesthetically designed" (Rancière 2004b, 18), then the question of the relation between aesthetics and politics is raised at "the level of the sensible delimitation of what is common to the community, the forms of visibility and of its organization. It is from this perspective that it is possible to reflect on artists' political interventions" (Rancière 2004b, 18). What is political about literature and art, then, is not reducible to thematic representations within the novel or the painting itself. The arts have political potential in their shifting of margins of exposure, in their heightening of visibility among, between, and beyond communities of writers and readers, artists, and viewers.

    2. The phrase "lines of fracture" is Rancière's.
    3. The classic distinction between constative and performative uses of language was first set out by J. L. Austin in the 1955 William James lectures at Harvard University. See Austin's *How to Do Things with Words* (1965). I discuss Austin's performatives in some detail in chapter 2, "Redrawing the Lines."

In the course of the discussion I draw attention to some suggestive points of contact between traditional, African philosophies of community and Jean-Luc Nancy's understanding of "Being 'itself' . . . *as community*" (Nancy 1991, 6). Two challenging questions arise: Do African philosophies of community have a contribution to make to current debates about "we" in continental philosophy? And what can be affirmed about the role of the novel in the transitional communities of postapartheid South Africa? Thoughts about the linguistic and ethical operation of "we" in this chapter extend the discussions of the pronouns "I" and "you" in chapter 2 ("Redrawing the Lines") and chapter 4 ("Intersections: Ethics and Aesthetics").

II

Several South African novels written after 1994 explore questions of personal identity as characters test their inherited values and beliefs in different and unfamiliar political contexts. The protagonists (from all sectors of a South African society) lament the erosion of communities that hold narratives of shared histories and memories, as they step into new and unchartered social, cultural, and political territory. The issue of belonging (to a culture, a history, a place) is poignantly focused in the insistent question "Who are 'we'?"—and it is through this question that each character confronts the contingency of his or her own way of being in the world. The examples are at once striking and subtly complex.

Aubrey Tearle—the protagonist in Ivan Vladislavić's novel, *The Restless Supermarket* (2001)—notices "rusted pipes, blackened bricks and outcrops of old foundations" that characterize empty plots in Johannesburg, as if "a civilization had gone to ruin here before we ever arrived" (Vladislavić 2001, 6). "What do I mean by 'we'?" Tearle goes on to ask, and he provides an answer at once pontifical and wry: "Don't make me laugh" (Vladislavić 2001, 6). Yet even this self-satisfied assertion of cultural unassailability comes with an admission that there have been prior claims to the place, and that the days of the Café Europa (Tearle's favorite haunt in Hillbrow) are "numbered" (Vladislavić 2001, 9). One day while Tearle observes a caged specimen of *Homo sapiens* in the Johannesburg zoo, he revisits the question of who "we" are, but this time with an ironic yet melodramatic, post-Darwinian angst:

> I felt—what would capture it—threatened? No, that was too reminiscent of "endangered." Certainly not merely affronted. I felt—I had to

stop myself from quaking—that we were *in mortal danger*. We were on the verge of extinction, I realized, and the fact seemed chillingly explicit. But what did I really mean? Who were "we"? The human race? People of good sense and common decency? The ragtag remnants of the Café Europa? Was it a royal "we"?

Vladislavić 2001, 154

The compass of Tearle's "we" contracts with sudden force to the level of "ragtag remnants" and ricochets off again to the "we" of an outmoded European imperial form. "We" does not simply affirm an easy intersubjectivity; instead it raises questions about the ephemeral and unstable limit of its reference.

Marlene van Niekerk's *Triomf* was originally written in Afrikaans and first published in 1994, the year of South Africa's first democratic elections. "We?" says Treppie, one of the protagonists. "We! What rubbish" (van Niekerk 1999, 46).[4] The Benades, the impoverished Afrikaners living in Triomf (formerly Sophiatown), console themselves that they have each other and a roof over their heads, but "'each other' [is] too little to live from" (van Niekerk 1999, 126), and besides, instances of community or family life in the novel are parodic at best, to the extent that "we," "together," and "each other" ("ons" and "mekaar") become catchphrases for incest—and, in political and socioeconomic terms, exploitation, nepotism, and corruption: "It's all in the family. All in the backyard. Community Development in the true sense of the word," Treppie cynically remarks. "And it's just their luck, or their lot, depending on which way you look at it, that the Benades themselves got counted into this community of Community Development."[5]

Neville Lister, the first-person narrator of Ivan Vladislavić's *Double Negative* (2010), is living in London at the time of South Africa's first democratic elections. In the queue at South Africa House in Trafalgar Square, the voters discover that they have become a tourist attraction. "Over on the right, ladies and gentleman," says the tour guide into her microphone from an

---

4. The original Afrikaans, "We, watse stront!" (van Niekerk 1994, 43), is difficult to render in English; "stront" could also be translated as "shit."

5. The translation here is mine. For the most part, Leon de Kock's translation of *Triomf* is excellent, but in this particular instance, the last sentence I have quoted does not appear in the English translation. Van Niekerk's Afrikaans prose is outrageously colorful, perhaps most especially in its rendition of a working-class vernacular studded with English words and phrases. Here is the passage just quoted in the original Afrikaans version: "It's all in the family. Gemeenskapsbou in die ware sin van die woord. / En dis net hulle luck, of hulle lot, hang af hoe jy daarna kyk, lat hulle Benades by hierie gemeenskap van Gemeenskapsbou ingereken geraak het" (van Niekerk 1994, 244).

open-top double-decker bus, "one of London's must enduring monuments, Nelson's column. . . . And over on the left, one of its newest and most transient attractions: South Africans voting" (Vladislavić 2010, 76). Neville reflects as he stands in line, "All around us principles I had nearly forgotten, togetherness, solidarity, engagement, glittered in the spring air." He comments on the speech of his fellow voters: "The broken shale of South African English, an abrupt concentration of flat vowels and sharp consonants, was assuring and threatening all at once. I wondered what my own speech, worn smooth by ten years of English weather, would sound like to an African ear. If I went home—*if*—would my compatriots think I was a foreigner?" (Vladislavić 2010, 76–77).

An awareness of social and cultural transience and questions (rather than complacent assumptions) about home, about belonging to a place or a community, are distinctive features in the writing of Ivan Vladislavić. *Portrait with Keys* (a work of nonfiction) includes an anecdote about Henion Han's film *A Letter to My Cousin in China*. After nearly sixty years of living abroad, Henion returns to his hometown on the island of Hainan in the South China Sea.

> But the homecoming is not what he expected. The island has changed, he cannot place friends from his distant childhood or recall the times they shared. The people he meets are equally unsure of him: he cannot explain where he has been or who he is. With the recognition that he does not belong here, that the gap between them will never be bridged, his bewilderment grows. After a day of frustrating questions and half-understood explanations, he is exhausted and confused. Rather than returning him joyfully to the remembered past, the visit has cast him adrift in an uncertain present.
>
> Vladislavić 2006, 98

To say "we" or "our" depends on this sense of a shared and remembered past, and when it is used without qualification or question, it has the effect of affirming a shared present. "We" is a linguistic "shifter," like "I," "you," "there," "before," "now," and "after." The referent is "picked out" by deixis, rather than by the "rigid designation" of a proper name. Since the referent of a shifter always changes, a situation where its repeated use is not questioned is indicative of a familiarity with the social, historical, and physical context, as Schalkwyk points out. Yet the examples from the novels I have cited are just a few of many instances in contemporary South African fiction where "we" emerges as a contested linguistic site, and the present—and hence the future—are uncertain. Ordinarily, inclusion in "we" is self-evident and participants need not be named, but in much current writing in South Africa, "we" is persistently qualified, modified, and questioned. Communal beliefs, histories, and bonds are by no means infrangible, let alone assured, and "we" in contemporary South African literature often has the effect of drawing attention to the tenuousness of presumed cultural limits. The use of the first-person plural may register acts of violence perpetrated against those excluded from the "we," and, in some instances, even against those coercively included within it. "We" does not simply reassert what we might like to take as being universally held. We see this particularly in the novels of J. M. Coetzee. In *Disgrace*, for example, David Lurie is appalled at Petrus's announcement that he will marry Lucy, David's daughter; David suspects that Petrus is somehow implicated in Lucy's rape. "This is not how we do things," snaps David. "*We*: he is on the point of saying, *We Westerners*" (Coetzee 1999a, 202).

Initially, at least, questions about "we" take the form "Who is summoned? Who is included or excluded by this 'we'?" In other words, *which referents* are in question? But (as in the discussions of pronouns in chapter 4, "Intersections: Ethics and Aesthetics") I would like to shift the ground of the inquiry so that it is no longer simply a matter of determining to whom "we" refers but a question of *how* "we" refers in the first place. In a sense, this line of discussion takes its cue from Aubrey Tearle in *The Restless Supermarket*. Rather than simply asking, "Who are we?" Tearle's more nuanced phrasing, "What do I mean by 'we'?" leads to a deeper formulation of the question. By asking the question in this way it becomes clear that a range of complex ethical implications are brought to bear. The question must be taken even further still—"we" and "our" cannot simply be contained in a reference to the characters inside the novel. The reader, necessarily present in the act of the novel's address, is caught up in these deictics too, so that any use of "I," "you," or "we" *activates* the reader's complicity in the utterance as interlocutor, conspirator, accomplice in a social—and political—contract of cultural recognition. Deictics (such as "here," "now," "you," "we," and "our") in novels have the curious interosculatory function of conflating the world of the book and that of the reader. An example of this is played out in the act of reading the title and subtitle of Njabulo Ndebele's most recent collection of essays. The front cover of the book reads: "Fine Lines from the Box: further thoughts about our country." The "fine lines from the box" refers to a box of banned books that Ndebele as a child discovered in his father's garage; "further thoughts about our country" tacitly alludes to a series of groundbreaking essays that Ndebele wrote in the 1980s and collected and published together in 1991 under the title *Rediscovery of the Ordinary: Essays on South African Literature and Culture.* The "our" in "our country" dramatically insists on a world shared by writer and reader, making it difficult to sustain a distinction between constative and performative effects of the text: The world spoken *about* is the very one that belongs to the reader, a world animated in each event of reading. The opening sentences of the preface create a thrilling scene:

> A turning point in my life occurred when I discovered a treasure trove of banned books in my father's garage. One day, alone at home and bored during the school holidays in the mid-1960s, I began to explore my home. There was that wooden crate at the front right corner of the garage. . . .
>
> Once I had removed everything from the top of the box, I opened it. Inside were many books on music, art, and poetry, and others that I thought my father must have used for his degree studies at the University of the Witwatersrand. But as I got closer to the bottom of the box, my heart leapt with disbelief! Here was *Down Second Avenue* by Ezekiel Mphahlele; and *Road to Ghana* by Alfred Hutchinson; and *Blame Me on History* by Bloke Modisane . . .
>
> Ndebele 2007, 9

The books break open the world of young reader Njabulo, lighting up "social and political realities"—protest against which an apartheid government had rendered illegal, invisible, mute. Yet what is striking for the boy reading *Down Second Avenue* and *Blame Me on History* for the first time is the realization that suffering under apartheid is not reducible to a collective abstraction: "No matter how much black people suffered under apartheid, they did not experience oppression in the same way. It struck me then that oppressed people were far more complex than the collective suffering that sought to reduce them to a single state of pain. This has been a consistent interest of mine: thinking about South Africa" (Ndebele 2007, 10).

What emerges, and what Ndebele's writing sustains, is a sophisticated tensile relation between, on the one hand, an invitation to the reader to recognize, participate, share, and belong (through the repeated use of "we" and "our") and, on the other hand, an appreciation of the difference and singularity of each human life represented and understood in writing. This tension between what is in common and what is unique, between the general and the specific, is played out, each time, in circuits of writing and reading. With particular reference to Ndebele's text: The boy reader, now a writer himself, having written about his own unique reading experience as a child, invites *us* to participate in that thrill of reading. The act of reading foregrounds lives not reducible to blanket "collective suffering" or to a "single state of pain," but at the same time, Ndebele writes, "these books spoke to me with a directness I had not encountered in many school books about South Africa" (Ndebele 2007, 10). Ndebele goes on to reflect: "It struck me that reading and writing are two sides of a coin I wish to call *the art of the fine line*. Writing is the one that compels the writer to explore and express complex feelings and thoughts through an attempt at simplicity and concreteness that are yet able to preserve the complexity" (Ndebele 2007, 10).

Again, the taut chord drawn in the art of the fine line—"pushing the boundaries of thought in *our* democracy and deepening intellectual engagement" (Ndebele 2007, 11, my emphasis)—marks out a tension between what is innovative, beyond preexisting thought, pushing the boundaries, and what is familiar, signaled in the "our" of a present that recognizes a shared history. This reminds me of Stephen Clingman's reflections on the boundary in *The Grammar of Identity*. The "boundary is also a horizon," writes Clingman, "a destination never quite reached, like the boundary of the world. The boundary of meaning, then, is a transitive boundary; the transitive is intrinsically connected with meaning; navigation depends on, and creates, the transitive boundary which itself may undergo change. In all these ways the boundary is not a limit but the space of transition" (Clingman 2009, 22).

Ndebele's project celebrates a passage from writing to reading and to writing again, a passage that generates new thoughts and challenges (an "antidote to orthodoxy and the comfort zones of populism"), at the same time creating bonds amongst "*us*," the writers and readers, heirs to words—and worlds—once outlawed: "This book is a tribute to my father's banned books: imprisoned thought now freely available, challenging *us* to build on the legacy," Ndebele writes (Ndebele 2007, 11, my emphasis). What of this "us," the "we" in "Now *we* struggle with the challenge of the future and face the necessity of hope" (Ndebele 2007, 11, my emphasis)? What are the historical, cultural, and semantic pressures of "we" in a time of political transition?[6] The act of perceiving the material printed letters on a page—the passage through writing and reading—creates a boundary of meaning: a horizon never reached, but one that comes into view thanks to an appreciation of what is recognized and shared.

III

As a way of opening this section, I consider uses of the word "we" from the perspective of African philosophies of community. What—if any—point of potential dialogue is there between African philosophy and contemporary Euro-modern discourses on community? What contribution could philosophies from Africa have to make to current Continental debates? Finally, and more specifically, what role could the African concept of *ubuntu* play in South Africa's new constitution in this time of transitional justice? This final question is revisited in the concluding chapter of this book.

The term "African philosophy" itself must be treated with caution, primarily because it rides roughshod over significant, if subtle, differences between various ethnic groupings. Further, the term "African philosophy" invites comparison with the written heritage of Western philosophy when in fact what we call "African philosophy" is more often than not a worldview constructed retrospectively out of an oral tradition of well-known proverbs and cultural practices.[7] The danger here is to create, through Western-tinted spectacles, an idealized vision of a supposedly static, traditional, and, by implication, "authentic" way of life, perhaps to the extent of ignoring the contemporary social, political, and philosophical scenes.

Nevertheless, an acquaintance with traditional African conceptions of self and community deepens our understanding of the intricacies of "we" in contemporary South African fiction—and perhaps contributes to cur-

---

6. Benedict Anderson discusses the use of "we" and "our" and the effects of "careful but *general* detail" in a story written by Indonesian communist nationalist Mas Marco Kartodikromo, in 1924: "Semarang Hitam" (Black Semarang). The hero is never named but referred to as "our young man," and there are no doubts about the reference. "Marco's 'our young man,' . . . *means* a young man who belongs to the collective body of readers of *Indonesian*, and thus, implicitly, an Indonesian 'imagined community'" (Anderson 2006, 32). See Anderson's detailed discussions of four different novels, where a "national imagination" is at work, fusing the world of the characters and that of the readers (Anderson 2006, 26–36).

7. For a rigorously detailed historical and philosophical account of various appropriations of the term "African Philosophy," see chapter 5 of V. Y. Mudimbe's *The Invention of Africa: Gnosis, Philosophy, and the Order of Knowledge* (1988). See also Kwasi Wiredu's "How Not to Compare African Thought with Western Thought" in *African Philosophy: An Anthology*, ed. Eze, (1998), 193–99.

rent debates about community in Continental philosophy. I begin with the problematic of the proper name, which marks the linguistic site, I shall argue, of a slippage from "I" to "we" (and its attendant ethical engagements) in a traditional Africanist view.

According to a popular Akan proverb, writes Kwasi Wiredu, a contemporary African philosopher,

> it is because God dislikes injustice that he gave everyone their own name (thereby forestalling any misattribution of responsibility). Along with this clear sense of individual responsibility goes an equally strong sense of the social reverberations of an individual's conduct. The primary responsibility for an action, positive or negative, rests with the doer, but a non-trivial secondary responsibility extends to the individual's family and, in some cases, to the surrounding community.
>
> Wiredu 1998, 308–9

The implications of Wiredu's observations are significant. One's proper name is the linguistic inscription of an accountability at once personal and social: The name marks the place at which a particular individual can be called to account in language, yet at the same time (as an element in a genealogical sequence), the name recalls the individual's kinship and ancestral ties. To respond to the call of one's name, therefore, is to respond on behalf of not only oneself but those kinsmen and ancestors who are, of necessity, voiced in that name. The ethical engagements that come with having a name extend beyond the notion of the self in a Western, atomistic sense: *"I" answers in his or her name as "we."*[8] Kenyatta writes about "Gikuyu ways of thinking," where "nobody is an isolated individual. Or rather, his uniqueness is a secondary fact about him; first and foremost he is several people's relative and several people's contemporary" (cited in Gyekye 1991, 318). It is telling that in several African languages, polite exchanges are conducted in the plural form, "we."

Yet even further, the force of this "we" is more radical in an African context than in ordinary Western uses of the word. It does not simply mean "myself and *others* whom I identify as the subject of my sentence"; instead it

---

8. Hegel's meditation on self-consciousness haunts me as I write this. He speaks of the "'I' that is 'We' and the 'We' that is 'I.'" But the philosophical context of Hegel's aphoristic formulation is very different. For Hegel, self-consciousness "is just as much 'I' as 'object.' . . . What still lies ahead for consciousness is the experience of what Spirit is—this absolute substance which is the unity of the different independent self-consciousnesses which, in their opposition, enjoy perfect freedom and independence: 'I' that is 'We' and 'We' that is 'I'" (Hegel 1977, § 177).

announces the self *as* an intersection of social relations. That is to say, individual identity is conceived as being *intrinsically* relational. In Okot p'Bitek's account,

> the central question "Who am I?" cannot be answered in any meaningful way unless the relationship in question is known. Because *"I" is not only one relationship, but numerous relationships*: "I" has a clan, and a shrine, a country, a job. "I" may or may not be married, may or may not have children. Is "I" a chief? Then he has subjects or followers, etc. etc.
>
> p'Bitek 1998, 74, my emphasis

It is at this point that I recall insights by contemporary French philosopher Jean-Luc Nancy—and most especially Nancy's claims about singularity and about "Being-as-relation." "Being 'itself,'" writes Nancy, "comes to be defined as relational, as non-absoluteness, and, if you will—in any case this is what I am trying to argue—*as community*" (Nancy 1991, 6). "*I*'s . . . are always *others* (or else are nothing)" (Nancy 1991, 15). Further: "Being *in* common means that singular beings are, present themselves, and appear only to the extent that they compear [*comparaissent*], to the extent that they are exposed, presented, or offered to one another. This compearance [*comparution*] is not something added on to their being; rather, their being comes into being in it" (Nancy 1991, 58).

For Nancy, he appearance-at-the-same-time of singular beings, rather than creating a unified communion of immanent selves, opens instead "a spacing within immanence" (Nancy 1991, 58). This *spacing* results in a delicate interplay of positions and dispositions ("dis-positions") that generate an experience of community:

> A single being is a contradiction in terms. . . . The very simplicity of "position" implies no more, although no less, than its being discrete, in the mathematical sense, or its distinction *from*, in the sense of *with*, other (at least possible) positions, or its distinction *among*, in the sense of *between*, other positions. In other words, every position is also dis-position, and, considering the appearing that takes the place of and takes place in the position, all appearance is co-appearance [*com-parution*]. This is why the meaning of Being is given as existence, being-in-oneself-outside-oneself, which *we* make explicit, we "humans," but which we make explicit, as I have said, *for* the totality of beings.
>
> Nancy 2000, 12

In Nancy's terms, then, a compearance with other singularities, which challenges assumptions about immanent, autonomous identities, is aligned with an inaugural coming-into-being of selves and communities, where, through their relation, each term itself is appreciated differently.

In less specialized terminology, but in a related conceptual field, African philosophies stress an *inherent relatedness* in definitions of the self. Across the African continent we find variations of the saying "A person is a person through people." For example, in Sepedi the saying goes, "Motho ke motho ka batho"; in Zulu, "Umuntu ngumuntu ngabantu"; in Shona, "Ndiri nokuti tiri; ndinorarama nokuti tinorarama." A literal translation of the saying in Shona is "I am because we are; I exist because the community exists."[9] Through *ubuntu*, the individual is at once the beneficiary and the bearer of the cultural resources of the community, and in a traditional African worldview, the notion of reciprocity and communal responsibility is intensified to result in an understanding of the self as an agent of cultural continuity, rather than primarily as an autonomous, Cartesian subject.[10] Yet in much contemporary South African fiction, the presupposition that cultural continuity, across time and different social contexts, is a good in itself becomes a question rather than something that can be taken for granted. This question haunts the characters in Phaswane Mpe's *Welcome to Our Hillbrow* (2001).

The novel tells a tale of fracture and discontinuity, of a yearning to reestablish some sense of community in an urban setting. At the same time, Refentše and his neighbors appreciate the limits and limitations of traditional values and beliefs in their inner-city world. The novel thus raises unsettling questions about individual identities and affiliations and, consequently, of individual responsibilities. Who, precisely, possesses and shares through the "our" of the novel's title—what is there to share? And how could this be done in a place that to each one is "elsewhere" rather than "home"? The "our" of the title ironically registers notions of *dispossession*: "There are very few Hillbrowans, if you think about it, who were not originally wanderers from Tiragalong and other rural villages, who have come here, as we have, in search of education and work. Many of the *Makwerekwere* you accuse

---

9. Sincere thanks to Sikhumbuzo Mngadi, Manie Groenewald, and Ebenezer Shoko for their assistance here.

10. Throughout *Ambiguities of Witnessing: Law and Literature in the Time of a Truth Commission* (2007), Mark Sanders discusses the concept of *ubuntu* in thoughtful and nuanced detail, with specific reference to South Africa's Truth and Reconciliation Commission. Sanders foregrounds the principle of reciprocity in *ubuntu*. See especially pages 24–33 and 95–97.

of this and that are no different to us—sojourners, here in search of green pastures" (Mpe 2001, 18).

Hillbrow finds definition not as a place of belonging but as a place of non-belonging, a disparate conglomerate of all the *Makwerekwere* (that is to say, strangers, foreigners, outsiders) of the continent. The Hillbrow of Vladislavić's *The Restless Supermarket*, too, is peopled by outsiders: "Germans. . . . Hungarians, Italians, Scots. Immigrants. Foul-weather friends" (Vladislavić 2001, 53). As a retired proofreader of telephone directories, the protagonist, Aubrey Tearle, is peculiarly sensitive to cultural drifts across the urban landscape: "An historic migration was afoot, comparable to the great scattering of the tribes before Chaka, the King of the Zulus" (Vladislavić 2001, 129).

Yet if the self, from a communitarian perspective, is tied up in notions of community, and if traditional communities and attendant values and belief systems are disintegrating, questions arise about the implications for one's sense of personal identity and personal obligations in a cosmopolitan present. Who are "we" now? Which is to say, who am "I," in the sense of: For whom do I/we speak? On whose behalf? Nancy's discussion implicitly insists on the performative force of "we," to the extent that the event of its saying is at an aporetic juncture of the singular and the plural: "'We' says (and 'we say') the unique event whose uniqueness and unity consist in multiplicity" (Nancy 2000, 5). In more detail: "'We' always expresses a plurality, expresses 'our' being divided and entangled: 'one' is not 'with' in some general sort of way, but each time according to determined modes that are themselves multiple and simultaneous (people, culture, language, lineage, network, group, couple, band, and so on)" (Nancy 2000, 65).

To view the self as "being singular plural" is to force shifters such as "I," "we," and "you" to challenge assumptions about social, and hence ethical, engagements. It is no longer simply a question of which subjects (as self-contained autonomous entities) are encompassed by "we"; rather, it is a matter of *which relations are brought to bear in my response*. In what ways am I called to position myself in this ever-fluctuating linguistic site of "we"? What are my margins of exposure to the other? Each use of "we" thus poses, at a radical level, a challenge to one's sense of the limit of one's self, to one's understanding of personal responsibility as the ability to respond. Each use of "we" relocates the site of response, and the ethical implications become increasingly complex, especially when we examine more closely the grammatical operations of the term.

IV

"We," as we all know, is the first-person plural. But the kind of plurality at stake is far from simple. It is not easily a case of "I plus I plus I." "'We' is not a multiplication of identical objects," writes the linguist Emile Benveniste, "but a *junction* between 'I' and the 'non-I'" (Benveniste 1971, 202). The "non-I" part of "we" can be "you" and/or "they," but it can, and often does, pointedly *exclude* "you," and especially "them," through the all-too-familiar formulation "us against them." It is easy to understand that a measure of violence can be registered against those not included in "we."

Nevertheless, "we" is ambiguous: it can mean "I and you" or "I and them" or even "I and you but not them." Yet what of the potential violence *within* "we," given that it is not a simple plurality? This is something that is not addressed in traditional African communitarian philosophies. For slightly different reasons, the question of violence *within* "we" is not a primary focus in Nancy: Nancy's complex and nuanced account of "community" cannot simply or readily be conflated with saying "we" in a conventional way. For the Nancy of *The Inoperative Community*,

> the true community of *I*'s that are not *egos* . . . is not a communion that fuses the *egos* into an *Ego* or a higher *We*. It is the community of *others*. . . . Community therefore occupies a singular place: it assumes the impossibility of its own immanence, the impossibility of a communitarian being in the form of a subject. In a certain sense community acknowledges and inscribes—this is its peculiar gesture—the impossibility of community. A community is not a project of fusion, or in some general way a productive or operative project—nor is it a *project* at all.
>
> Nancy 1991, 15

But the question of violence *within* "we"—or within community in a more ordinary sense (as an operative project)—is the central preoccupation in several instances of uses of the word "we" in contemporary South African fiction. To return to the passage I cited from Marlene van Niekerk's *Triomf* in section II of this chapter: Treppie is speaking about the apartheid government's racist social program for poor white Afrikaners when he says, "It's all in the family, all in the backyard . . . and it's just their luck, or their lot, depending on which way you look at it, that the Benades themselves got counted into this community of Community Development." The gesture of an all-inclusive "we" is not necessarily an ethically laudable one. Benveniste points out that the components of "we" are not equivalent: "In 'we' it is always 'I' which predominates since there cannot be 'we' except by starting with 'I,' and this 'I' dominates the 'non-I' element" (Benveniste 1971, 202).[11] In "we," "I" speaks *on behalf of* "non-I," yet the "non-I" (especially when this "non-I" is in the position of a third person) need not be present to the site of the discourse. Thus even in the absence of the "non-I," the subject position instantiated by the "I" in a performative "we" *still takes effect*.[12]

But because "we" is not simply a plural "I," there is no first person *plural* speaker.[13] "We" simultaneously announces the presence of a speaking position, and the absence of those co-opted into it. As we have learnt from Benveniste, "I" (not "you" or "them"—the "non-I" constituents of "we") am by definition the one "who utters the present instance of discourse" (Benveniste 1971, 218). Any instance of "we," then, rests on "*political* presuppositions involved in 'doing something together,'" as van Roermund points out (van Roermund 2003, 235), because it instantiates a relation between "I" and "non-I," between the one in the speaking position of the utterance and those who are absent yet presented in it. Thus the "non-I" of a "we" may well be "represented" (Nancy's term), but *at the same time* the supposed speaking position of a "non-I" is necessarily "usurped," "appropriated" (the terms that Christodoulidis uses), by the "I" who dominates in the "we" of the utterance. Thanks to the performative force of "we," Christodoulidis argues (perhaps following Lyotard here), this assumption of the speaking position by the "I" can only ever be countered by the "non-I" "*after the event*, after the invocation has already been effected" (Christodoulidis 2004, 200) and, by implication, in a different utterance altogether. In the event of "we," the place of "the speaker" is a non-site, an aporia of absence *and* presence,

---

11. In *Alice's Adventures in Wonderland*, the heroine finds herself unthinkingly speaking to a mouse about her pet cat, Dinah. The mouse is visibly upset:

"—oh I beg your pardon!" cried Alice again, for this time the Mouse was bristling all over, and she felt certain it must be really offended. "We won't talk about her any more, if you'd rather not."

"We, indeed!" cried the Mouse, who was trembling down to the end of its tail. "As if *I* would talk on such a subject!" (Carroll 1998, 21–22).

12. In *Being Singular Plural*, and in a different context, Nancy presents the "on behalf of" (that comes with a speaking position) in positive terms: "*The speaker speaks for the world, which means the speaker speaks to it, on behalf of it, in order to make it a 'world.' As such, the speaker is 'in its place' and 'according to its measure'*" (Nancy 2000, 3, emphasis in the original).

13. This part of the paper owes much to memorable conversations I had with Emilios Christodoulidis, Bert van Roermund, Johan van der Walt, Scott Veitch, and Andrew Schaap in Cape Town in December 2004. See Christodoulidis (2004), "The Objection That Cannot Be Heard: Communication and Legitimacy in the Courtroom," and Van Roermund (2003), "First-Person Plural Legislature: Political Reflexivity and Representation." More specifically, see Christodoulidis (2004, 200) reading van Roermund (2003) at 240–41.

nonspeaker *and* speaker. Further, I would say that these terms (absence/presence, nonspeaker/speaker) are not exactly commensurate with "non-I" and "I" within the we: In a certain sense, "non-I" is necessarily a speaker (performatively engaged by "we"), and "I" is a nonspeaker, always speaking, to some degree, in the name of the other. It is thus that the full political—and philosophical—import of van Roermund's question hits home: "Who is the speaker?" (van Roermund 2003, 240).

Because I dominate with respect to our utterance, the political implications proliferate: How do you, the addressees, *hear* different pitches in the vibration of complicity and distance between "I" and "non-I," in a "we" that sounds an even note? Given that there is no first-person plural *speaker*, how do you locate sites of responsibility within an authorizing "we" of legal or political discourse, a "we" in which you yourself so often seem to be inexorably complicit? Further, how to *say* "I am not the we of anyone"? (Coetzee 2005b, 193).

It is in this context that the self-questioning and protean nature of the parameters of "we" registered in the novels I have cited can be viewed as a potential margin for cultural renewal. In the concluding section of this chapter I suggest that the very act of reading a literary text instantiates, as much as it shifts, this margin.

v

Apart from any thematized content, let us consider the performative fiat of the text itself, that is to say, the physical "event" of its being read. To look at a text as performance has implications for the reader—*we* readers. And since it is a question of "we readers," the implications, in the light of what I have been saying about an inexorable "on behalf of" in "we," are ethical—as much for the "I" as for the "non-I." What I have to say now about performance applies to the notion of a text, utterance, enunciation, or address in the very broadest sense.

My example is a San poem called "The Broken String." It was dictated (in the Katkop dialect) to Willem Bleek in July 1875 by Díä!kwāin, who in turn heard the poem from his father, who sang it in lament at the death of his friend, a magician and rainmaker.[14] Now that the string is broken (Bleek

---

14. For the name Díä!kwāin, I use Willem Bleek's spelling and diacritical marks as far as typesetting allows. The symbol "!" denotes a cerebral click; "˷" (which originally appears above the dash of the

provides us with an explanation), the former "ringing sound in the sky" is no longer heard by the singer, as it had been in the magician's lifetime:

The Broken String
People were those who
Broke for me the string.
Therefore,
The place became like this to me,
On account of it,
Because the string was that which broke for me.
Therefore,
The place does not feel to me,
As the place used to feel to me,
On account of it.
For,
The place feels as if it stood open before me,
Because the string has broken for me.
Therefore,
The place does not feel pleasant to me,
On account of it.
Bleek and Lloyd 1968, 237

We do not speak from or to a void: Any text is always already, and at once, a response and a vocative address. Thus, even if at the level of representational "content" the text in question constitutes a testament to a sense of loss, at the level of performance it anticipates and inaugurates a "community" of listeners, viewers, or readers. In Nancy's phrasing, "Regretting the absence of meaning itself has meaning" (Nancy 2000, 1). The poem "The Broken String" ostensively asserts a loss of coherence in place and time ("The place feels as if it stood open before me"; "The place does not feel to me / As the place used to feel to me"), but already, if still within the world of the poem, the syntax of relentless causality ("therefore," "on account of it," "for," "because") underwrites the inevitability of the speaker's response to events in his world, and hence his connectedness with it.

Yet further still (and beyond the internal world of the poem now), through our recognition that this poem constitutes an address to us as potential readers or listeners—which is to say, through the prior fact of the poem's ad-

---

second "a") denotes a nasal pronunciation of the syllable, and "˵" (under the second "a"), a "rough, deep pronunciation" (Bleek and Lloyd 1968, viii).

dressivity (before any internal, thematic content)—*we* are instantiated as addressees, and hence "*we* are meaning in the sense that we are the element in which significations can be produced and circulate" (Nancy 2000, 2). To take this further: The boundaries of this "we" are no longer quite what they were just a moment ago. There is a new "we": we who have just read this San poem. Each "I" within this "we" is now inscribed differently—*in relation to my fellow readers*. Each "I" is relocated in this new "we," exposed in a different way, by means of different margins of exposure, through the performance of the text. This is the extraordinary potential of literature: In our recognition of its addressivity, our receptiveness to its address, the text retraces the limits of "we," and in the process it challenges our assumptions about the location and the limit of the self.[15]

In an interview with Derek Attridge (which I have cited in a slightly different context in section II of chapter 2), Jacques Derrida speaks of the singularity of literature. "An absolute, absolutely pure singularity, if there were one," he says,

> would not even show up, or at least would not be available for reading. To become readable, it has to be *divided*, to *participate* and *belong*. Then it is divided and takes *its part* in the genre, the type, the context, meaning, the conceptual generality of meaning etc. It loses itself to offer itself. . . . There would be no reading of the work—nor any writing to start with—without this iterability. . . . I would say that the "best" reading would consist in *giving oneself up to* the most idiomatic aspects of the work while also *taking account* of the historical context, of what is *shared* (in the sense of both participation and division, of continuity and the cut of separation). . . . And any work is singular in that it speaks singularly of both singularity and generality.
>
> Derrida 1992a, 68

The accent on participating (in all the complexity of that term) in no way devalues or overrides the insistent theme of loss that is expressed in each of the novels and that I have discussed in this chapter and the preceding one. With a further twist, the physical existence of the novels themselves is not

---

15. Jacques Rancière makes strong claims for the subversive potential of literature in its "negation of any relationship of necessity between a determined form and a determined content" (Rancière 2004b 14). Rancière goes on to say: "Yet what is this indifference after all if not the very equality of everything that comes to pass on the written page, available as it is to everyone's eyes? This equality destroys all of the hierarchies of representation and also establishes a community of readers as a community without legitimacy, a community formed only by the random circulation of the written word" (Rancière 2004b, 14).

simply the *consequence* of a recalibrated social order in South Africa: Instead, it presupposes and inaugurates this new order in each event of reading. Each reading demands, on the part of the reader, a responsiveness to the work, a giving over of oneself to the call of the text. That gesture, in itself, constitutes an act of sharing in the sense that Derrida speaks of it in the passage just cited. This sharing affirms something in common, but in its responsiveness to hearing of other landscapes besides my own, *in* the here and now, it also crosses supposedly intransigent cultural limits. In giving myself over, I am no longer simply in the place I always thought I was.

Thanks to Nancy and to African accounts of self and community, we come close to asking whether "I" ever really precedes "we." How can we not be "in community?" Nancy writes, "We are meaning in the sense that we are the element in which significations can be produced and circulate" (Nancy 2000, 2). If this is so, then the realm of the aesthetic—making *sense* of a world—is the medium in which a community comes into being. At the same time, every "I" is always already a "we," interpellated each moment in any number of communities, always speaking "on behalf of," and instantiated, again, in each response.

Conclusion

I

In what has become a seminal paper in South African jurisprudence, former Constitutional judge Yvonne Mokgoro writes about *ubuntu* in an interesting way. "*Ubuntu*, a Zulu word with *botho* as its *sesotho* equivalent," Mokgoro explains, "has generally been described as a world-view of African societies and a determining factor in the formation of perceptions which influence social conduct" (Mokgoro 1998, 15). Of interest here is Mokgoro's appreciation of the way in which a world-view is integrally bound up in the "formation of perceptions"; bound up in what is socially *perceived*. Taking this further: What are the conditions under which a particular world-view takes hold? This brings us back to one of the originary meanings of "aesthetics" (mentioned in the introduction of this book)—namely, "the science of the conditions of sensuous perception" (*OED*). In more specific terms: Could South Africa's new Constitution be understood to provide a context in which an African world-view is valued alongside occidental law? In other words, to what extent could the Constitution be taken as an "aesthetic act" (in Rancière's sense) in its potential to change social perceptions of who and what ought to be seen and heard, to change what is perceived to be just and/or legally binding?

In the last chapter I spoke of the performative effect of the word "we" as resting on a perception of something shared. The taking hold of meaning—that is to say, making *sense* of a world—is also supervenient on shared perceptions, whether these are social, literary, political, or legal perceptions. Jean-Luc Nancy draws attention to this in a nuanced way: "There is no meaning if meaning is not shared, and not because there would be an ultimate or first signification that all beings have in common, but because *meaning itself is the sharing of Being*" (Nancy 2000, 2).

Nancy's translator, Robert Richardson, tags a footnote to "shared"—the word translating Nancy's verb *partager*, which has the further meanings of "to divide" or "to share out." Richardson's footnote continues: "It is also worth bearing in mind that the adjective *partagé* is used to describe, among other things, a requited love, a shared meal, and a divided country" (Richardson in Nancy 2000, 194). Perhaps less well known to the English reader than Nancy's *partage* is Jacques Rancière's use of this term: The French source for Rancière's phrase (most readily translated as) "the distribution of the sensible" is *le partage du sensible*—which carries all the semantic freight of sharing, dividing, participating, partaking, belonging, sharing out.

II

Yvonne Mokgoro in her essay on *ubuntu* and the law proposes what we might take to be a new "distribution of the sensible"—one in which the African philosophy of *ubuntu* would be part of the new constitution. Mokgoro acknowledges that a clear definition of ubuntu is "unattainable," and yet she sets out "to put forward some thought-provoking ideas on *ubuntu* and its relation to South African law in general, the South African Constitution, and customary law in particular, as a way to initiate debate for *ubuntu/*ism in a new jurisprudence for South Africa" (Mokgoro 1998, 15).[1] In other words, *ubuntu* is a term that would once again be seen and heard in debates about the law. Mokgoro's essay can perhaps be read as responding to the fact

---

1. Mokgoro cites Kunene's warning against taking *ubuntu* simply as a "social ideology." Instead, says Kunene, "we prefer to call it the potential of being human" (Kunene 1996, cited in Mokgoro 1998, 16).

that *ubuntu* features in the preamble to South Africa's Interim Constitution of 1994 but was then dropped from the Constitution of 1996.

Section 39(3) of the South African Constitution reads: "The Bill of Rights does not deny the existence of any other rights or freedoms that are recognized or conferred by common law, customary law or legislation, to the extent that they are consistent with the Bill" (*Constitution* 2010, 23). Mokgoro's argument is more specific, and more radical: She proposes incorporating "*ubuntu* into mainstream jurisprudence" so that "age-old African social innovations and historical cultural experiences are aligned with present day legal notions and techniques." This is necessary, Mokgoro argues, "*if the intention is to create a legitimate system of law for all South Africans*" (Mokgoro 1998, 18, my emphasis). That is to say, the very legitimacy of South African law, for Mokgoro, depends on the inclusion of customary law and on the appreciation that a legitimate system of law is something that needs to be *created*; it is not simply a natural given.

When we take a step back, though, the philosophy of *ubuntu* itself (even before we consider its incorporation in South African law) appears strikingly different from an occidental view of the sovereign, autonomous self as key player in national and other social structures. In *No Future Without Forgiveness*, his book on South Africa's Truth and Reconciliation Commission, Archbishop Desmond Tutu writes about *ubuntu* in ways that draw this out:

> *Ubuntu* is very difficult to render into a Western language. It speaks of the very essence of being human. When we want to give high praise to someone, we say, "*Yu, u nobuntu*"; "Hey, so-and-so has *ubuntu*." Then you are generous, you are hospitable, you are friendly and caring and compassionate. You share what you have. It is to say, "My humanity is caught up, is inextricably bound up, in yours." We belong in a bundle of life. We say, "A person is a person through other persons." It is not, "I think therefore I am." It says rather: I am human because I belong. I participate, I share."
>
> Tutu 1999, 31

In the concluding sentences cited here, an appreciation of what it is to be human rests in the perception of "I belong. I participate, I share"—and it is this realization, for Rancière, that is an incipient moment in politics, most especially when an ostensibly universally shared humanity is not legally recognized by a partisan ruling elite. "Politics revolves around what is seen and what can be said about it," writes Rancière, "around who has the ability to see and the talent to speak, around the properties of spaces and the possibilities of time" (Rancière 2004b, 13). In his afterword to Rancière's *Politics of Aesthetics*, Slavoj Žižek puts the argument across in more specific terms:

> Political struggle proper is . . . not a rational debate between multiple interests, but, simultaneously, the struggle for one's voice to be heard and recognized as the voice of a legitimate partner: when the "excluded," from the Greek *demos* to Polish workers, protested against the ruling elite . . . the true stakes were not only their explicit demands (for higher wages, work conditions etc.), but their very right to be heard and recognized as an equal partner in the debate. . . . Furthermore, in protesting the wrong (*le tort*) they suffered, they also presented themselves as the immediate embodiment of society as such, as the stand-in for the Whole of Society in its universality, against the particular power-interests of the aristocracy or oligarchy ("we—the 'nothing,' not counted in the order—are the people, we are All against others who stand only for their particular privileged interests").
>
> Žižek 2004, 69–70[2]

If the term *ubuntu* can be translated as "shared humanity," and if making sense of our surroundings is dependent on the perception of a world shared, then *ubuntu* finds itself in an interstitial zone of "meaning, morality and materiality."[3] Questions of human aesthetic endeavor and questions of social justice are inextricably linked.

III

In book 10 of Plato's *Republic*, poets and artists are banished from the ideal state: Aesthetic considerations are explicitly announced to be inimical to the pursuit of justice. Perhaps as a response to this, my core preoccupation in this book has been to make a plea for the value of the aesthetic in questions of social justice. Across the seven chapters I hope to have drawn a line that

---

2. In a deft summation of Rancière's position, Žižek writes: "This identification of the non-part with the Whole, of the part of society with no properly defined place within it (or resisting the allocated subordinate place within it) with the Universal, is the elementary gesture of politicization" (Žižek 2004, 70).
3. The phrase is John Comaroff's. He used it in a creative and conceptually invigorating way in his chairing of the panel "Critical Theory and Ethnography" at the Ubuntu Project colloquium, Pretoria, August 2011.

reconnects these two seemingly distant points. In this sense my project can also be understood as a response to an essay by Albie Sachs, former chief justice of the Constitutional Court. In "Art and Freedom," Sachs writes:

> Art and justice are usually represented as dwelling in different domains: art is said to relate to the human heart, justice to human intelligence. Rationality is sometimes seen as inimical to art, and passion as hostile to justice. Our building shows how art and human rights overlap and reinforce each other. At the core of the Bill of Rights and of artistic endeavour represented in the Court is respect for human dignity. It is this that unites art and justice.
>
> Sachs 2008, 23

For Sachs, the fulcrum of art and justice is the "respect for human dignity"; human dignity itself is presented in the Constitution and in the Bill of Rights as being innate. Section 10 of the Bill of Rights in the Constitution states that "everyone has inherent dignity and the right to have their dignity respected and protected" (*Constitution* 2010, 6). Yet matters are not quite this straightforward: To accept a human value as innate, a natural given, runs the risk of underplaying the discriminating and creative act—an aesthetic act—of attributing value in the first place. The performative opening sentence of the Bill of Rights reads: "The Bill of Rights is the cornerstone of democracy in South Africa. It enshrines the rights of all people in our country and affirms the democratic values of human dignity, equality and freedom" (*Constitution* 2010, 5).

The Bill of Rights—a document that is itself the product of human creativity—is the cornerstone, the enshrinement, and the affirmation of democratic value. That is to say, a human value that "*all* people in *our* country" *share*. Yet this endeavor of participation and veneration depends on a creative and collective attribution of value, and *hence* on a drawing of lines—between what is enshrined as law and what is not, between humans and other animals, between "all people in our country" and those beyond its borders . . . These lines are testament to a fiat of the human imagination.

Drucilla Cornell in *Philosophy of the Limit* is deeply attentive to the dangers of setting boundaries with complacent assurance. "The care for difference needs a generosity that does not attempt to grasp what is other as one's own," writes Cornell. She goes on to say: "The danger of certainty is that it turns against the generous impulse to open oneself up to the Other, and to truly listen, to risk the chance that we might be wrong. The move to non-closure, then, can and should be understood ethically" (Cornell 1992, 57). Nevertheless I would argue that the gesture of drawing the line, too, should be understood ethically, precisely because it comes *in the teeth* of recognizing that we might be wrong: The decision of where to draw the line is contingent (we could draw it somewhere else) as much as it is an everyday necessity. With the drawing of lines comes the recognition of difference, and, in Stephen Clingman's terms, "difference is not the barrier but the *prompt*, the very *ground* for transition and meaning"; it is the "space of crossing" (Clingman 2009, 241). With the discernment of difference comes the attribution of value, and also the possibility of change. It is through the appreciation of differences and shared values that we are able to create meaningful worlds.

This brings me back to the quotation from G. K. Chesterton where this book started out. Chesterton laments those who "seldom draw the line anywhere"; it amounts to "living on prejudices and never looking at them" (Chesterton 1928, 780).[4] Without drawing any lines, asserting a "view of life," Chesterton argues, you have no ground from which to question your assumptions and prejudices and will blindly follow tradition.

Throughout this book I have discussed novels, speeches, artworks, scholarly essays, legal documents, philosophical works, a walk through the city, my daily encounters at the traffic lights, in ways that have led me to reflect on the modes of articulating relationships between what can be seen, and heard, and made—and hence thought—in a time of transition. My discussions have ranged across topics such as land arrogation as a foundation for law, the ethics of address, literature as a way of thinking through the relations between humans and other animals, and the resonances between constitutive acts of law and literary acts of human signification. A discussion of the ways in which we draw the lines that stratify and set the limits that define an emergent democracy is enriched when aesthetic considerations are brought to bear on a conversation that would more readily be associated with legal or political philosophy. In the meaningful projection of a more just future, how do we imagine, make sense of, and perhaps redraw these lines?

---

4. Philip Howard in his book *The Lost Art of Drawing the Line* puts matters this way: "Today, Americans believe that fairness to individuals is the goal of justice. . . . But what does it mean to be fair? What's fair, as most adults know, depends on your point of view. The reason we know American justice is fair, unassailable in its fairness, is that it avoids anyone's point of view. American justice is neutral. Fairness in America comes not from asserting beliefs, but from avoiding them" (Howard 2001, 8).

References

Adorno, Theodor. 1977. "Commitment." In *Aesthetics and Politics*, edited by Ronald Taylor, 177–95. London: NLB.
Anderson, Benedict. 2006. *Imagined Communities: Reflections on the Origin and the Spread of Nationalism*. Revised ed. London and Brooklyn: Verso.
Anti-Apartheid Movement, ed. 1985. *Drawing the Line: Cartoonists against Apartheid. A Selection of Illustrations from 20 Years of "Anti-Apartheid News."* London: Anti-Apartheid Movement.
Aristotle. 1974. *The Politics*. Translated by Thomas Sinclair. Harmondsworth: Penguin.
Attridge, Derek. 2004. *The Singularity of Literature*. London and New York: Routledge.
———. 2005. *J. M. Coetzee and the Ethics of Reading: Literature in the Event*. Scottsville, South Africa: University of KwaZulu-Natal Press.
Attwell, David. 2002. "Race in Disgrace." *Interventions* 4 (3): 331–41.
Austin, John L. 1965. *How to Do Things with Words*. Oxford: Clarendon.
Bakhtin, Mikhail. 1986. *Speech Genres and Other Late Essays*. Translated by Vern W. McGee. Edited by Caryl Emerson and Michael Holquist. Austin: University of Texas Press.
Barthes, Roland. 2001. "The Death of the Author." Translated by Stephen Heath. In *The Norton Anthology of Theory and Criticism*, edited by Vincent Leitch, 1466–70. New York and London: Norton.
Bates, Robert Latimer and Julia Jackson, eds. 1980. *Glossary of Geology*. 2nd ed. Falls Church, Va.: American Geological Institute.
Beavon, Keith. 2004. *Johannesburg: The Making and Shaping of the City*. Pretoria: Unisa Press.
Beer, Gillian. 1983. *Darwin's Plots*. London: Routledge & Kegan Paul.

Benveniste, Emile. 1971. *Problems in General Linguistics*. Translated by Mary Elizabeth Meek. Coral Gables, Fla.: University of Miami Press.

Bernasconi, Robert, 1988. "'Failure of Communication' as a Surplus: Dialogue and Lack of Dialogue between Buber and Levinas." In *The Provocation of Levinas: Rethinking the Other*, edited by Robert Bernasconi and David Woods. London: Routledge.

Blanchot, Maurice. 1982. *The Space of Literature*. Translated and edited by Ann Smock. Lincoln: University of Nebraska Press.

Bleek, Willem, and Lucy Lloyd. 1968. *Specimens of Bushmen Folklore*. Cape Town: Struik.

Boire, Gary. 2004. "Symbolic Violence: Law, Literature, Interpretation—an Afterword." *Ariel: Law, Literature, Postcoloniality* 35 (1–2): 231–45.

Borges, Jorges. 1964. *Dreamtigers*. Translated by Mildred Boyer and Harold Morland. New York: E. P. Dutton.

Boshoff, Willem. www.willemboshoff.com.

———. 2003. *Licked*. Exhibition catalogue. Cape Town: Michael Stevenson Contemporary.

Bosman, Herman Charles. 2000. *Old Transvaal Stories*. Edited by Craig MacKenzie. Cape Town: Human & Rousseau.

———. 2006. "Unto Dust." In *The Complete Oom Schalk Lourens Stories*, edited by Craig MacKenzie, 262–26. Cape Town: Human & Rousseau.

Buber, Martin. 1970. *I and Thou*. Trans. Walter Kaufmann. Edinburgh: T & T Clark.

Butler, Judith. 1999. *Gender Trouble: Feminism and the Subversion of Identity*. New York and London: Routledge.

———. 2004. *Precarious Life: The Powers of Mourning and Violence*. London and New York: Verso.

Carroll, Lewis. 1998. *Alice's Adventures in Wonderland* and *Through the Looking-Glass*. London: Penguin.

Cavalieri, Paola, with Matthew Carlaco, John M. Coetzee, Harlan B. Miller, and Cary Wolfe. 2009. *The Death of the Animal: A Dialogue*. New York: Columbia University Press.

Cazeaux, Clive, ed. 2000. *The Continental Aesthetics Reader*. London and New York: Routledge.

Celan, Paul. 1986. *Collected Prose*. Translated by Rosmarie Waldrop. Manchester, U.K.: Carcanet.

Cheim, John, Diego Cortex, Carmen Gimenez, and Klauss Kertess. 1993. *Drawing the Line against AIDS*. New York: American Foundation for AIDS Research.

Chesterton, Gilbert K. 1928. "Our Notebook: Drawing the Line Somewhere." *Illustrated London News*, May 5, 780.

Christodoulidis, Emilios. 2000. "'Truth and Reconciliation' as Risks." *Social and Legal Studies* 9 (2): 179–204.

———. 2004. "The Objection That Cannot Be Heard: Communication and Legitimacy in the Courtroom." In *Truth and Due Process*. Vol. 1 of *The Trial on Trial*, edited by Antony Duff, Lindsay Farmer, Sandra Marshall, and Victor Tadros, 179–202. Oxford: Hart.

———. 2007. "Against Substitution: The Constitutional Thinking of Dissensus." In *The Paradox of Constitutionalism: Constituent Power and Constitutional Form*, edited by Martin Loughlin Neil Walker, 189–208. Oxford: Oxford University Press.

Christodoulidis, Emilios, and Scott Veitch. 2007. *Introduction to Law and the Politics of Reconciliation*, edited by Scott Veitch, 1–8. Aldershot: Ashgate.

Clark, Graeme. 2012. "Determination Paid Off." *The Big Issue* 192: 20.

Clarkson, Carrol. 1999. "Dickens and the Cratylus." *The British Journal of Aesthetics* 39 (1): 53–61.

———. 2003. "'By Any Other Name': Kripke, Derrida, and an Ethics of Naming." *Journal of Literary Semantics* 32: 35–47.

———. 2005. "Locating Identity in Phaswane Mpe's Welcome to Our Hillbrow." *Third World Quarterly* 26 (3): 451–59.

———. 2008. "Ancient Antagonisms." *English Academy Review* 25 (2): 101–10.

———. 2009. *J. M. Coetzee: Countervoices*. Houndmills: Palgrave.

Clingman, Stephen. 2009. *The Grammar of Identity: Transnational Fiction and the Nature of the Boundary*. Oxford: Oxford University Press.

———. 2010. "Writing the Treason Trial." *Current Writing* 22 (2): 37–59.

Coetzee, J. M. 1977. "Achterberg's 'Ballade van de gasfitter': The Mystery of I and You." *PMLA* 92 (2): 285–96.

———. 1983. *Life & Times of Michael K*. Johannesburg: Ravan Press.

———. 1992. *Doubling the Point*. Edited by David Attwell. Cambridge, Mass.: Harvard University Press.

———. 1993. "Homage." *The Threepenny Review* 53: 5–7.

———. 1999a. *Disgrace*. London: Secker & Warburg.

———. 1999b. *The Lives of Animals*. Princeton, N.J.: Princeton University Press.

———. 2005a. "Roads to Translation." *Meanjin: Tongues Translation: Only Connect* 64 (4): 141–51.

———. 2005b. *Slow Man*. London: Secker & Warburg.

Coetzee, J. M., and Tony Morphet. 1987. "Two Interviews with J. M. Coetzee, 1983 and 1987." *Tri-Quarterly: From South Africa* 69: 454–64.

The Constitution of the Republic of South Africa. 2010. Ninth ed. Cape Town: Juta.

Comaroff, John. 2011. *Chair's talk for the panel "Critical Theory and Ethnography." Conference of the Ubuntu Project*, August 3, University of Pretoria.
Corcoran, Steven. 2010. *Introduction to Dissensus*, by Jacques Rancière, translated by Steven Corcoran, 1–24. London and New York: Continuum.
Cornell, Drucilla. 1992. *The Philosophy of the Limit*. New York and London: Routledge.
———. 2008. *Moral Images of Freedom*. Lanham, Md.: Rowman and Littlefield.
Craig-Martin, Michael. 1995. *Drawing the Line: Reappraising Drawing Past and Present*. London: South Bank Centre.
Damasio, Antonio R. 1996. *Descartes' Error: Emotion, Reason, and the Human Brain*. London and Basingstoke: Papermac.
———. 2004. *Looking for Spinoza: Joy, Sorrow, and the Feeling Brain*. London: Vintage.
Danson, Edwin. 2001. *Drawing the Line: How Mason and Dixon Surveyed the Most Famous Border in America*. New York: Wiley.
Darwin, Charles. 1901. *The Descent of Man and Selection in Relation to Sex*. 1871. London: John Murray.
———. 2009. *On the Origin of Species by Means of Natural Selection; or, The Preservation of Favoured Races in the Struggle for Life*. 1859. London: Penguin.
Davidson, Donald. 1980. "Mental Events." In *Readings in Philosophy of Psychology*, edited by Ned Block, 1:107–19. London: Methuen.
Davies, Margaret. 1996. *Delimiting the Law: Postmodernism: and the Politics of Law*. London: Pluto Press.
———. 1998. "The Proper: Discourses of Purity." *Law and Critique* 9 (2): 143–73.
de Certeau, Michel. 1984. *The Practice of Everday Life*. Translated by Steven F. Rendell. Berkeley and Los Angeles: University of California Press.
Derrida, Jacques. 1967. *De la Grammatologie*. Paris: Les Éditions de Minuit.
———. 1978a. "Force and Signification." In *Writing and Difference*, translated by Alan Bass, 3–30. Chicago: University of Chicago Press.
———. 1978b. "Violence and Metaphysics: An Essay on the Thought of Emmanuel Levinas." In *Writing and Difference*, translated by Alan Bass, 79–153. Chicago: Chicago University Press.
———. 1982. "The Ends of Man." In *Margins of Philosophy*, translated by Alan Bass, 109–36. Chicago: Chicago University Press.
———. 1986a. "Declarations of Independence." *New Political Science* 15: 7–15.
———. 1986b. *Schibboleth pour Paul Celan*. Paris: Galilée.
———. 1987. "The Laws of Reflection: Nelson Mandela, in Admiration." In *For Nelson Mandela*, edited by Jacques Derrida and Mustapha Tlili, 13–42. New York: Seaver Books.

———. 1988. *Limited Inc*. Evanston, Ill.: Northwestern University Press.

———. 1989. "Psyche: Inventions of the Other." In *Reading de Man Reading*, translated by Catherine Porter, edited by Lindsay Waters and Wlad Godzich, 25–65. Minneapolis: University of Minnesota Press.

———. 1992a *Acts of Literature*. Edited by Derek Attridge. New York and London: Routledge.

———. 1992b. *Given Time: Counterfeit Money*. Translated by Peggy Kamuf, Chicago: Chicago University Press.

———. 1994. *Specters of Marx: The State of the Debt, the Work of Mourning, & the New International*. Trans. Peggy Kamuf. New York and London: Routledge.

———. 1995a. *The Gift of Death*. Translated by David Wills. Chicago: University of Chicago Press.

———. 1995b. "Passions: 'An Oblique Offering.'" Translated by David Wood. In *On the Name*, edited by Thomas Dutoit, 1–31. Stanford: Stanford University Press.

———. 2001. *On Cosmopolitanism and Forgiveness*. Translated by Mark Dooley and Michael Hughes. London and New York: Routledge.

———. 2002. "Force of Law: The 'Mystical Foundation of Authority.'" In *Acts of Religion*, 230–98. London: Routledge.

———. 2004. "For a Justice to Come." Interview with Lieven Cauter. http://www.brusselstribunal.org/pdf/Derrida_EN.htm.

Derrida, Jacques, and Nancy, Jean-Luc. 1991. "'Eating Well,' or the Calculation of the Subject: An Interview with Jacques Derrida." In *Who Comes after the Subject?* edited by Eduardo Cadava, Peter Connor, and Jean-Luc Nancy, 96–119. London and New York: Routledge.

Dlamini, Jacob. 2009. *Native Nostalgia*. Johannesburg: Jacana.

Dyzenhaus, David. 2001. "'With the Benefit of Hindsight': Dilemmas of Legality in the Face of Injustice." In *Lethe's Law: Justice, Law, and Ethics in Reconciliation*, edited by Emilios Christodoulidis and Scott Veitch, 65–89. Oxford; Portland, Ore.: Hart.

Eze, Emmanuel Chukwudi, ed. 1998. *African Philosophy: An Anthology*. Oxford and Malden, Mass.: Blackwell.

Fitzpatrick, Peter. 2001a. "Law like Poetry: 'Burnt Norton.'" *Liverpool Law Review* 23 (3): 285–88.

———. 2001b. *Modernism and the Grounds of Law*. Cambridge: Cambridge University Press.

———. 2004. "Juris-fiction: Literature and the Law of the Law." In "Law, Literature, Postcoloniality," edited by Cheryl Suzack and Gary Boire. Special issue, *Ariel* 35 (1–2): 215–29.

Forster, Edward Morgan. 1982. *A Passage to India*. Harmondsworth: Penguin.

Fynsk, Christopher. 1996. *Language and Relation:... That There Is Language.* Stanford, Calif.: Stanford University Press.

Gilmartin, Sophie. 2000. "Geology, Genealogy, and Church Restoration in Hardy's Writing." In *The Achievement of Thomas Hardy*, edited by P. Mallett, 22–40. Houndmills, Basingstoke, and London: Macmillan.

Goldblatt, David. 2010. *TJ: Johannesburg Photographs, 1948–2010*. Cape Town: Umuzi.

Gyekye, Kwame. 1991. "Person and Community in African Thought." In *Philosophy from Africa: A Text with Readings*, edited by P. H. Coetzee and A. P. J. Roux, 317–36. Cape Town: Oxford University Press Southern Africa.

Hacking, Ian. 2002. *Historical Ontology*. Cambridge, Mass.: Harvard University Press.

———. 2008. "Deflections." In *Philosophy and Animal Life*, 139–72. New York: Columbia University Press.

Hardy, Thomas. 1984. *The Life and Work of Thomas Hardy*. Edited by Michael Millgate. London: Macmillan.

———. 2000. *Tess of the d'Urbervilles*. Ware: Wordsworth.

Hartley, Leslie Poles. 1984. *The Go-Between*. Harmondsworth: Penguin Books.

Hegel, Georg. 1977. *Phenomenology of Spirit*. Translated by A. V. Miller. Oxford: Oxford University Press.

Heidegger, Martin. 1991. *Nietzsche: The Will to Power as Art*. 2 vols. Translated by David Farrell Krell. New York: HarperCollins.

———. 1993. "The Origin of the Work of Art." Translated by Albert Hofstadter. In *Basic Writings*, edited by David Farrell Krell, 143–212. New York: HarperCollins.

———. 1998. "On the Question of Being" [Concerning "The Line"]. Translated by William McNeill. In *Pathmarks*, edited by William McNeill, 291–322. Cambridge: Cambridge University Press.

Honderich, Ted, ed. 1995. *The Oxford Companion to Philosophy*. Oxford: Oxford University Press.

Howard, Philip. 2001. *The Lost Art of Drawing the Line: How Fairness Went Too Far*. New York: Random House.

Ingold, Tim. 2007. *Lines: A Brief History*. London and New York: Routledge.

Isaacson, Walter. 2011. *Steve Jobs*. London: Little, Brown.

Jakobson, Roman. 1990. *On Language*. Edited by Linda R. Waugh and Monique Monville-Burston. Cambridge, Mass.: Harvard University Press.

Jespersen, Otto, 1922. *Language: Its Nature, Development and Origin*. London: Allen and Unwin.

Kafka, Franz. 1988. *Metamorphosis and Other Stories*. Translated by Willa and Edwin Muir. London: Penguin Books.

Kant, Immanuel. 1996. *Groundwork of the Metaphysics of Morals: Critique of Practical Philosophy*. Translated and edited by Mary J. Gregor. Cambridge: Cambridge University Press.

———. 1998. *Critique of Pure Reason*. Translated and edited by Paul Guyer and Allen W. Wood. Cambridge: Cambridge University Press.

Kentridge, William and Angela Breidbach. 2006. *William Kentridge Thinking Aloud: Conversations with Angela Breidbach*. Johannesburg: David Krut.

Kertzer, Jonathan. 2010. *Poetic Justice and Legal Fictions*. Cambridge: Cambridge University Press.

Kripke, Saul. 1980. *Naming and Necessity*. Oxford: Basil Blackwell.

Krog, Antjie. 1998. *Country of My Skull*. London: Jonathan Cape.

Krog, Antjie, Nosisi Mpolweni, and Ratele Kopano. 2009. *There Was This Goat: Investigating the Truth Commission Testimony of Notrose Nobomvu Konile*. Scottsville, South Africa: University of KwaZulu-Natal Press.

Kunene. 1996. "The Essence of Being Human—an African Perspective." Inaugural lecture, University of Natal, Durban, August 16.

Langenscheidt's Standard Dictionary of the English and German Languages. 1970. 6th ed. London: Hodder and Stoughton.

Leist, Anton. and Peter Singer, eds. 2010. *J. M. Coetzee and Ethics: Philosophical Perspectives on Literature*. New York: Columbia University Press.

Lenta, Patrick. 2010. "Introduction: Law and South African Literature." *Current Writing: Text and Reception in Southern Africa* 22 (2): 1–18.

Levinas, Emmanuel. 1974. *Autrement qu'être ou au-dela de l'essence*. The Hague: Martinus Nijhoff.

———. 1979. *Totality and Infinity: An Essay on Exteriority*. Translated by Alphonso Lingis. The Hague: Martinus Nijhoff.

———. 1981. *Otherwise than Being; or, Beyond Essence*. Translated by Alphonso Lingis. The Hague: Martinus Nijhoff.

———. 1989a. "Reality and Its Shadow." Translated by Alphonso Lingis. In *The Levinas Reader*, edited by Sean Hand, 129–59. Oxford: Basil Blackwell.

———. 1989b. "Time and the Other." Translated by Richard Cohen. In *The Levinas Reader*, edited by Sean Hand, 37–58. Oxford: Basil Blackwell.

———. 1996a. "Is Ontology Fundamental?" Translated by Simon Critchley, P. Atterton, and G. Noctor. In *Emmanuel Levinas: Basic Philosophical Writings*, edited by Adriaan Peperzak, Simon Critchley, and Robert Bernasconi, 1–10. Bloomington: Indiana University Press.

———. 1996b. "Paul Celan: From Being to the Other." In *Proper Names*, translated by Michael B. Smith, 40–46. Stanford, Calif.: Stanford University Press.

———. 1996c. "Transcendence and Height." Translated by Tina Chanter, Simon Critchley, and Nicholas Walker. Revised by Adriaan Peperzak. In *Emmanuel Levinas: Basic Philosophical Writings*, edited by Adriaan Peperzak, Simon Critchley, and Robert Bernasconi, 11–31. Bloomington: Indiana University Press.

Levinas, Emmanuel, and Richard Kearney. 1986. "Dialogue with Emmanuel Levinas." Translated by Richard Kearney. In *Face to Face with Levinas*, edited by Richard Cohen, 13–33. Albany: State University of New York.

Levinas, Emmanuel, and François Poirié. 2001. "Interview with François Poirié." Translated by Jill Robbins and M. Coelen with T. Loebel. In *Is It Righteous to Be? Interviews with Emmanuel Levinas*, edited by Jill Robbins, 23–83. Stanford: Stanford University Press.

Levinas, Emmanuel, with Tamra Wright, Peter Hughes, and Alison Ainley. 1988. "The Paradox of Morality: An Interview with Emmanuel Levinas." Translated by Andrew Benjamin and Tamra Wright. In *The Provocation of Levinas*, edited by Robert Bernasconi and David Wood, 168–80. London and New York: Routledge.

Lindahl, Hans. 2007. "Constituent Power and Reflexive Identity: Towards an Ontology of Collective Selfhood." In *The Paradox of Constitutionalism: Constituent Power and Constitutional Form*, edited by Martin Loughlin and Neil Walker, 9–26. Oxford: Oxford University Press.

Lingis, Alphonso. 1968. *Translator's preface. The Visible and the Invisible, by Maurice Merleau-Ponty*, edited by Claude Lefort, xl–lvi. Evanston, Ill.: Northwestern University Press.

Locke, John. 1997. *An Essay Concerning Human Understanding*. Edited by Roger Woolhouse. London: Penguin.

Lyotard, Jean-François. 1988. *The Differend: Phrases in Dispute*. Translated by Georges van den Abbeele. Minneapolis: University of Minnesota Press.

MacKinnon, Catherine. 1996. "Law's Stories as Reality and Politics." In *Law's Stories: Narrative and Rhetoric in the Law*, edited by Peter Brooks and Paul Gewirtz, 232–37. New Haven, Conn.: Yale University Press.

Mandela, Nelson Rolihlahla. 1994a. *Long Walk to Freedom: The Autobiography of Nelson Mandela*. Randburg, South Africa: Macdonald Purnell.

———. 1994b. *The Struggle Is My Life: His Speeches and Writings, 1944–1990*. Cape Town and Johannesburg: Mayibuye Books, David Philip.

———. 14 April 2004. Live television news broadcast: SABC.

Marks, Jonathan. 2002. *What It Means to Be 98% Chimpanzee: Apes, People, and Their Genes*. Berkeley and Los Angeles: University of California Press.

McDonald, Peter. 2009. *The Literature Police: Apartheid, Censorship, and Its Cultural Consequences*. Oxford: Oxford University Press.

Merleau-Ponty, Maurice. 1962. *Phenomenology of Perception*. Translated by Colin Smith. London: Routledge & Kegan Paul.

———. 1964. *Sense and Non-sense*. Translated by Hubert L. Dreyfus and Patricia Allen Dreyfus. Evanston, Ill.: Northwestern University Press.

———. 1968. *The Visible and the Invisible*. Translated by Alphonso Lingis. Edited by C. Lefort. Evanston, Ill.: Northwestern University Press.

Michaels, Anne. 2009. *The Winter Vault*. New York: Bloomsbury.

Miller, J. Hillis. 1968. "'Wessex Heights': The Persistence of the Past in Hardy's Poetry." *Critical Quarterly* 10 (4): 339–59.

———. 1992. *Ariadne's Thread: Story Lines*. New Haven, Conn.: Yale University Press.

———. 2009. *For Derrida*. New York: Fordham University Press.

Mokgoro, Yvonne. 1998. "Ubuntu and the Law in South Africa." *Buffalo Human Rights Review* 4: 15–23.

———. 2008. "The Utility of Ubuntu." Talk, University of Cape Town, July 30.

Monk, Ray. 1990. *Ludwig Wittgenstein: The Duty of Genius*. London: Vintage.

Moraru, Christian. 2000. "'We Embraced Each Other by Our Names': Levinas, Derrida, and the Ethics of Naming." *Names* 48 (1): 49–58.

Morris, Alan. 1999. *Bleakness and Light: Inner-City Transition in Hillbrow, Johannesburg*. Johannesburg: Witwatersrand University Press.

Motha, Stewart. 2007. "*Reconciliation as Domination*." In *Law and the Politics of Reconciliation*, edited by Scott Veitch, 69–91. Aldershot: Ashgate.

Mpe, Phaswane. 2001. *Welcome to Our Hillbrow*. Pietermaritzburg, South Africa: University of Natal Press.

———. 2003. "'Our Missing Store of Memories': City, Literature, and Representation." In *Shifting Selves: Post-Apartheid Essays on Mass Media, Culture, and Identity*, edited by H. Wasserman and S. Jacobs, 181–98. Cape Town: Kwela Books.

Mudimbe, V. Y. 1988. *The Invention of Africa: Gnosis, Philosophy, and the Order of Knowledge*. Bloomington: Indiana University Press.

Nancy, Jean-Luc. 1991. *The Inoperative Community*. Translated by Peter Connor, Lisa Garbus, Michael Holland, and Simona Sawhney. Minneapolis: University of Minnesota Press.

———. 2000. *Being Singular Plural*. Translated by Robert Richardson. Stanford: Stanford University Press.

Ndebele, Njabulo. 1991. *Rediscovery of the Ordinary: Essays on South African Literature and Culture*. Johannesburg: COSAWU.

———. 2007. *Fine Lines from the Box: Further Thoughts about Our Country*. Edited by Sam Raditlhalo. Cape Town and Johannesburg: Umuzi.

Norris, Christopher. 1984. "Deconstruction, Naming, and Necessity: Some Logical Options." *Journal of Literary Semantics* 13 (3): 159–80.

Nuttall, Sarah. 2003. "City Forms and Writing the 'Now' in South Africa." http://wiser.wits.ac.za/content/city-forms-and-writing-now-south-africa-10137.

[*OED*]. *The Shorter Oxford English Dictionary on Historical Principles*. 1973. Edited by William Little, H. W. Fowler, and Jessie Coulson. Revised by C. T. Onions. Oxford: Oxford University Press.

p'Bitek, Okot. 1998. "The Sociality of the Self." In *African Philosophy: An Anthology*, edited by Emmanuel Chukwede Eze, 73–74. Oxford: Blackwell.

Pickover, Michelè. 2005. *Animal Rights in South Africa*. Cape Town: Double Storey.

Plato. 1970a. *The Cratylus*. Translated by Benjamin Jowett. In *The Dialogues of Plato*, edited by R. M. Hare and D. A. Russell, 3:129–94. London: Sphere Books.

———. 1970b. *The Laws*. Translated by Trevor Saunders. Harmondsworth: Penguin.

———. 2003. *The Republic*. Translated by Desmond Lee. 2nd ed. London: Penguin.

Proust, Marcel. 1954. *Un Amour de Swann*. Paris: Gallimard.

Pollard, Natalie. 2012. *Speaking to You*. Oxford: Oxford University Press.

Posner, Richard. 1988. *Law and Literature: A Misunderstood Relation*. Cambridge, Mass.: Harvard University Press.

Rabbethge-Schiller, Hella, ed. 2006. *Memory and Magic: Contemporary Art of the !Xun & Khwe*. Johannesburg: Jacana.

Rancière, Jacques. 1999. *Disagreement*. Translated by Julie Rose. Minneapolis: University of Minnesota Press.

Rancière, Jacques. 2004a. *The Flesh of Words: The Politics of Writing*. Translated by Charlotte Mandell. Stanford, Calif.: Stanford University Press.

———. 2004b. *The Politics of Aesthetics*. Translated by Gabriel Rockhill. London: Continuum.

———. 2010. *Dissensus: On Politics and Aesthetics*. Translated and edited by Steven Corcoran. London and New York: Continuum.

Robinson, A. M. Lewin. 1974. Introduction. *South African Journal*. Cape Town: South African Library Reprint Series, 4 (1).

Ross, Fiona. 2003. *Bearing Witness: Women and the Truth and Reconciliation Commission in South Africa*. London: Pluto.

Rosenblatt, Roger. 2011. *Unless It Moves the Human Heart: The Craft and Art of Writing*. New York: HarperCollins.

Russell, Bertrand. 1940. *An Inquiry into Meaning and Truth*. London: George Allen and Unwin.

Sachs, Albie. 2008. "Art and Freedom." In *Art and Justice: The Art of the Constitutional Court of South Africa*, edited by Bronwyn Law-Viljoen, 17–30. Johannesburg: David Krut.

Sanders, Mark. 2007. *Ambiguities of Witnessing: Law and Literature in the Time of a Truth Commission*. Stanford, Calif.: Stanford University Press.

Sartre, Jean-Paul. 1978. *What Is Literature?* Translated by Bernard Frechtman. London: Methuen.
Saussure, Ferdinand de. 1960. *Course in General Linguistics.* Translated by Wade Baskin. London: Peter Owen.
Schaap, Andrew. 2007. "The Time of Reconciliation and the Space of Politics." In *Law and the Politics of Reconciliation*, edited by Scott Veitch, 9–31. Aldershot: Ashgate.
Schalkwyk, David. 1995. "Saussure, Names, and the Gap between Word and World." *Journal of Literary Semantics* 24 (2): 127–48.
———. 1996. "Knowledge, Ethics, and the Limits of Language: Wittgenstein and Lyotard." *Journal of Literary Studies* 12 (1–2): 86–109.
———. 2000. "'What's in a Name?': Derrida, Apartheid, and the Logic of the Proper Name." *Language Sciences* 22: 167–91.
———. 2002. *Speech and Performance in Shakespeare's Sonnets and Plays.* Cambridge: Cambridge University Press.
———. 2004. *Literature and the Touch of the Real.* Newark: University of Delaware Press.
Schmitt, Carl. 2003. *The Nomos of the Earth in the International Law of the Jus Publicum Europaeum.* Translated by G. L. Ulmen. New York: Telos Press.
Sebald, W. G. 2001. *Austerlitz.* Translated By Anthea Bell. London: Penguin.
Segal, Lauren, ed. 2006. *Number Four: The Making of Constitutional Hill.* Johannesburg: Penguin.
Simone, AbdouMaliq. 2004. "People as Infrastructure: Intersecting Fragments in Johannesburg." "Johannesburg: The Elusive Metropolis Public." Special issue, *Culture* 16 (3): 407–29.
Smith, Anna H. 1971. *Johannesburg Street Names: A Dictionary of Street, Suburb, and Other Place-Names, Compiled to the End of 1968.* Cape Town and Johannesburg: Juta.
Spinoza, Benedict de. 1891. *De Intellectus Emendatione—Ethica.* Translated by R. H. M. Elwes. Vol. 2 of *The Chief Works of Benedict de Spinoza*. London: George Bell and Sons.
Staten, Henry. 1985. *Wittgenstein and Derrida.* Oxford: Basil Blackwell.
Tinzi, Mzwe Themba. 2012. "*Dreams Have Come True.*" *The Big Issue* 192: 22.
Tolstoy, Leo. 1930. *What Is Art? And Essays on Art.* Translated by Aylmer Maude. Oxford: Oxford University Press.
Tomasello, Michael. 1999. *The Cultural Origins of Human Cognition.* Cambridge, Mass.: Harvard University Press.
Trier, Jost. 1942. "Zaun und Mannring." *Beiträchen zur Geschichte der deutschen Sprache und Literatur,* 66: 232–64.
Tutu, Desmond. 1999. *No Future without Forgiveness.* New York: Doubleday.

Ulmen, G. L. 2003. Introduction. *The Nomos of the Earth in the International Law of the Jus Publicum Europaeum*, by Carl Schmitt, 9–34. New York: Telos Press.

van Niekerk, Marlene. 1994. *Triomf.* Cape Town: Queillerie.

———. 1999. *Triomf.* Translated by Leon de Kock. Johannesburg: Jonathan Ball.

Van Roermund, Bert. 2003. "First-Person Plural Legislature: Political Reflexivity and Representation." *Philosophical Explorations* 6 (3): 235–52.

Veitch, Scott. 2001. "The Legal Politics of Amnesty." In *Lethe's Law: Justice, Law, and Ethics in Reconciliation*, edited by Emilios Christodoulidis and Scott Veitch, 33–45. Oxford and Portland, Ore.: Hart.

———, ed. 2007. *Law and the Politics of Reconciliation.* Aldershot: Ashgate.

Vismann, Cornelia. 1997. "Starting from Scratch: Concepts of Order in No Man's Land." In *War, Violence, and the Modern Condition*," edited by Bernd Hüppauff, New York and Berlin: Walter de Gruyter.

Vladislavić, Ivan. 1998. "Street Addresses, Johannesburg." In *Blank Architecture, Apartheid and After*, edited by Hilton Judin and Ivan Vladislavić, 305–13. Cape Town: David Philip; Rotterdam: NAi.

———. 2001. *The Restless Supermarket.* Cape Town: David Philip.

———. 2004. *The Exploded View.* Johannesburg: Random House.

———. 2005. *Willem Boshoff.* Johannesburg: David Krut.

———. 2006. *Portrait with Keys: Joburg & What-What.* Roggebaai: Umuzi.

———. 2010. *Double Negative.* Cape Town: Umuzi.

Wicomb, Zoë. 2006. *Playing in the Light.* Roggebaai: Umuzi.

Wilson, Edward Osborne. 1978. *On Human Nature.* Cambridge, Mass.: Harvard University Press.

Wiredu, Kwasi. 1998. "The Moral Foundations of an African Culture." In *Philosophy from Africa: A Text with Readings*, edited by P. H. Coetzee and A. P. J. Roux, 306–16. Oxford: Oxford University Press.

Wittgenstein, Ludwig. 1922. *Tractatus Logico-Philosophicus.* Translated by C. K. Ogden. London and New York: Routledge.

———. 1994. *The Blue and Brown Books: Preliminary Studies for the "Philosophical Investigations."* Oxford: Blackwell.

———. 2001. *Philosophical Investigations: The German Text, with a Revised English Translation.* Translated by G. E. M. Anscombe. Oxford: Blackwell.

Young, Dudley. 1992. *Origins of the Sacred: The Ecstasies of Love and War.* London: Little, Brown.

Žižek, Slavoj. 2004. "The Lesson of Rancière." Afterword. In *The Politics of Aesthetics by Jacques Rancière*, translated by Gabriel Rockhill, 67–79. New York: Continuum.

Index

Adorno, Theodor, 83
aesthetics, 2, 4, 11, 89, 181; aesthetic act, 2–3, 6, 18–21, 25, 47, 67, 108, 132–133, 182, 185; aesthetic discourse, 16; aesthetic experience, 5, 12; and ethics, 20, 43, 92, 102, 105, 110, 163, 166; and politics, 5, 6, 162, 184; of law, 27; of reconciliation, 83; of transitional justice, 2, 20, 89. *See also* Rancière, Jacques
Africa, 20, 44, 46–49, 57–60, 70, 146, 159, 163, 169–174, 181–182
African National Party (ANC), 44, 48, 53, 59, 85
African nationalism, 46, 49, 57, 58, 60
African philosophy, 169, 169n7, 182
Afrikaans, 30, 69, 83, 85, 96, 149, 150, 164
agent, 172
alterity, 51, 96, 98, 102, 127, 128, 130, 131
"ancient antagonism," 6, 127, 131
Anderson, Benedict, 169n6; *Imagined Communities*, 3, 20
animal ethics, 108, 126, 127
animals, 2, 20, 34, 49, 98, 107–114, 119–134, 185–186
apartheid, 7, 8, 19, 29, 30–31, 48–62, 69, 70, 84, 85, 107, 167, 174
Aristotle, 4; *The Politics*, 4, 18
art, 1, 2, 6, 9, 13–18, 33, 37, 47–49, 52, 65–66, 73–75, 80, 81, 83, 92, 100–102, 105, 108, 133, 134, 162; creative arts, 6, 38; dramatic arts, 8, 37; and justice, 17, 19, 36, 37, 39, 66, 74–76, 185; language arts, 67, 70, 80, 159; of reconciliation, 87; visual arts, 2, 66, 72, 75, 108
Attridge, Derek, 6n6, 178
Attwell, David, 41; "Race in Disgrace," 44n7
Auden, W. H., 38
audience, 49, 52, 56, 58, 66, 130
Austin, J. L., 95n10; *How to Do Things with Words*, 47, 162n3
author, 40, 41, 44, 74, 84, 137
authority, 7, 8, 41, 44, 47, 49, 52, 55, 57, 67, 100n14, 131
authorship, 19, 40, 41, 44, 45
autobiography, 84, 86

Bakhtin, Mikhail, 19, 51–52
Barthes, Roland, "The Death of the Author," 124
Beavon, Keith, *Johannesburg: The Making and Shaping of the City*, 150n2
Beer, Gillian, 112n2
Beethoven, Ludwig van, 39
Benjamin, Walter, 75
Benveniste, Emile, 61, 97, 103; "Subjectivity in Language," 59, 93–94, 174–175
Bernasconi, Robert, 97n11, 98n12
Blanchot, Maurice, 39
Bleek, Willem, and Lloyd, Lucy, 176–177
Blond, Louis, xi, 100n14
Boire, Gary, 4n5, 25
Borges, Jorge Luis, 32
Boshoff, Willem, xi, xiii, 3, 20, 67, 69–70, 80–82, 84, 86
Bosman, Herman Charles, 19, 27, 30–32; "Unto Dust," 30, 44, 45

Botha, P. W., 54–55
Breidbach, Angela, 65–66
British settlers, 7
Buber, Martin, 95, 97n11, 98, 106n17; *I and Thou*, 94
Butler, Judith: *Gender Trouble*, 3n3, 47n1, 55n4; *Precarious Life*, 100n14

Calarco, Matthew, 109, 126–127; "Toward an Agnostic Animal Ethics," 126
Cape, 7, 30
Cape Colony, 7
Cape Town, 56, 59, 60, 61, 85, 88, 90n1, 91n3, 99, 106, 156, 175n13
Carroll, Lewis, 32, 175n11
Cavalieri, Paola, *The Death of the Animal*, 20, 109–110, 123–128, 130–133
Cazeaux, Clive, 2, 11
Celan, Paul, 60, 73, 74, 79, 80, 103, 105, 106; "The Meridian," 19, 79, 104
censorship, 3. *See also* literature: and censorship
Chesterton, G. K., xiv, 1, 18, 186
Christodoulidis, Emilios, xi, 56, 86n21, 175n13; "Against Substitution: The Constitutional Thinking of Dissensus," 77n11
Clarkson, Carrol, *J. M. Coetzee: Countervoices*, 93n6
Clingman, Stephen: *The Grammar of Identity*, 168–169, 186; "Writing the South African Treason Trial," 50n2
Coetzee, J. M., 16, 19, 27, 41, 44–45, 92, 93n6, 109, 110, 127, 128, 129, 132–133, 176; "*Achterberg's 'Ballade van de Gasfitter': The Mystery of I and You*," 94n8; *Disgrace*, 20, 42, 44, 107, 166; *Life & Times of Michael K*, 42–43; *The Lives of Animals*, 71n6, 130, 131
colonialism, 19, 25, 29, 30–32, 42, 44–45, 108, 122
Comaroff, John, 184n3
community, 3–5, 20, 26, 68, 74, 76, 78, 82, 113, 116, 123, 126, 149, 154, 158, 162–174, 177–179
Constitutional Court, 3, 19–20, 67, 78, 80, 85–86, 91, 106, 185
Copernicus, 11
Corcoran, Steven, 55n4
Cornell, Drucilla, xi, 16, 32; *Moral Images of Freedom*, 18; *Philosophy of the Limit*, 19, 185

critical and legal theory, 4, 17, 33, 47n1, 74n8, 77n11, 82, 157, 161; preliminary note, 184n3
culture, 2, 20, 46, 47, 49, 82, 163, 173; cultural production, 2, 102

Damasio, Antonio, 111, 112
Danson, Edwin, *Drawing the Line: How Mason and Dixon Surveyed the Most Famous Border in America*, 25–26n1
Darwin, Charles, 20, 110, 112–113, 121, 127, 163; *The Descent of Man*, 110, 119, 122; *On the Origin of Species by Way of Natural Selection*, 110, 112–113, 114–119
Davies, Margaret, *Delimiting the Law: Postmodernism and the Politics of Law*, 37
death sentence, 54
deconstruction, 16n13, 32, 49, 50, 75, 105n16
Defoe, Daniel, 44
democracy, 50, 58, 67, 85, 107, 168, 185, 186
Derrida, Jacques, 12, 13, 14, 20, 32, 37, 39, 49–50, 51, 53, 67–68, 72, 76–77, 79, 80, 86–87, 94n9, 105n16, 125–126, 154, 178–179; "Acts of Literature," 6n6; *On Cosmopolitanism and Forgiveness*, 51n3, 73; "Deconstruction and the Possibility of Justice," 67–68; "Force of Law," 19, 67–68, 72–73, 75, 77, 79, 84; "Force and Signification," 19, 67, 72, 75, 79, 83–84; *The Gift of Death*, 55n5, 91n4; *Limited Inc.*, 14; "The Laws of Reflection: Nelson Mandela, in Admiration," 86n20; *Schibboleth: Pour Paul Celan*, 60n7; *Specters of Marx*, 115–116
diachrony, 116–119
dialogic discourse, 53
dialogic response, 52
"distribution of the sensible," 3n3, 3–5, 48, 55, 182
Dyzenhaus, David, 58

Eliot, T. S., 38, 39
emigrants, 7
ethics: of address, 20, 73, 93, 98, 100, 186; of naming, 12n10
Europe, 19, 29, 32, 152, 164; European philosophy, 50
existentialism, 16

Fairbairn, John, 7
fences, 19, 28–32, 42–43, 45

Fischer, Bram, 54, 58*n*6
Fitzpatrick, Peter, 26–29, 32–33, 36–41, 45, 51, 69*n*4, 161; *Modernism and the Grounds of Law*, 4*n*4, 25, 27*n*2, 28, 33, 36, 39, 40, 41
forgiveness, 51*n*3, 53, 73
Forster, E. M., *A Passage to India*, 39, 123–124
Foucault, Michel, 5, 10, 39
freedom, 17, 18, 50, 58, 66, 78, 100–102, 170*n*8, 183, 185
Freud, Sigmund, 39–40
Fynsk, Christopher, *Language and Relation . . . That There Is Language*, 60*n*7, 61

Greek philosophy, 2
Group Areas Act, 31, 146
Gyekye, Kwame, 170

Hacking, Ian, 10, 19, 131*n*6; "Deflections," 130
Hardy, Thomas, xi, 112, 113, 115, 124, 128
Hartley, L. P., 154
Hegel, Georg, 170*n*8
Heidegger, Martin, 19, 37, 39, 66*n*1; *Nietzsche: The Will to Power as Art*, 36; "On the Question of Being," 19, 70–72; "The Origin of the Work of Art," 27, 33–35
Homer, 6, 8, 16
human, 9, 10, 14–15, 20, 28, 31, 34, 42, 44, 55*n*4, 58, 71*n*6, 84, 95, 98, 106–115, 119–121, 124–134, 147, 157, 160, 162, 164, 168, 171, 182*n*1, 183–186

"I" and "you," 58–62, 92–94, 97–99, 103–106 163, 173–175
imagination, 17–18, 43*n*6, 109–110, 119, 169, 185
immigrants, 146, 173
Immorality Amendment Act, 31
individual, 4, 37, 58, 59, 93, 106, 113, 117–119, 151–152, 154, 159, 170, 172, 186*n*4
Ingold, Tim, *Lines: A Brief History*, 1*n*1, 19, 29*n*3

Jakobson, Roman, 19, 48, 92–93, 95, 97
Jespersen, Otto, 92
Johannesburg, xi, 67, 78, 79, 82, 90, 137, 146, 148, 149–152, 156–157, 159–163
Johannesburg Art Gallery, 147

judgement, 84, 89
"just state," 6–8, 18, 37, 108, 184. *See also* Plato
justice, 2, 6, 14, 17–19, 46, 49–50, 51, 56–58, 69, 74–76, 80, 89, 112, 147, 169, 184, 186*n*4; deconstruction and justice 53, 67–68; injustice, 68, 75, 170; and the law, 19–20, 32, 45, 66, 72–73, 84; symbol of justice, 50–51, 57–58; transitional justice, 2, 19, 20, 74–75, 80, 89, 169. *See also* art: and justice

Kafka, Franz, "The Burrow," 43*n*6
Kant, Immanuel, 5, 6, 11, 16–17, 100, 101; *Critique of Pure Reason*, 10–12; "Fundamental Principles of the Metaphysics of Morals," 17
Kaross, 46–49, 52, 57
Kentridge, William, 3, 20, 65–66
knowledge, 2, 8, 9, 10, 14, 17, 41, 65, 66, 75, 76, 95, 115, 125, 162
Kripke, Saul, 161*n*1
Krog, Antjie, 74*n*9
Kunene, 182*n*1

Lacan, Jacques, 41
language, 9, 10, 12–16, 19, 20, 25, 47, 50–53, 57, 60*n*7, 61, 66–75, 79–82, 96, 101, 104, 106, 125, 130, 133, 162*n*3, 170, 73, 183
law, 7, 10, 18, 25–29, 31–33, 36–39, 44, 47, 49, 51, 55, 57, 58, 61, 62, 66–70, 72, 74, 84, 107, 111, 117, 159, 181–186; and art, 74, 76, 77, 86; customary law, 182–183; as fence, 28–32; and justice, 19–20, 66, 67, 72–73; and literature, 4, 6–7, 19, 27, 38, 45, 172*n*10; natural law, 20; and politics, 19, 48, 56, 77, 85; rule of law, 6, 7, 8, 26
legality, 2, 16, 19, 21, 25–26, 28–29, 32, 38, 43–44, 48, 53–57, 58, 61, 66, 69, 70, 72, 73, 75, 76, 78*n*13, 79, 85, 146, 167, 176, 182–183, 186; legal discourse, 27, 57; legal identity, 2; legal reasoning, 65–66, 72; legal responsibility, 62
Lenta, Patrick, 4
Levinas, Emmanuel, 20, 91–122, 126–127, 133; *Otherwise than Being*, 96, 105, 118; "Reality and its Shadow," 92, 101–104; *Totality and Infinity*, 95, 97, 115, 118
Lindahl, Hans, xi, 77*n*11
Lingis, Alphonso, 151, 157

literature, 2, 15, 19, 25, 45, 100, 124, 127, 134, 162, 166–167, 178, 186; "acts of literature," 6; and censorship, 8; and philosophy, 13–14, 20, 108–109, 129–130, 133. *See also* law: and literature
litigation, 55
Locke, John: *An Essay Concerning Human Understanding*, 9, 10, 12; "Lockean imperative," 10, 19
Lyotard, Jean-François, 175; *The Differend: Phrases in Dispute*, 99–101, 103

Malan, D. F., 30
Mandela, Nelson, 47–62, 78, 84–86; *Long Walk to Freedom*, 46, 49, 53, 84, 85
Marks, Jonathan, 124
McDonald, Peter, *The Literature Police*, 7n7, 8n8
Merleau-Ponty, Maurice, 20, 87, 149, 155; *Phenomenology of Perception*, 148, 151, 155, 157; *Sense and Non-sense*, 155, 157; *The Visible and the Invisible*, 151, 152, 157, 158
Michaels, Anne, 34
Miller, J. Hillis, xi, 55n5, 91n4, 112n2; *Ariadne's Thread: Story Lines*, 19, 35
Mokgoro, Yvonne, 91, 106, 181, 182
Monk, Ray, 14
morality, 184; and art, xiv, 1, 18, 121, 83; moral authority, 100n14; moral community, 76n10; moral opposition, 52–53, 85; moral philosophy, 7, 127; moral sense, 120–121; moral status, 123–128; and reason, 132
Moraru, Christian, "We Embraced Each Other by Our Names: Levinas, Derrida, and the Ethics of Naming," 94n9
Morris, Alan, *Bleakness and Light: Inner-City Transition in Hillbrow, Johannesburg*, 137, 146
Motha, Stewart, xiii, 82
Mpe, Phaswane, 3, 16, 20, 137, 147, 148, 152, 158; *Welcome to Our Hillbrow*, 146, 148, 151, 154, 157, 172
Mudimbe, V. Y., *The Invention of Africa*, 106, 106n18, 169n7

Nancy, Jean-Luc, 51, 125, 163, 171–174, 175, 179, 182; *Being Singular Plural*, 171, 177–178; *The Inoperative Community*, 20, 163, 173–174

"narrated event," 48, 51, 54, 92–95, 97
nation, 3–4, 55, 59, 78, 108
Nationalist Party, 30
natural science, 7, 122
Ndebele, Njabulo, 16, 167–168; *Fine Lines from the Box*, 19, 166–167; *Rediscovery of the Ordinary*, 167
newspaper, 4, 90
Nietzsche, Friedrich, 36, 66n1
nomos, 10, 19, 25–29, 32, 33, 36–37
Norris, Christopher, 12
novel, 4, 16, 148, 149, 159, 162–163, 165, 166, 186
Nuttall, Sarah, "City Forms and Writing the 'Now' in South Africa," 157

Old Fort. *See* Constitutional Court
oppressor, 50, 57

painting, 11, 87, 89, 100, 162
partage, 51, 182
p'Bitek, Okot, "The Sociality of the Self," 171
"the people," 4, 58, 77, 184
performative, 18, 41, 47–48, 52, 54, 58–59, 69, 76, 84, 95–98, 130–131, 158, 160, 162, 167, 173, 175, 176, 182, 185
philosophers and poets, 6, 9, 13, 18, 108, 110, 127, 129, 131, 133–134
philosophical discourse, 9, 16, 131
"philosophy of the limit," 19, 32, 33
photography, 147–148, 152, 153n4, 155
Plato, 6–9, 14–18, 37–39, 95, 108–109, 159, 127–133, 184; *Laws*, 18; *Republic*, 6, 9, 14, 16, 18, 37, 108, 127–128, 131, 159, 184
pleasure and pain, 7–9, 37–38, 109, 133, 158, 167–168
poet, 6–9, 13–14, 16, 18, 37–38, 73, 94n8, 102–103, 105, 108–112, 127–129, 131–133, 134, 159, 184
poetry, 6–9, 14, 37, 38, 40, 60, 69, 73–74, 79, 94n8, 103, 128–129, 131, 133, 159, 167
politics, 2, 17, 29, 57, 70, 127, 159, 182; political community, 3, 4, 76n10; political protest, 19, 30, 55, 56, 84, 184; political responsibility, 62; political subjectivity, 2. *See also* Rancière, Jacques
Pollard, Natalie, xi, 94n8
Population Registration Act, 31

postapartheid, 2, 18, 20, 44–45, 48, 66, 86, 162–163; jurisprudence, 45, 182
Pringle, Thomas, 7
Prohibition of Mixed Marriages Act, 31
pronouns, 92, 97–98, 163, 166. *See also* "I" and "you"; we

racism, 20, 32, 44, 53, 58, 85, 156, 160, 174
Rancière, Jacques, 2–5, 19, 25, 47, 48, 49, 52, 108, 132, 149, 160, 162, 178, 182–184; *Disagreement*, 4–5; *Dissensus*, 5, 55n4; *The Flesh of Words*, 158, 159; *The Politics of Aesthetics*, 2, 5, 49, 52, 160, 162, 178n15, 183–184
rationality, 6–7, 37, 65, 71, 127–128, 132–133, 184–185
reader, 2, 20, 41, 44, 48, 70, 80–83, 86, 92, 100–105, 124, 146, 149, 158, 160, 162, 166–168, 169n6, 176–179
reason, 37, 65–66, 71–72, 97, 108, 109, 119, 121, 124, 127–129, 131–133
"Republic of Letters," 7
Riss, 33, 35, 37, 41
Rivonia Trial, 3, 19, 46–49, 51, 53, 55–58, 60–61, 84–86
Robinson, A. M. Lewin, 7
Ross, Fiona, 74n9
Russell, Bertrand, 13, 14, 16, 161n1; *The Philosophy of Logical Atomism*, 129

Sachs, Albie, 78, 185; "Art and Freedom," 185
Sanders, Mark, *Ambiguities of Witnessing: Law and Literature in the Time of a Truth Commission*, 4n5, 74n9, 172n10
Sartre, Jean-Paul, 66, 105; *What Is Literature?*, 20, 100–101
Saussure, Ferdinand de, 10, 12, 14
Schaap, Andrew, 76, 76n10, 77, 78n13, 82, 82n16, 175n13
Schalkwyk, David, 15, 26; *Speech and Performance in Shakespeare's Sonnets and Plays*, 161
Schmitt, Carl, 29–30; *The Nomos of the Earth*, 19, 26, 27, 28, 33
Sebald, W. G., 42
segregation, 9, 70
sensory experience, 5, 9
sensory perception, 2, 3, 5, 83, 89, 152, 181
Shakespeare, William, 13, 161
shifters, 92, 161–162, 173

Singer, Peter, 109, 126, 131n6
Socrates, 6–8, 15–18, 37, 128, 131
Somerset, Lord Charles, 7, 8
Sousa Santos, Boaventura de, 32
South Africa, 4–8, 16, 19–20, 44–45, 50, 69, 74, 85, 89–100, 108, 146, 150, 157, 160, 163–168, 174, 179–185
South African Communist Party, 31, 59
South African Journal, 7, 8
South African letters, 7
"speech event," 48, 51, 54, 60–62, 68, 92–97
Spinoza, Benedict de, 110–111
Staten, Henry, 13n12
Stevens, Wallace, 38, 39
street hawker, 20, 88
Suppression of Communism Act, 31

testimony, 54, 85
"thinking in action," 51
Tinzi, Mzwe Themba, 90n1
Tolstoy, Leo, 133–134
Transkei, 58
Transvaal, 27, 30, 31
Trek (journal), 30
Trier, Jost, 28–29
Tutu, Desmond, 183
Tuynhuys, 54

ubuntu, 16, 20, 91, 106, 169, 172, 181–184
Ulmen, G. L., 29
utterance, 47–48, 52, 57, 59, 61, 75, 92, 93–94, 103–105, 158–159, 166, 175–176

van Niekerk, Marlene, 3, 20; *Triomf*, 148–149, 156, 164, 174
Veitch, Scott, xi, xii, 57, 74n8, 86n21, 175n13
Vismann, Cornelia, 26, 28; "Starting from Scratch: Concepts of Order in No Man's Land," 26
Vladislavić, Ivan, 3, 34; *Double Negative*, 164–165, 178; *The Exploded View*, 90n2; *Portrait with Keys*, 179; *The Restless Supermarket*, 151, 156, 162, 164, 166, 170, 173, 177; "Street Addresses, Johannesburg," 153n4

we, 67, 108, 161–179, 182, 184
Wicomb, Zoë, 3; *Playing in the Light*, 104n2

Wilson, E. O., 111
Wiredu, Kwasi, 170; "How Not to Compare African Thought with Western Thought," 169*n*7
Wittgenstein, Ludwig, 13–15, 92; *Philosophical Investigations*, 13, 14, 27–29; *Tractatus*, 15, 29, 92

writer, 2, 19, 41, 44, 48, 66, 101–103, 124, 129, 167–168; "new writing," 50; South African writer, 3, 16, 69, 162

Young, Dudley, 37, 43

Žižek, Slavoj, 184

just ideas

Roger Berkowitz, *The Gift of Science: Leibniz and the Modern Legal Tradition*

Jean-Luc Nancy, translated by Pascale-Anne Brault and Michael Naas, *The Truth of Democracy*

Drucilla Cornell and Kenneth Michael Panfilio, *Symbolic Forms for a New Humanity: Cultural and Racial Reconfigurations of Critical Theory*

Karl Shoemaker, *Sanctuary and Crime in the Middle Ages, 400–1500*

Michael J. Monahan, *The Creolizing Subject: Race, Reason, and the Politics of Purity*

Drucilla Cornell and Nyoko Muvangua (eds.), *uBuntu and the Law: African Ideals and Postapartheid Jurisprudence*

Drucilla Cornell, Stu Woolman, Sam Fuller, Jason Brickhill, Michael Bishop, and Diana Dunbar (eds.), *The Dignity Jurisprudence of the Constitutional Court of South Africa: Cases and Materials, Volumes I & II*

Nicholas Tampio, *Kantian Courage: Advancing the Enlightenment in Contemporary Political Theory*

Carrol Clarkson, *Drawing the Line: Toward an Aesthetics of Transitional Justice*

Jane Anna Gordon, *Creolizing Political Theory: Reading Rousseau through Frantz Fanon*